Love Lifted Me

...from sharecropping to Harvard!

Bessie W. Blake
12/13/2022

Dr. Bessie W. Blake

Lit Lore - New York

Love Lifted Me
...from sharecropping to Harvard!
Copyright 2022
By Dr. Bessie W. Blake

Blake, Bessie W.
Love Lifted Me
ISBN: 978-0-9835699-0-9 (paperback)
First printing

Composition and Design: Bessie W. Blake

Cover Design: James Carter
Photos: Front cover - James Reynolds
          Back cover - Gwendolyn G. Flowers

Library of Congress Control Number: 2021948569

Published by Lit Lore
URL: www.litlorepublishing.com
email: lore@litlorepublishing.com

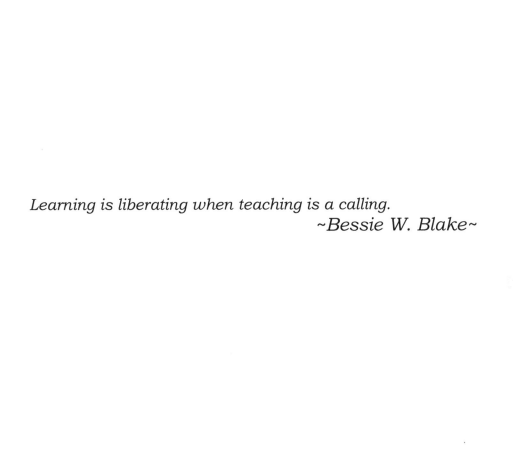

Learning is liberating when teaching is a calling.
                    ~Bessie W. Blake~

Preface

Love Lifted Me is dedicated to my four children—Kanari, Shango, RiShana and Takbir. It is the third of three volumes of the Waites-Blake saga. The first book evolved from a short biographical sketch intended to arouses memories; evoke the telling of powerful ancestral stories and, ultimately, to motivate future generations of achievers in my extended family. As it turned out the publication was destined for a far wider audience.

Of three volumes of oral history, the debut award-winning book, *Speak to the Mountain*, reaches seven generations back into slavery and provides the backdrop for Tommie Martin Waites' rocky road from motherless child and tormented wife to caring nurse and fiery minister; and, to the amazing woman that my children adore as MamMaw and I cherish as Mama. The second volume, *God's Bad Boy*, is about my husband's shattered family; the years he and his siblings spent in children and foster homes; as well as about his transformative years as an activist social worker and college professor. The third book chronicles my journey as learner, teacher and writer.

"Dr. Blake, when are you going to write your story?" was the frequent question raised at book talks. This persistent urging by readers and the nudging of family inspired the writing of *Love Lifted Me*. As you read, it is my sincere desire that you celebrate my successes; reflect on the stops and starts; learn from my failures; and heed the lessons of joy and pain. May your rough roads lead to love that lifts you to higher ground.

When I was seven dreams drifted on the wind. I lay on a rickety little porch inhaling the nutty smell of cotton and yearning to reach the sky.

"Fly!" I whispered and *Swish!* Loops and twirls sent me sailing through clouds until, *Thump!* A low-gliding crop duster jolted me back to earth. Powder spewed over my house. I coughed but did not care. I had never seen an airplane. If the man in the plane could lift wings and fly, maybe I could flee my cotton-field front yard.

My playful garden was Mama's sweaty work camp. The smell of snowy cotton sent my heart on gleeful flights, but turned her beautiful smile into a twisted frown. In 1949, I did not know that we lived on a Gilliam, Louisiana sharecropper plantation. All I knew was Mama worked sunup to sundown while a gun-toting boss watched her every move. Thorny bolls scraped and slashed her hands with each rip of cotton from the stalks. Her bones ached from pulling heavy cotton sacks up one gritty row and down another. Sometimes, when she thought I was not looking, she cried. Her unkind garden sprouted a new dream: to dry my mother's tears. With a child's worry and no hope on the horizon, I fretted constantly about Mama's sadness.

In late October, after crops had been gathered, the school year got underway on the plantation and my dream for Mama inched closer to reality. Thelma, a year older than me, led the way over rows of dry cotton stalks that leaned against the wind. In frayed wool coats and no

1

gloves, my sister and I crossed the empty field. Nearly frostbitten, we entered the one-room schoolhouse.

The teacher soaked our half-frozen hands in a cool pan of water before leading us to the wood-burning stove to warm them. Then, she made warm cups of weak tea flavored with Pet milk and sugar. Only after the tea was finished, were we required to join in the lesson. At the end of the school day, I rushed home to sing Miss Anderson's praises.

"Mama, she's kind. Ask her to help us," I said.

"Bessie, your teacher can't get involved in our problems," she answered. "God is going to make a way."

"I know she'll help us," I pestered Mama almost every day.

Finally, on a cold November day, she and my younger brother, Edgar, plodded across the barren field to school with Thelma and me.

In hushed tones Miss Anderson and Mama spoke in the corner of the classroom near my desk. I overheard bits of rapid-fire instructions: "Danger!" "Don't tell a soul." "Pack tomorrow." "Watch from your window." "At midnight..." "Move fast!" Did she say, "...a car with no lights?" A scary plot was taking shape.

The next night, I tried to stay up to see the plan unfold, but Mama woke me and, in hushed tones, ordered, "Get up! Run outside jump in the car get down on the floor and don't make a sound!"

Sandwiched between Thelma and Edgar, I lay on the floor behind the front seat. Mama threw a blanket over us. Muffled grunts and groans were heard as she and the driver pushed the car through the quiet of a pitch black night.

Images of the overseer with his rifle galloped in my head. My heart pounded wildly. Fear shook my body. The slimy taste of terror crawled from my stomach up to my throat. Just when I was about to puke, car doors slammed and the engine roared. The *whoosh* of great speed calmed my panic.

"Come on out now," Mama gently tugged at the blanket, "We free."

We children crawled from under the sweaty covering and onto the back seat of the unheated car. I drew a deep breath of chilled November air as safety wrapped its arms around my family. At lighting speed we zipped to Shreveport, Louisiana.

In worlds where dreams give rise to freedom, anything is possible. Fantasy flights above fluffy rows of cotton led to a plan that taught me people will sometimes help when they hear your story.

*W*hen Daddy left us on the Gilliam plantation, he had promised, "I'ma go look for work. Be back to git y'all." Months went by without Mama hearing from him. It was not the first time he abandoned his family.

Before the Gilliam escape, our family fled from Smithland, Texas under the threat of death. Like children of migrant farm workers, I had been snatched away from everything and everyone familiar. Left behind were loving grandparents, aunts, uncles and cousins who were playmates. Because of my father's debts, armed men looking for money had chased us into the backwoods of Red Water, and from there to Texarkana but Daddy had moved on to Fort Worth. "Looking for work," he had said. During his absence, my mother took odds jobs to earn money for food and rent for the cramped room where she, Thelma, Edgar and I slept in one bed.

One day while Mama was at work, we heard noise on the stairs and scurried under the bed like she taught us. Two men broke through the door of our second floor room. I lay on the dusty floor holding my breath but my eyes followed cowboy boots stumping around the bed. There was no closet to search, just things piled in boxes against the wall and beneath the one dingy window.

"Ain't nothing here," the man gave up without bothering to look under the bed. He, and a partner who stayed just outside the room, started down the stairs. The scraping sound of brass tip boots and spinning spurs faded in the distance but my sister, brother and I could not be sure the men were gone. For hours, we lay frozen under the bed until Mama came home from work.

Fleeing from place to place was a frightful way to live. I never knew when I would be snatched out of bed or who was chasing my family. Thoughts of night flights left me jumpy. Sometimes the sound of clinking cowboy boots rang in my ear; other times the picture of a galloping horse popped into my head. Each memory called up scary hunters with guns: one with a pistol, the other a rifle. I lived in constant fear of being caught and badly hurt.

By the time my family arrived in Shreveport, I had enrolled in four schools. Three in Texas included Smithland—where I was born, followed by Red Water and Texarkana. The fourth was on the Gilliam, Louisiana plantation. The sad thing is I never stayed in one school long enough to get to know a single child other than my sister, Thelma.

When I enrolled in Hollywood Elementary School, I was a farm girl out of place in another new town. City children teased me because I talked funny, dressed different and looked like I was afraid someone might sneak up any moment and say, *Boo!* My very presence drew bullies who giggled at my shabby clothes, threatened to beat me, and labelled me, "Scare-dee-cat!"

Mama made things worse when she took it upon herself to promote me to third grade. In the flight from

Gilliam, school records had been left behind and Mama provided the needed information about Thelma's and my school history. We were not tested and few questions were asked; she simply gave name, address, age and grade for each of us.

Mama knew our skills better than anyone. After all, back in Smithland, before we were on the run, she had been my first teacher. Nestled deep in the woods, the front bedroom of a crumbling three-room house had been the classroom. With me at her knee and my baby brother, Edgar, on her lap, Mama got my older sister ready for first grade. Squiggly letters cut from old cardboard boxes crowded the floor where Thelma and I lay on our stomachs lost in play. Under the strokes of our busy little fingers, piles of stiff paper grew into a carpet of yellow, blue, red and purple letters. Mama tacked them around the top edge of the wall near the ceiling. Pointing to the bright patchwork ribbon, she sang, *"A, B, C, D, E, F, Geee / HIJKLMNOPeee!"* The musical sounds tickled my ears as vibrant colors danced in my eyes. I fell in love with the alphabet and, later, with the words they made.

I watched, listened and learned as Thelma read from her first grade primer, "Run, Spot, run. See Spot run." By the time I entered first grade, I had finished my sister's *Dick and Jane* books and was eager for new readers. So, the teacher assigned second grade work to keep me busy. At the end of the year, I was reading level three *Bobbsey Twin* stories but was passed to second grade along with my class. Mama went straight to school and argued for putting me in third grade, but her plea fell on deaf ears. Though she did not give up, the struggle to skip me a grade was cut short when we were chased out of East Texas because of Daddy's debts.

Upon arrival in Shreveport, not only were we free from plantation life, it gave Mama another chance to correct the unfair decision made by my Smithland teacher. With no report cards from previous teachers or other records, Hollywood Elementary School depended on my mother to tell them about her children's past learning.

"What grade is Bessie?" they asked.

"Third," she answered and erased the thin line between fact and truth. The truth is I was ready for third grade work. The fact is I had never attended second grade. Mama was determined, though, that my progress would not be slowed by repeating lessons already learned.

In grade three, I did well in my studies but my classmates were a year older and had the upper hand when it came to horsing around. Slowly, my personality changed. The spunky little girl who inspired the Gilliam escape became quiet and withdrawn.

I felt unsafe. Strict rules and routines did not help. Obedience to teachers was required. Good manners were expected at all times. Students never spilled into the sandlot schoolyard that surrounded the five gray wooden buildings of Hollywood Elementary. We marched in a straight line and once outside, every aspect of play was supervised. Still, butterflies swirled in my stomach.

I wanted to stay on the sideline but took part in rough and tumble games at the orders of teachers. Shaking nervously, I stretched out sweaty palms for *Pop the Whip*—a game where ten to fifteen children grabbed hands, formed a chain, and then ran fast-fast-fast before bending into a curve that snatched students senseless— especially those at the end of the line. Had my hand slipped from my classmate's, I would have been slung to kingdom-come. I held on for dear life.

Before I caught my breath, I was bobbing up and down in *Hot Peas and Butter*. The activity should have been called extreme jump rope. It left ditches in the ground, dust in my hair and whelps on my legs from fast

6

turning ropes that had once tied horses to hitching posts. I was tortured by such play.

Quiet recess games like *Ring-Around-The-Roses* were more my speed. All I had to do was stroll in a circle and squat quickly on demand. Though shy, I loved *Little Sally Walker*. There was something magical about rising from a make-believe saucer. Boy did I, *put my hands on my hips and let my back bones slip/aahhh shake it to the east/shake it to the west/ shake it to the one you love the best.* Even the calming effect of these gentle games did not last. I feared a funny move might draw attention that would lead to teasing after school.

I had been giddy-happy on the night my family arrived from Gilliam. We entered the city in the wee hours before daybreak just after a fast moving rain shower. Flickering traffic signals threw fuzzy splashes of color onto shiny wet pavement. Stylish manikins in well-lit shop windows offered promises of store-bought dresses. I could feel my body shedding homemade clothes for the frilly outfits showcased along the main street.

By Easter, Mama had earned enough money to buy dresses for Thelma and me. My heart pumped joyful beats as we stepped off the downtown bus. Just inside the door of a dress shop on Texas Street the yellow eyes of tiny white daisies twinkled from the brim of a pretty straw hat. I reached out but...

"Gal, don't touch that!" the voice snapped.

I jumped back.

"You want 'a buy it?" the woman behind the counter continued her twangy attack.

"Ma'am, first we want to see if it fits," Mama grabbed my hand with a soothing squeeze.

"Niggers don't try on nothing!" the clerk flung an angry, confusing word at Mama. Instantly, a mistrust never felt toward an adult drew a sharp dividing line between the woman and me.

I did not know that she was White and I was Black. Even on the sharecropper plantation, as best I could tell at age seven, the difference between my mother and the overseer was he had a rifle and she did not. It was his would-be violence that I feared; but strange as it may sound, the woman standing among pretty store-bought clothes scared me more. I sensed from my mother's rapid exit from the store that an army of attackers would appear at her call.

In the farm village of Smithland, Texas where I lived until I started school, I had never witnessed such ugly behavior. I played carefree games among people with light, dark and in between skin colors like brown and tan. When Mama took us children to Mosley's General Store, the light skinned man behind the counter drawled, "How you folks doing today?" His hands slid spicy ginger treats into mine. I did not know that he was White. An even paler woman had silky hair worn in a long braid that swung to her waist, but my great Aunt Emily was Black. Closest to Aunt Emily's skin tone was our near neighbor, Mr. Shirley Durham, who enjoyed hot cups of java and biscuits on Grandma's front porch. Mr. Shirley and his family owned the land our family farmed as well as most of the fields and woods that we children roamed. I was too young, too innocent to know that Mr. Shirley's skin color entitled him to an ownership denied my uncles and grandfather.

Protected by a loving extended family of mother, grandparents, uncles, aunts and older cousins, the sting of racism had escaped me until I heard the word, *Nigger*. While eyeing a pretty Easter bonnet, hate wiped the sparkles off everything and I stood shaking.

Once outside the store, Mama grumbled, "Ignorant woman!"

Hand in hand, she, Thelma and I headed home. I noticed the people in the front of the bus looked like the mean woman in the store. Those in the back looked like me. Among frilly dresses, a glare of hatred had caused my first conscious steps into places pre-assigned by society. Perplexing questions gurgled in my belly. I wondered about the shabby clothes I wore; my seat assignment on the bus; and, about the names used to describe me and the neighborhood where I lived. *Did people hate me for no reason?*

In Shreveport people referred to my family and my neighbors as Negroes; but I had not entered the Texas Street dress shop, as a Negro. I was simply a schoolgirl who wanted to wear a lacy store-bought dress. Instead, the label Negro had easily slid to Nigger on the tongue of an angry woman who knew nothing about me.

Seventy years later it is still hard to bear the sound of the hateful word so casually floated among misguided teenagers (and many adults) as if its use gives them swag. Growing segments of the American population attempt to blunt the impact of the slur by saying, "N-word," as if the demeaning term does not pop immediately into everyone's head. Even worse than off-handed references are the ways in which the racial insult is still brandished in hateful exchanges. Most troubling, though, are mixed groups of teens—the bearers of the future—who try to relate across racial lines with: "Yo, my *Nigger.*" "What's happenin' *Nigger?*" "Myyyy *Nigger!*" I hear them and tumble back to age seven.

With my ears still burning, Mama, Thelma and I reached Hollywood—a "Negro" neighborhood. I trailed behind the two of them into Harris Dry Good Store. The owner greeted us with a warm welcome. On display were shoes, cotton underwear, coarse knitted sweaters, wool coats, and bolts of fabric but no dresses. Mama purchased a pattern and two yards of fabric for another set of twin home-made outfits for my sister and me. I groaned. A flowered print dress, trimmed in white rick-rack edging was sure to cause another round of teasing at school.

The more I tried to hide in my homemade dress, the bolder the bullies. However, I was not totally without spunk. The teacher had turned her back handing out papers to the class and I cleaned the blackboard with a prissy-missy. The busybody girl had smooth black skin and a puff of soft hair tied with a red, white and green plaid ribbon. I hated the days she and I were paired because she always made fun of my clothes. That day at the board she went too far. She wiggled her pointing finger into my braid down to the scalp and whispered a nasty word.

Bop! Before I could stop it, a white eraser mark landed in the middle of her navy blue store-bought sweater.

She was shocked and so was I. She looked from me to the dusty spot and in a split second, it hit us both. There was no time to lose. With quick pats she brushed little clouds of chalk from her sweater. I wanted to help but did not dare touch her again.

Had the teacher noticed the spat, I would have been in double trouble. Mama had two strict rules: No lying. No fighting. "Would Jesus do that?" was the question that separated right from wrong. In fact, in the Deep South where I grew up, lessons learned at church also guided public school behavior. Neither Prissy-Missy nor I wanted to explain ourselves to the teacher. She was at fault for starting the squabble. I was guilty of hitting her. Punishment would have come from the stinging licks of a wooden ruler until our palms turned red; and another whipping would have been waiting for me at home.

Because the teacher had not seen the blackboard tit-for-tat, Prissy-Missy and I did not get a licking. However, we were doomed to spend the rest of the day as partners. At the wash basin, during the afternoon lavatory break, she whispered, "I'ma git you after school!" My mind leaped forward to the walk home. It was the one time of day with no grown-ups around. I guessed, *That's when she gon' jump me.* The rest of the day was spent worrying about a way to avoid the fight.

When school let out, I stepped into the yard ready for a foot race. Searching for the best route, I cranked my head in every direction. No blood thirsty mob of children had gathered in the distance. Prissy-Missy, a popular girl seen by all at dismissal, was nowhere in sight. *Amazing!* The bully-turned-coward had disappeared. I hurried home anyway.

Prissy-Missy never bothered me again. The strong whack in the chest had ended her bullying days. Still, victory over one tough girl did not give me confidence to stand and fight. I feared a student who was full of mischief might jump me at any time.

*H*asty exits from school were suspended on days Thelma walked home with me. My sister did not shy away from fights. One afternoon, with big-sister protection, I followed behind a band of schoolmates. The most popular boy in the group eyed a man in the ditch. "Look! It's a drunk," he shouted.

"Let's go see," a second student egged us on.

You see a crowd, don't be nosey; run the other way, darted through my head. I ignored Mama's warning. I was lonely and wanted to belong. I took off running with the other children.

"Ha-ha-ha, he's falling down," someone yelled.

"Look! He broke his eggs," another pointed.

Panting with excitement, I pushed forward to see, *Daddy!* I froze. Staggering in the ditch was my father dragging a slimy string of egg white that leaked from the brown paper bag he carried.

My would-be pals were hot on the heels of helpless prey and did not notice Thelma and I pull away in shame. Mocking jeers in the distance underlined my failure to fit in with other children. My father had showed up in Shreveport just in time to spoil my first attempt at being a regular student.

Most every school day I faced cruel choices. When I should have been paying attention in class, I worried about how to make it home without crossing my father's path. Or, I fretted over how to dodge bullies.

In that first year at Hollywood Elementary School, the only bright spot shined at the Friday "Heaven and Hell" party. My heart danced as I pulled straws. The short straw sent me to hell for delicious homemade chili, crackers and a cold bottle of Coke; the long one sent me to heaven for ice cream and cake. A lasting love of vanilla ice cream formed at those parties; but the memories of teachers all but faded.

If he had not been the only man in the school, I probably would not remember that Mr. Hall taught long division in sixth grade. Other than him, the names and faces of elementary school teachers vanished—that is until recently. In the middle of the night a teacher leaped from hiding. "Miss Ogilvy!" I bolted upright. "She was my third grade teacher." Like a skeleton, the weird fact rattled around without fleshy details.

I asked Thelma, "Was Miss Ogilvy my third grade teacher?"

"Yeap," she answered. "That ole fat witch pulled your dress up and whipped you. Made me mad!"

"Why?" I asked. "I was always a good girl. Why did she do that?"

Thelma answered, "I don't know. Just mean, I guess; but Mama went to school and got her straight. She didn't bother you anymore."

I thought my father and bullies had turned me into a nervous little schoolgirl. Maybe all along it was Mrs. Ogilvy's whipping that made me unsure in any classroom and left me without a single friend at Hollywood Elementary School.

I tried to fit in, failed, and tried again. I longed for a kinder-garden where living and learning were wrapped in one big bundle of love. In her little East Texas bedroom, Mama had made learning fun; but fear and loneliness hounded my early schooldays in the city.

Sister Lucille Anderson

Photo: The Kermit Anderson collection, circa 1990s.

ᘓᘔ

Words matter! They are seeds of hope and despair that shape lives for better or worse.

Daddy's words were explosive forces in my childhood. His anger flashed like lighting in a nasty storm. "I'm the damn king in this house!" he thundered with an accusing finger pointing across the room. In the split second it took for him to catch his breath, my body froze but my eyes darted to the sign on the wall above Mama's calm face. A navy blue velvet poster trimmed in gold read: *In this house Jesus is King.*

"That," he ordered, "better be gone when I get back!" Then, snatching his hand to his side and spinning around, away he went. The minute the door slammed to our little three-room shot-gun apartment, my sister, brother and I leaped to our feet and huddled around Mama.

"Awww, don't y'all pay your daddy any mind," she said, rose, brushed the wrinkles from her cotton skirt and calmly removed the tacks from the sign. Left on the sun-bleached wall was a dark square where kind words had lived.

Men of the neighborhood took on any odd jobs to put food on the table for their families. They were janitors, delivery truck drivers, street sweepers, "yard boys," junk peddlers, jackleg mechanics and dayworkers in hot fields just outside the city limit. Not my father. He huddled on street corners and shared bottles of cheap wine with small groups of idle men. *Daddy is lazy,* I concluded.

I knew nothing about the war years except the glimpse of a faded brown tone picture of him with one arm around a White woman's shoulder. Daddy never talked about the picture or anything else about World War II; nor did he speak of the battles he had waged to hold onto a job once he returned home. All I knew was the two personalities shown me. When he needed a drink, he ripped through the house like a tornado. After the drink, he floated in like a soft breeze. On any given day, I did not know whether to expect the irritated or the gentle father.

Hateful, threatening words of Angry Daddy left me breathless. Had he been one of the fourth grade bullies at school, and Thelma was by my side like when we were home, I might have mumbled under my breath, *Sticks and stones may break my bones but talk don't bother me.* The truth is Daddy's words hurt Mama and they hurt me because they hurt Mama. His fury said: *You can't help your mother. You're useless.*

Tipsy Daddy—the one half-drunk from cheap wine— came home in a mellow mood. He let us children comb his hair, sit on his lap and dig in his pockets for loose change. Though I loved to buy two-for-a-penny rubboard cookies, most times I refused to pat him down on the days he had shouted awful words at Mama before he got high. Sometimes he would plead: "Girl don't look at me like that." When he followed up with a corny joke, "Come on, smile; I'd laugh at a dying man if he wiggled funny," and then winked, I could not hold back the smile that broke through my anger. Though it felt like a betrayal of Mama, my giggles blew love bubbles splashed with shiny rainbows.

By morning, the bubbles popped. With his face twisted in frowns, Daddy went searching for the next drink. It was painful to grab at straws of affection and have them snatched away quickly. Thankfully, his ugly words were balanced by a vocabulary of hope.

$\mathcal{H}$ollywood Church of God in Christ was Mama's safe haven. She had joined Reverend J. K. Anderson's church the week we came to Shreveport. He was the husband of my teacher, Mrs. Lucille Anderson, who had arranged the escape from the Gilliam sharecropper plantation. A few months after my family arrived in the city, just as Mama had foretold, Sister Anderson had gotten a job in Shreveport. However, she was never one of my schoolteachers; nor did she provide religious instruction at church.

As First Lady, Sister Anderson looked out for the physical needs of young people in the congregation. She found shelter for families who needed housing; fed us children when we were hungry; and clothed us when we were cold or raggedy. I have fond memories of twin baby blue and pale pink sill-sucker summer dresses; and of the velvet-covered buttons, collar and cuffs on a winter coat that her daughter, Kermit, had outgrown. At one of the First Lady's clothing drives, Sister Lee Etta Robins dazzled me with purple suede shoes that replaced the brown high top Brogans worn from Gilliam. Though it was Sister Anderson who gradually brightened my drab attire, I adopted Sister Robins as godmother.

As a teacher in the school system, Sister Anderson also informed parents of free lunch and free school supplies. Notices regarding vaccinations for polio and other childhood diseases were passed out after Sunday and mid-week services. No, the First Lady did not provide religious instruction. She made sure our stomachs were full, our bodies were warm and healthy and that we arrived at church ready to learn. Teaching was placed in the capable hands of others.

Women who could not read and sometimes signed their names with an *X* taught Sunday and Vacation Bible School at Hollywood Church of God in Christ. Their distant voices still echo, "Okay chulluns, today we gon' learn you 'bout God's love." "Now baby, what do that mean?" "Put that verse in yo' words." "All you need is a tee-nine-chee bit of faith the size of a little ole mustard seed."

We children giggled at phrases like "gon' learn you" and made-up words like "tee-nine-chee." Some of our tutors used sentences like, "Us gon' read this hinh." Out of respect, we did not dare correct their speech, but muffled snickers rumbled along the pew. Silly kids! We did not think they knew we were laughing at them.

The sisters took turns teaching Sunday school but I liked Sister Robins the best, not because she was my godmother, but because she had spunk and was a good listener. Sister Robbins, also a church usher, strutted to the back corner of the tiny church sanctuary and slid sideways between two pews to face her six students.

"Today, we gon' learn about the Sermon on the Mount," she said and flashed a card the size of a baseball card. On the front was a picture of Jesus sitting on a mountainside with a big crowd; on the back was a Bible verse.

"Hinh Bessie, you start," she handed me the card.

I stood and read, "Blessed are the merciful for they shall obtain mercy."

"Now put that verse in yo' own words," she said.

"It means, if I'm good to people they will be good to me."

The next student repeated the reading and answered, "If you be kind to people, they'll be kind to you."

The third said, "That ain't so. I was kind to this boy in school and he punched me in the face."

We squabbled back and forth and Sister Robins listened patiently before saying: "Well, maybe the mercy ain't comin' from the boy. Maybe it come from you 'cause you didn't punch him back. Or, maybe it come from yo' teacher. Mercy don't always come from the one you give it to. Ask God to show you where the mercy comin' from. You can ask yo' mama and daddy too." Then, she called on the next child.

When every child had a turn reading, "Blessed are the merciful...," Sister Robin moved to the next question, "Now that you read this hinh verse, how you gon' change?"

Down the row, we answered: "I'ma stop fighting." "I'll be kind." "I'ma get mercy from my teacher." "I'ma love everybody and I'll get love."

I thought, *I need mercy at home and at school*, but I said, "I'ma pray for mercy."

Sister Robins summed up the lesson, "This ole world would be a better place if everybody lived by this hinh Word?"

Probing Sunday school questions exposed my grief one layer at a time. Most adults saw me as a child with small problems. Not my Sunday school teachers. They helped me talk about pain; and then soothed it with kind words and warm hugs snuggled against soft bellies.

At church, students and teachers learned together. The instructors enjoyed listening to us read scriptures they would have had to memorize. We students took pride in showing off our reading skills. That way, learning was multiplied when loving women of faith connected with eager young minds.

Not only did Bible knowledge make me feel better, my reading and critical thinking skills improved as I developed a hefty vocabulary. Plenty of words in the Bible and in church programs were hard to pronounce. When I got home, Mama broke them into small parts that I could handle. I repeated after her, "De-spite-ful-ly, rec-i-ta-tion, ren-di-tion." Before long, the words despitefully, recitation and rendition flew from my mouth with ease. Later, I looked the words up in the dictionary Sister Anderson kept at church.

Sunday school classmates sneered, "Listen at Bessie. She thinks she so smart; always using them big words."

Well, they read the same Bible; knew the meanings of the same words. Just because they did not hear the music that flowed in longer words was no reason to spoil my fun. I was not a show-off. I simply liked the melodic sounds that rolled through big words. Also, church was a safe place to practice fancy new expressions because the sisters permitted only so much teasing. Did I use big words in school? Never! Someone might have punched me in the mouth.

Memorization, the dreaded Sunday school activity, ended up being the most helpful. I was eager to memorize, "Suffer little children to come unto me, and forbid them not; for such is the kingdom of heaven." The verse was a personal invitation of friendship from Jesus himself. *Forget the bullies. Jesus is my friend*, I said to myself. Later I memorized, "If anyone slaps you on the right cheek, turn to him the other," and my fear of fighting became godly rather than cowardly. I hid the two verses in my heart and carried them to school. They did not stop the bullying but they eased the pain.

The rewards of memorization were also on display in church programs. Though I never recited James Weldon Johnson's "The Creation," each line of the poem flooded my heart with hope:

And God stepped out on space,
And he looked around and said:
I'm lonely—
I'll make me a world...

I was a lonely ten-year-old with a vivid imagination. I could see God reaching down into the "cypress swamp" and rolling the darkness back so light could shine through. With light, I saw that it was possible to create a world different from the one I knew. Johnson's poem was by far my favorite dramatic recitation.

Did I memorize songs? Yes and, at choir practice, I sang loud and off key, *"The Jesus in me/ Loves the Jesus in you/ You're easy to love."* My every note was misery to my peers in the youth choir.

"Make Bessie be quiet!" one of them grumbled.

"Her singing is like fingernails scratching a blackboard," another complained.

"That's okay baby; the Bible says, 'Make a joyful noise unto the Lord,'" my mother, who was a great songster, encouraged me at home.

The other children never stopped complaining and I never stopped singing. On Monday mornings, I returned to school with praise-songs ringing in my head and my two favorite Bible verses tucked in my bosom. Though it was easy to talk to Sunday school teachers, it never occurred to me to tell them about the bullies that tormented me. I thought public school classmates were beyond being scolded by "sanctified holy-rollers." So, the bullying continued while I grew strong enough to ignore it.

The real struggle was at home. My body went rigid searching for relief from my father's cruelty. I was taught, "Love your enemies, bless them that curse you, do good to them that hate you, and pray for them that despitefully use you." In my young mind, Daddy was an enemy. Surely he hated me. Still, I wanted to forgive him. Whispering over and over, "Bless them that curse you," I prayed but those attempts to bless my father were short-lived. I was trapped in a house where Daddy raged; Mama retreated behind a wall of calm; while my sister, brother and I trembled with fear and anger that were slowly turning to hate.

Chaos reigned for months before my mother decided it was time to go. "Y'all get dressed; we leaving. Get the cedar chest," she said in her usual quiet manner.

A wide grin crossed my face as Thelma and I rushed to her bedroom. We dragged out the wooden trunk that Daddy's hands had built with love in a cabinet-making veteran's program at the end of World War II. With white oak, he had carefully carved a "T" and laid it in one lid, and a "W" in the other lid. The letters reminded me of good times in Mama's classroom back when I had held the alphabet in my hands. I ran my fingers over the initials and whispered, "Tommie Waites," my mother's name.

Mama packed the treasured chest that followed her everywhere. It had sneaked away with her when we fled to Red Water seeking safety from my father's armed creditors. It journeyed to Texarkana and onto Fort Worth in my mother's search for work. The hope chest held her most prized possessions during scary months on the sharecropper plantation and was the only piece of furniture brought from Gilliam to Shreveport. On a night when love was cold, Mama prepared the cedar chest for yet another flight to freedom.

I watched nervously from the sofa while precious minutes ticked away. *Hurry up before he comes back*, I wanted to shout but kept quiet.

Whew! The chest finally sat on the backseat between Thelma and me. With Edgar up front beside her, Mama cranked the car. We were on our way! *Goodbye and good luck!* I thought as I looked back at our lonely little house.

One block down, Mama made a right turn; and then another right turn at the corner. *Grandpa's house!* The third right turn raised an eyebrow but..., *Wait!* The fourth turn was downright alarming. We rode one square block before the car pulled back into our yard.

What did we forget? I wondered.

Mama walked toward the back fender with her shoulders slumped.

She better hurry up before Daddy comes back, I was thinking when she opened the door on Thelma's side of the car. "Y'all gone on in and get ready for bed," she sighed. "We can't go anywhere tonight."

"Awwwww!" the three of us children groaned in unison.

I wanted to scream, *We can go live in Texas with Grandpa! Why we got to stay in angry ole Louisiana? Why can't we live with Grandpa? He always fixes everything.*

Only after Mama testified at the mid-week prayer meeting, did I understand. She did not have enough gas in the car to carry us the forty miles to Smithland. Even with a full tank, leaving that night would have caused her to lose her job. Her testimony ended, "It makes me sad to see my children angry with their father." The words stuck like tiny darts in my heart.

After the prayer meeting, I focused on Mama's needs the way I had done back on the plantation. I helped out around the house; and, for her sake, I tried to hide my attitude toward Daddy. Sunday school lessons comforted me the way testimony services strengthened Mama. When bad feelings about my father crept in, I murmured under my breath, "Love those that despitefully use you." More than any other scripture, Matthew 5:44 shaped my early understanding that Christian love involves suffering. The verse helped me see how my mother was able to keep calm during my father's outbursts.

Instead of a bunch of rules to follow without questioning, The Bible was Mama's guide for daily living. Testing scriptures was a faith-building process that led to hope in desperate situations. She often said to us children, "Let's try this verse and see how it helps with the problem."

In my pre-teen years, Bible studies with Mama and weekly Sunday school classes molded a church-girl who depended on God for everything. No matter how difficult life became, I believed I could achieve the desires of my heart because the Bible said so. I did not have to be the loudest or strongest person in the group. If easygoing women who did not read or write could understand difficult English text in the Bible, all things were possible. In addition to hope, reading the King James Version of the Bible trained my ear for poetry. With strong critical reading and critical listening skills and a good-sized vocabulary, I was ready to "plow new ground," as the old church mothers would say.

"Finders keepers," I shouted with glee. Mama had brought home an old wooden cabinet from the house where she was the maid. Eagerly, I searched inside for an old doll or used toy. A dingy brown book lay on the top shelf of the musty cupboard. I picked it up, rubbed the dust off the cover and read, *The Romantic Poets*. I flipped through the yellowing pages and claimed it as mine. The only other book in our house, *The Holy Bible*, belonged to Mama. In the summer following my fifth year of school, I became the proud owner of my first book.

I read all the time. During the day, my mother startled me with the stern order, "Bessie, get your head out of that book!" At night, I crawled under the covers with a flashlight and drifted to exciting new places. Romantic poets of the eighteen hundreds swept me from a dull and stressful household into the world of ideas, beautiful gardens and loving relationships. *"I wandered lonely as a cloud"* with William Wordsworth; whispered, *"How do I love thee? Let me count the ways,"* with Elizabeth Barret Browning; and I watched Thomas Gray's *"...plowman homeward plod his weary way,"* without once thinking of death and dying. Instead, Gray's poem called to mind my grandfather who was alive and well and farming in East Texas.

Writers of the nineteenth century caused my sixth grade school year to zoom by. Like cloud-sailing on the rickety front porch back in Gilliam, lively flights of fancy took hold of me again. As poetry awakened my young mind, I was swept up by throbbing rhythms and rhymes. Fantasies of travel, glamor and puppy love fluttered in my pre-adolescent heart. With each line of verse, harsh reality faded. I trampled through the English countryside inhaling the sweet fragrance of daffodils and wild flowers. Left behind were comic books, Golden Book fairy tales and picture-reading of movie magazines on the wire rack at the checkout counter of the Big Chains Supermarket.

Added to my prized volume of English literature were the Black publications Daddy kept around the house like *Sepia,* (a mostly picture magazine with occasional romance stories); *Jet* (a pocket size national magazine that reported on the social lives and successes of Black people); and old copies of *The Shreveport Sun* (the local weekly newspaper for and about African Americans). Through my father's reading list for "lazy days" when he could not find a drink, finally, he and I had something in common. Reading became our joint means of escaping an unbearably miserable household.

The Holy Bible and *The Romantic Poets* prepared me for writers who would influence me in years to come. Poetry introduced me to worldly ideas and scripture to religious principles. The two ways of thinking set the stage for a future battle for my mind. However, a more immediate impact of my readings was the respect I gained from advanced skills that allowed me to sort through the most difficult texts.

At home, Mama asked me to help my sister and brother with their homework whenever she worked evenings. The effort was wasted. Thelma rejected my "meddling" with alarming threats and Edgar simply ignored me. Among classmates it was a different story. I helped other students with tough assignments and their opinions of me changed from an odd girl to be bullied to an egghead to be valued. This shift in attitudes by peers made me keenly aware of the power of words to help as much as they could hurt.

Though fear of my classmates had vanished by the time I left Hollywood Elementary School, I remained a lonely little girl watching fun-filled activities from the sidelines. Like crop dusters buzzing in a plantation sky, a loving father and a close circle of friends were out of reach. Words were the constant companions throbbing in my heart.

ild and wonderful are headlong leaps of freedom.

"Over yonder," Nick pointed to a low hanging tree branch near the fence. Heads swirled. He stooped down and everyone squatted around a half buried hump in the sand. He gave it a quick thump, nodded, "Yep," and raised a clinched fist that landed like John Henry's sledge hammer. Oozing red meat lay bare. Thelma, Edgar and I gorged out pieces of the heart. Like tigers tearing into raw meat, we gobbled down chunks. From our hands, sticky streams trickled along skinny arms, off boney elbows and made red splotches on the ground. Once the heart was devoured, the prowl was on for the next target. Our exploits left a bloody trail across the watermelon patch.

The Fearsome Foursome's summer of plundering was underway. On the brink of adolescence, my cousin (Marvin Harper whose nickname was Nick), my sister, brother and I roamed the East Texas countryside of the early 1950s. Nick was our leader. He had lived in the little three room farm house with our grandparents since preschool and knew every inch of the surrounding woods and fields. What Nick said, we did. Where he went, Thelma, Edgar and I followed. He directed the hunt as we ate on the move. After we filled our bellies with watermelon, we stormed the peach orchid for its golden fruit.

Several raids later, Cuttin' Mex showed up on his tractor. "Them children destroying my crops," our cousin complained.

"Dat-gum-it! They at it again? Don't you worry, I'll see to them," Grandpa promised but only gave us a mild scolding. He was a big ole softie. I had never seen or heard of him whipping any of his grandchildren. Well, maybe I should count the pretend whipping he gave my sister and I back when I was six.

Once a week Uncle 'Lijah delivered fresh milk to Grandma. She sat a tall thick crock between her legs and churned the wooden paddle up and down until butter rose to the top. After hours of preparation, she poured buttermilk into a deeply carved white pitcher and placed it gently on the scarf with hand embroidered roses that covered the top of the old peddle-operated sewing machine in the bedroom where Thelma and I slept.

Grandma was a plain and simple woman who did not fret over material goods. She cherished two things: the chicken she summoned, "Here babies. Here babies," for twice-a-day feedings; and the once-weekly pitcher of milk that was used for cooking after it curdled to clabber.

A tiring day of churning and household chores had sent her to bed early. Her sleepy voice called out several times to my sister and me, "Y'all go to bed."

"Yas'sum," Thelma and I answered; but kept tipping through the door that separated our bedroom from the kitchen where Edgar and Nick slept on cots. When we heard our grandmother's call, we would dash back to the bed in time to answer, "Yas'sum, Grandma."

Back and forth we ran in the dark until, *Crash!* My foot got caught under the wrought iron peddle of her sewing machine. Milk and glass splashed everywhere.

Grandma and Grandpa got up. She busied herself cleaning up the mess and he dealt with Thelma and me.

"Y'all come on in here," he called. The kerosene lamp he lit threw threatening shadows against the kitchen wall. Edgar and Nick played possum in their cots while my sister and I answered to Grandpa. I stood before him drenched in buttermilk. My sister, the guilty silent partner, stood beside me.

"You heard your grandma, didn't you?

"Yas'suh," I nodded.

"But you didn't listen, did you?"."

"Naw'suh."

"Now we won't have cool buttermilk to drink this week and no fluffy biscuits, or..." On he went describing the good eating that always followed milk day.

My head hung in heavy sadness. I did not notice the small switch in his hand until he asked, "What y'all think I ought to do?"

"Whip me?" I answered his question with a question; it was not a suggestion. No man had ever raised his hand to hit me, not even Daddy in his worst outbursts. I could not imagine my loving Grandpa whipping me.

When he motioned, "Come on over here," I almost fainted. The three gentle licks to the tail of my nightgown never touched my skin but I let out wrenching wails the moment Grandpa raised his hand. I sobbed until my body shook. My sister took her shirttail licking like a soldier and then shot an angry *Bessie-what-you-got-to-cry-about* look in my direction and went straight to bed.

Grandpa was the perfect father that I longed for—the one who always spoke in soft tones. His raised hand struck blows at the idea of a loving family. I cried until my eyes were swollen and Grandpa stayed up half the night petting me. By the time I fell asleep his image as the superhero who fixed everything had eased back into place.

Next morning, Grandma served a breakfast we children did not deserve. Somehow, she managed to make biscuits as fluffy as ever. We sopped up Brer Rabbit syrup laced with swirls of fresh clotted butter. Grandpa added my favorite treat of warm water, Pet milk and sugar spiked with three tablespoons of coffee. The make-believe cup of java was his way of apologizing for the pretend-whippings of the previous night.

Yes, Grandpa was an ole softie. That is why years later his pre-teen grandchildren continued to raid Cuttin' Mex's fields and orchids.

After gobbling up watermelon and peaches in the heat of the day, the Fearsome Foursome went skinny dipping in Ole Man Whatley's pond. Honestly, it was more mud-crawling than swimming. "Stop clouding that water! My cows have to drink there," Mr. Whatley sent us racing into the woods.

At the abandoned pulpwood mill we zoomed from the top of the sawdust pile in makeshift sleds of cardboard boxes. I was clueless about hidden air pockets in the dusty mound that could have swallowed me alive. I did not know how to swim either but, with no fear of drowning or snakes or snapping turtles or other swimming critters, I whizzed downward into the creek at the bottom of the sawdust hill where Nick waited in waist-deep water to catch me. He was my guardian angel in every situation.

Summers were spent mostly unchecked in a world absent of daddies and mamas. Even grandparents existed on the rim of our lives. In unbridled spaces, we developed curious minds, lively imaginations and strong wills. While elementary school had failed to teach me these aims of a good education, Nick, Thelma, Edgar and I learned them in the wilds of East Texas. Our return from daily outings in one piece was also proof that *God protects babes and fools.*

The Fearsome Foursome headed out on the highway on half-day treks to Mosley's General Store for ice cold soda pops or bear-track and stage-plank gingerbread treats. In the cool of the morning, we strolled in the middle of U.S. Route 49 but there was little danger of being run over. Our chatter and laughter echoed in the quiet of a sparsely populated countryside. Any approaching car could be heard long before it was visible. By the time a vehicle appeared on top of one of the rolling hills, we had scattered to the road's shoulder and were rambling among the growth. We climbed pine saplings, bent them toward the ground and rode our make-believe ponies until they snapped. We searched the grass for marble-sized blue bird's eggs. They bobbled in our hands until the delicate shells cracked and splattered on the ground. Tiny baby birds floated in a clear jell with little specks of blood. Though awed by the glimpse at life before birth, we were soon on our way.

The distant humming of motors, the sounds of metal wheels scrapping against pavement, and the smell of horse droppings floated to us. In the mid-fifties, wagons still shared the roads with cars. Almost always a Black farmer who knew us eased over the hill and groaned, "Whoaaaa," as he pulled up on the reins. We jumped aboard for a bumpy ride to the center of the tiny village of Smithland.

The sun was high in the sky by the time we arrived in the little shopping area. A blinking orange light cautioned the occasional car or truck to slow down for people who might be crossing the road from Mosley's General Store over to the Post Office and the Dry Goods Store. Before going inside Mosley's, Nick reached into the red metal cooler with a frosted Coca-Cola pictured on its front. Glass bottles clinked against ice as he searched for a Royal Crown Cola for Thelma, Nehi Strawberry for me and Cokes for Edgar and him. Tiny chips of ice dripped from the bottles as we headed inside; passed the twenty-five pound sacks of flour stacked on the floor and stepped up to the counter.

"How y'all doing today?" one of the Mosley men greeted us.

"Fine," we answered.

"You Ed's children from over there in Shreveport, ain't you?"

"Yas'suh."

"Tell your daddy it's 'bout time we get in some fishing."

"Yas'suh."

We gave him a nickel each for the sodas. He called out, "Say howdy to Mr. Tommy," as we left. The greeting was for my grandfather, Tommy Martin, who was a respected member of the village.

Mr. Mosley's children went to the segregated White school. His family and neighbors also attended separate churches from Blacks. Still, I never experienced in his or the other two Smithland stores the unfair treatment I had faced in a Shreveport dress shop back when I was seven. The unspoken rule in the three Smithland stores was first come, first served. While waiting their turn, Blacks and Whites chatted about crops, the need for rain and whether or not the fish were biting. The polite behavior of country people said the races could live together in peace.

Years later, when in my teens, I heard of a tent burning because a few Blacks and Whites were worshiping together. Later still, the new Brick school building for Black children mysteriously burned to the ground. However, on the many trips to the general store, incidents of violence or heckling never occurred.

Our excursion to purchase soda pops ended with Nick, Thelma, Edgar and I sitting on wooden crates in front of the store and drinking in peaceful bliss. With each gulp, fizz shot through my young nostrils like steam. I did not know the tingle was produced by traces of cocaine that should have been removed from soda water years earlier.

The midday trek back to Grandpa's house was way too hot for mischief. The temperature soared above a hundred degrees. We squinted down the highway and argued about whether the pools of water up ahead were real. It was obvious to Nick that a "heat mirage" was shining on the pavement in the distance.

"See. It moves when we move," he said. It made sense to me but in her usual struggle against Nick's authority, Thelma decided, "I'ma run up and cool off in the water."

"Don't run in this heat!" he yelled.

She kept going. He chased after her while Edgar and I lagged behind in weak little trots.

It was not a new scene. Edgar and I were Nicks devoted followers. He was the commander of our treks through fields, streams and woodlands; but Thelma challenged his leadership almost every day.

I was about to collapse in the heat but Nick kept hollering after Thelma, "Y'all from the city. Y'all don't know the country like me."

"You twelve. I'm twelve. I don't do no minding of twelve-year-olds. Anyhow, I'm the oldest."

"Yeah, sixteen days might make you older; but I'm the strongest."

Two-thirds the way home, the heat finally shut them up. Everyone was too tired and too busy searching for shady spots. To cool our bare feet, we trooped in low-cut grass at the edge of the road. We scanned the hillside for trees, and scurried to them for shade. Thank God, we made it home without anybody passing out.

As we neared the yard, Grandpa rose from the cane bottom chair on the porch; went to the backyard; drew a bucket of cold well water and passed the dipper around to cool us children down. Tired, sweaty and itchy, I crawled onto the front porch and napped the rest of the afternoon away while gentle breezes stirred in Grandma's Mulberry tree.

Summers were the best times. For three months, I lived in the peaceful home of loving grandparents and enjoyed exciting ventures with the Fearsome Foursome. They were more than kin; they were friends who included me in every activity.

*O*n a rare idle day on the front porch, Nick told how he came to live with our grandparents. He was the youngest of three children born to Aunt Too-Too before she married the uncle with the initials O.C. for a first name. Maybe because he was too young to work, my cousin suffered awful beatings from his stepfather. For her baby's protection, Aunt Too-Too sent him to live with Grandpa.

Whenever Mama visited her sister's house, Uncle O. C. flashed wads of cash and bragged about how he took good care of my aunt and the children. He never mentioned beatings or brandishing a pistol in her face. Those were whispered secrets overheard when two sisters poured out their hearts to one another. I had also witnessed my uncle's cruelty firsthand.

"What you doing eating my food?" he roared; and etched in my memory the words, "If you don't pay up, I'ma get my gun."

I almost choked. A picture of his nickel-pistol flashed in my head. I had seen the gun in the bedroom. Its metal reminded me of the five-cent coin used to buy Cub sodas at Mosley's General Store.

"Scared pic-a-ninnies," he ended his twisted teasing with belly laughs.

From that moment, I was never at ease at my aunt's dining room table. There was no telling when her husband might appear. Aunt Too-Too made the best crispy fried chicken and her homemade ice cream had chunks of peaches fresh off the tree; but nervousness about the possibility of Uncle O.C.'s sudden arrival made it impossible to enjoy her cooking.

Before Nick told his story, I had considered him the luckiest boy in the world because he lived with Grandpa. I had been wrong. He worried about the safety of his mother as well as his sisters and brothers. Our grandparent's house was as much a haven for Nick as it was for my siblings and me. Truly, Grandpa was the father of us all.

Hard times were not the only subject of porch talk. Like on the Gilliam plantation, dreams sprouted during sky-gazing days.

"When I grow up, I want to live just like Grandma and Grandpa," one of us said but all agreed.

"Yeah, here in the woods of Texas," Thelma offered.

"We can build a house and live together," Nick added.

Edgar and I nodded.

"We'll have our own sections. Mine will be big enough for my wife and children," Nick continued.

"Your sisters and brothers will have houses nearby and we won't have to go back to Louisiana," I said. Thoughts of a forever-land that did not require going home to parents sent my imagination reeling out of control. I blurted, "The house will be shaped like a great big wagon wheel."

The others shot funny looks at me before breaking out in laughter. They poked fun: "A wheel?" "A wagon wheel?" "Nobody can't live in no wagon wheel!"

"No, no, let me tell you," I pleaded. They were doubtful but quieted while I described our dream house: "It will be shaped like a wagon wheel. Four huge spokes with a bunch of rooms will shoot from the axle down between the pines trees in different directions. Nick you'll have the most rooms for your family. Thelma, Edgar and I will live in separates spokes with our own families. All we have to do is open our doors and walk into this huge round room in the middle of the wagon wheel whenever we want to visit one another. We can be together forever."

"Yeah! Together forever! Together forever," the four of us chanted.

We were preteens who knew nothing about African compounds where extended families live under one roof. Yet, an idea as old as the African blood in our veins had crossed an ocean of woes and showered the Fearsome Foursome with dreams of an ancient way of life. Like cloud-sailing in Gilliam, wild and wonderful times in East Texas had freed us to imagine new possibilities for our lives.

The summer of 1954 began with the usual adventures. The day started with early morning frolicking in the sun. Thelma, Edgar and I trailed behind Nick as we headed to Mosley's General Store for jumbo gingerbread cookies. On the way we spotted an old half demolished house. No workers were around. We detoured, climbed up on the roof and surveyed open fields bordered by baby trees. It did not take long before the downward slope from the roof's apex caught Nick's eye.

"I'ma jump," he said and dashed into a running leap. "Come on! It's easy," he yelled back to the rest of us.

Thelma was quick to follow and Edgar went right behind her. Still a scare-dee-cat, I stalled trying to figure out how to crawl down.

Grumbles from below drifted upward: "Shoot, Bessie make me sick." "She always spoiling the fun." "Let's leave her." "No. Grandpa might whip us." "Come on Bessie!" The last shout contained an undeniable threat. For fear of being left behind I stumbled into a blind leap.

"Oooooh! Ouch! Ouch!" The board fastened like a ski to the bottom right foot caused my whole body to twitch. A rusty nail in one of the planks had plunged into the sole, pushed between the bones and pierced the skin on top. The nail plugged a wound where blood should have been flowing.

"It hurrrts! Oooooh!" I screamed to the top of my lungs; but the wailing did not muffle the sound of metal scraping against bone as Nick tugged at the board. Once my foot was free, he carried me in his arms the mile back to Grandpa's house.

Electricity and telephones had not reached most homes of Blacks in East Texas in the mid-1950s. Grandpa had to saddle up the chestnut mare and ride to the general store to call Mama. By the afternoon she arrived to take me to the Charity Hospital back in Shreveport. Thelma and Edgar were angry and I was sad. Vacation had barely started before it ended.

As usual Edgar sat up front with Mama. Nick, who came along for a week's stay in the city, climbed into the back seat behind the driver. Thelma sat next to him and I took the other window seat in order to block anyone from bumping into my foot. While the car sped pass farmland, familiar ponds and fruit archers, Thelma and Nick poked at me because I had spoiled an entire summer.

"Lockjaw," Thelma said and the pain in my foot raced to throbbing.

"Yeah. Lockjaw," Nick echoed and added, "She gon' have a stiff leg."

They scared me real good but nothing was as shocking as Nick's next comment. "Aunt Tommie is pregnant," he announced with a want-to-be-grown smirk.

"No, she ain't!" I shot back.

"Yes, she is."

"My mama don't get pregnant. Your mama, Aunt Minnie and Aunt Emily get pregnant!" I named my mother's other two sister who, like Aunt Too-Too, had six or more children while Mama only had three.

"You'll see," he said with an air of superior wisdom.

"I'ma ask Mama when we get home," I ended the squabble and returned to the throbbing foot that held my attention for the rest of the ride back to the city.

We spent most of the night in the dingy Colored waiting room of the Charity Hospital. When the doctor finally looked at my foot, the pain was so bad I did not feel the stab of the needle as he said, "To protect against lockjaw."

I hobbled to the car leaning on Mama whose soothing words eased the pain. "I prayed for you through the whole thing," she said. "Everything is going to be okay. You won't have a stiff leg."

Next day, I asked straight out, "Mama, you pregnant?"

"Yes, I'm going to have a baby."

The skinny mother mistaken for my big sister is having a baby? Instantly, I pictured a huge belly trying to hide beneath, "A sloppy blouse!" I said.

"A maternity smock," she corrected.

"A sloppy blouse," I repeated and crossed the line of respectful conversation between mother and child. Maybe Mama let me get away with it because of my foot injury. I continued, "Can you stay out of sight? I don't want my classmates to see you."

Clearly, I was out of control but Mama answered with a chuckle, "I plan to go to work so you can eat."

With those sobering words, I shut my fresh mouth but moped around the house sulking and blaming Nick for bringing the bad news of a baby on the way. His visit to Shreveport zipped by and I was glad to see him go. At the same time, I was jealous of his return to the heavenly realm of Smithland, Texas. The remaining two months of summer were filled with anger over the shortened vacation; and grief over Mama's pregnancy. I acted like the family faced an imminent death rather than new life.

In the spring of 1955, my baby sister, Honorene, was born and silly notions that Nick or Mama had ruined my life flew right out the window. I fell under the spell of mesmerizing big beautiful eyes that followed my every move conveying unconditional love and confidence that she could depend on me.

With Honorene's birth, visits to Texas were reduced to holidays. The happy-go-lucky days of childhood had vanished but I had no regrets. Blissful summers were replaced by attempts to take good care of my baby sister. At the end of Mama's workday, I made sure she entered a clean house and that Honorene was bathed, powered, fed and sleeping peacefully. "Bessie, you're a good little helper," she would say. My chest pulsated with pride. Though wild and wonderful Texas summers lingered in my heart, caring for Honorene brought a new kind of delight.

Central Colored High School

Photo: close-up of salt shaker from Blake Collection of
Central High School memorabilia.

ᏣᎦ

$\mathcal{S}$*plendor* swept the landscape in a flurry of change.

In the fall of 1954, the national junior high school movement begun in the 1940s, finally reached shabby little Negro schools of Shreveport. Ordinarily, I would have gone directly from elementary into high school at grade nine. In an abrupt change, I was assigned a different school for seventh grade. Unaware of the historic nature of the transfer, I dreaded leaving Hollywood Elementary just when I was beginning to make friends.

Of all places, I was sent to the frightful neighborhood visited annually with my church family. Actually, all of the city's Churches of God in Christ assembled once a year in Holy Convocation at Whites Temple in Mooretown. Parents, pastors and church elders issued stern warnings to youth about fights, stabbings and generally sinful living in the area. They did not dare let us out of their sights.

On the first day of school in Mooretown, I braced myself for dangers that church elders had taught me to fear. I might have relaxed at the sight of the familiar sandlot schoolyard with a cluster of gray wooden buildings, but a skinny little girl was looking me up and down. I dared not return her stare but caught sidewise glimpses of her advancing on me. Shallow breaths did not calm the flutters in my heart.

"What's your name?" she asked.

She's trying to pick a fight, I thought but answered, "Bessie Waites." The fact is bullying was the last thing on her mind. It was her first day in a new school too; but she was spunky enough to reach out for friendship.

41

"What grade?" her questioning continued.

"Eighth." I said.

"Teacher?" I gave the name of a teacher I do not now recall; and a smile crossed the girl's face. The tightness in my chest eased. "What's your name?" I asked.

"Armanda Clarkson," she said. Within weeks, Armanda and I were fast friends forever. I also realized Mooretown was no less safe than Hollywood, Allendale, Cedar Grove or other Black communities—except maybe Stoner Hill and the Bottom.

After one term at Mooretown, the entire eighth grade transferred to a school back in my neighborhood of Hollywood. Joined by students from Little Hope Elementary School of Cedar Grove, we formed the first class to attend the brand new Union Street Junior High School.

As if someone had waved a magic wand, I stepped into the future. Two-room wooden school buildings were replaced by a sprawling one-story ranch-style brick structure nestled in a green meadow. Its three wings had spacious outdoor corridors called breezeways and the entire complex was framed by concrete sidewalks, and a paved parking lot.

Living directly across the street from the school presented bonuses for my family. Our entire block was upgraded during the school's construction. A paved street and sidewalk ran right pass our rundown shotgun house all the way to the corner bus stop. The concrete surfaces were magical new additions that eliminated the need to scrub tar and mud from white penny-loafers and black and white saddle oxfords.

Children lucky enough to live on the block also got a free unofficial roller skating rink. On weekends Thelma and bolder youth zipped along the breezeways at top speed. Daredevils raced down outdoor ramps leading to

42

brick walls. Sharp turns were made just before crashes occurred. Too cautious to risk scraped elbows and knees, I inched along never quite gaining enough speed to say that I was actually skating. Still, it was great fun.

Could anything be more fantastic than a new school building? Yes! Come autumn, football—the ultimate thrill in sports—arrived with all the trappings. On game day, the team, the band, the cheerleaders took to the playing field dressed in dazzling royal blue and white outfits. I sat in the stands with the booster squad wearing my white sweater and baby blue pleated wool skirt. With royal blue and white pom-poms in hand, I shouted, "Go Eagles!"

My heart lifted with each beat as the band played classical parade anthems. Dressed like a toy soldier, the drum major twirled his baton. Majorettes followed closed behind swishing short skirts and frilly gold tassels on the front of white cowboy boots. The pageantry of the sport rocked my world.

$\mathcal{I}$ was more excited than the average student. Prior to the opening of Union Street Junior High, I had been inside only two types of brick buildings: dress shops like the one where I could not try on clothes before I purchased them; and the ranch style homes my mother cleaned as a maid. So enchanting was my new brick school that the 1954 Brown v Board of Education desegregation decision almost slipped by without my noticing. Though jolts of the U. S. Supreme Court ruling must have been felt by adults in the neighborhood, no explanations were given concerning the rapid changes in my life.

Little by little, bits and snatches of hushed conversations drifted from women who huddled after church: "All deliberate speed, hump!" an elderly sister grumbled. Then, the perplexing phrase, "separate but unequal," floated my way. The fact that I had been attending "unequal" schools was a surprise to me. Until I entered junior high school, I thought all school children attended little wooden buildings.

Over time, I heard rising frustration in the women's voices. They murmured: "We don't want our children to go 'cross town to their schools." "My child don't have to sit next to a White kid to learn." "Just give us the same as them." "We gon' lose our Black teachers with this hinh integration." "How they gon' teach somebody they don't love?"

Integration! What does that mean? My continuing fascination with words caused me to look the term up in the dictionary. Under "Integrate," I read, "unity, oneness, and togetherness." That did not seem bad to me but the women's complaints piled up.

"We gon' lose a lot of other jobs too; you wait and see." "White people gon' be scrubbing the school floors before this thing is over. They'll give it some fancy name and take those jobs." "You sho' right." "Not enough jobs as it is." "We don't need to be losing jobs."

Something big was happening but parents and teachers never spoke openly. Even our pastors—the most respected leaders in the community and the sources of all good news—were quiet about the huge changes. So, information of behind-the-scenes integration activities never reached me. I relied on developments that unfolded in plain sight. New school buildings popped up in Black neighborhoods throughout the city. Within two years, my sister, brother and I were transferred from over-crowded frame buildings to modern school facilities.

Edgar went to the new brick Hollywood Elementary School in Bellaire—a low income housing complex built in the community. Thelma, who had spent the fall semester at Booker T. Washington, was transferred back to Union Street to complete the ninth grade before returning to high school in her tenth year. As for me, I was assigned to Union Street Junior High School for the spring term of grade eight and stayed through ninth grade.

The shuffling of students from school to school and neighborhood to neighborhood must have been crazy for parents and teachers, but they showed no signs of stress. If adults in my life were aware of legal steps to secure equal educational opportunities, not a word of it reached my ears. For me, attendance at Union Street Junior High School was a delightful surprise, like a giant Christmas present in bright foil wrapping.

*T*here was nothing stormy or stressful about studying in a spanking new brick school. A dignity was breathed into life that said I had left the cotton fields of Gilliam. Teachers emerged from shadowy back regions of my mind and challenged me to rise above my circumstances. This increased awareness of teachers can be traced, in part, to the modern setting in which I studied; but there was a less obvious source of the shift in my attitude.

Bustling from one classroom to the next, I realized the flaw was not in teachers; it was in me. My family lived like nomads. Though we remained in Hollywood, by junior high school my Shreveport address changed six times in five years. Such instability created a restlessness that put me at odds with a schedule that required sitting all day in one classroom. In elementary school I felt trapped. It was hard to focus on teachers and their lessons when all I wanted was to get up and get moving.

The opposite was true in junior high school. When the bell signaled, the merriment of movement whizzed along airy corridors. I floated from Math, to Social Studies, from Science to Language Arts. During the changing of classes, I inhaled fresh air and exhaled bottled up tension. The flurry of students between classes matched the seesaw pattern of my life outside of school and had a calming effect on my day. Every hour or so, I got a break from the droning of one teacher's voice and arrived at the next class ready to pay attention.

Of course, my interest was not always on my studies. With the sweet smell of honeysuckles drifting through an open classroom window, I swooned over my eighth grade math teacher. Mr. Holt was light-skinned, freckle-faced, sandy-haired and short; but to me he was tall, tan and handsome. From the desk of my first period class, I watched him zoom into the sun-drenched parking lot and bounce from his fancy car. In a short sleeve shirt, dress slacks and shiny shoes, he strolled into the building. *Boy was he cool!*

More than cool, Mr. Holt knew his Math and he knew how to reach students. With a talent for making difficult problems simple, he coaxed, "Relax. Multiplication is just rapid addition." Immediately, the problem seemed small enough to solve. Other times, humorous word-problems, with student names inserted, contributed to the liveliness of his classroom.

Two junior high school friends recently praised Mr. Holt. Minnie V. (Lee) Fontenot described him as an excellent teacher who "talked to us on our level. You know, he joked around with us but he was determined that we would learn."

Armanda Clarkson added, "He sometimes went to classes where a student excelled in the subject and got permission from that teacher to tutor them in Math for a few minutes. After several sessions, one student told him, 'Mr. Holt, I still don't understand.' He answered, 'That's okay. Some of us never do;' and he continued to tutor the student until Math became her best subject." That was Mr. Holt. Students fell in love with him and with his beloved Mathematics.

Though we took her class in different periods, Mrs. Walker taught ninth grade Language Arts to Minnie V., Armanda and me. "Strikingly beautiful," they said but I could not picture her. What I remember is her lasting influence on my life.

Mrs. Walker introduced me to project learning and team work. Small groups of students created charts that demonstrated how words developed into sentences and paragraphs. In addition to being a pushover for the written word since age five, I loved the class because we were active learners who discussed topics among ourselves instead of addressing all our answers to the teacher. The room had an orderly buzz. Quiet muttering of ideas electrified the environment. Groups of four chatted and then moved out of our seats to tack completed team projects on the bulletin boards. Mrs. Walker's two-hour class period always ended too soon.

Ninth grade is most remembered, however, for the loyal friendships that developed. Armanda, Minnie V. and I became an inseparable trio. Though our only time to socialize was during the lunch period, strong bonds formed while the three of us ate, whispered about crushes on teachers or football players and giggled away the minutes. My newfound friends also stood with me and against any threatening classmates; and they encouraged me when I told sad stories about my home life. At dismissal, *no lollygagging around the building after school* was an unwritten but strictly enforced rule. Armanda rushed back to Mooretown; Minnie V. headed home to Cedar Grove; and I strolled across the street to a rundown house for all to see.

Ninth grade is also the year, Mrs. Walker chose me for the leading role in the spring play. Set in the drab kitchen of a poor family, the plot was centered on the life of a shy girl who dressed in rags and had little food at home. The dialogue was heart wrenching and I loved it. Practicing the lines reminded me of pre-school days when words took on physical form and lived in the world. Equally as enjoyable was rehearsal time spent in a spacious nearly empty school building away from the crammed three-room apartment where I live with six family members.

As we prepared for the big event, my thoughts often strayed to images of pastors, teachers, parents and students all assembled in one place to see us perform. "Ignore the audience," Mrs. Walker coached, "Just listen for the cues from one another. You'll be fine!" After a few weeks of rehearsal, the minute I stepped on stage nothing and no one existed but my fellow actors. When the curtain rose on opening night, I got lost in character. At the end of the play, the cast held hands, bowed, and bathed in the applause of our community.

Delighting in my moment of stardom, I sailed out of the auditorium on a euphoric cloud of possibilities. On the way home, I overheard a parent praise my performance as "Terrific! She is going to..."

Yes! I'm going to be an act...

"That wasn't acting. She IS poor!" her son silenced the mother's praise and smothered my dream while it was still forming.

For weeks afterwards, I was haunted by a play that has since lost its title. Nagging questions caused me to wonder whether I was chosen for the leading role because I lived right across the street from school and was available for rehearsals. Or, was it something more disturbing? Did Mrs. Walker pick me in order to solve a wardrobe problem? After all, I was already dressed for the part. Or, could it be she had seen a hidden talent in me others had not noticed? I could not be sure.

It would take decades to realize how shifting the blame away from personal circumstances and onto my teacher was an unfair but typical response. The same is true today: many societal ills are placed at the feet of teachers. Either our first teacher, our mother, or some poor teacher at school is blamed for all kinds of failings. In junior high school my anxieties were not the making of Mrs. Walker. She was a teacher who cared enough to volunteer after her workday ended. She provided programs that enriched my life. She was not responsible for my poverty, but I buried her memory as painful and moved on.

At the end of ninth grade, I was promoted to high school. In 1950s Shreveport, every academic milestone was not celebrated. No kindergarten "moving-up" ceremonies and elementary or junior high school graduations were held. Educators were skeptical about creating illusions of success. They pushed students to keep their eyes on the "real graduation" that would occur at the completion of high school.

Though I left without fanfare, I enjoyed almost everything about Union Junior High School. It is the place where a positive attitude toward learning was revived. A splendid school setting, magnificent teachers, and good friends defied the "storm and stress" of adolescence.

My first day of high school was an eye-opener. I followed Thelma into the corner store across from the bus stop. She purchased a five-cent dill pickle from the jar on the counter; jammed the wooden stick of a strawberry lollypop down its center; wrapped the sweet and sour treat in a small brown paper bag; and slid it into her pocket. She was a junior in high school and knew the ropes. So I prepared my pickle too. We smelled like vinegar when we boarded the city bus but one nibble on the juicy treat and the odor did not matter. Besides, most of the students had a little brown paper bag with a pickle to last them throughout the day.

For half an hour the bus weaved in and out of *have-not* and *have-even-less* neighborhoods of poor Whites and Blacks. At the last stop on the top of the hill in Lakeside, Thelma and I changed buses for the short ride down Milam Street. She pointed out large homes that belonged to "Negro" doctors, lawyers, ministers and teachers. Before I could absorb the economic status suggested by such housing, she announced, "We here."

I stepped off the bus in front of a little whitewashed hamburger shop with a sign that invited me in for a frosty coke float. My stomach grumbled but I turned away; and, in complete majesty, the absolute best school in Shreveport stood before me. Though Bird and Fair Park high schools enrolled Whites only, neither matched the grandeur of Booker T. Washington.

I had been wrong in thinking that Union Street Junior High School was the first and only brick building for children who looked like me. Not only did my high school exceed the splendor of my junior high school, it had been built five years earlier. The construction of Booker T. Washington was completed in 1949 and its doors had opened to students in 1950.

A special edition entitled, "U. S. Schools," published October 16, 1950 in *Life Magazine*, applauded Booker T. Washington High School as one of the most modern schools in the country. The capture beneath a photograph of the expansive building described career and technical shops with cutting edge features costing $1.5 million to build and $230,000 to equip and furnish.

Seven years after its opening, the majestic structure rested gracefully on a sloping hill that glided to a football field with half-moon seating. Once inside the school building, I marveled at novelties such as central heating, florescent lighting, moveable classroom desks, and individual hallway lockers for students. The facility rivaled many of the nation's small colleges of the period.

How was it I did not know about the grandest building in the Black community? On the way home, I asked Thelma, "Why didn't you tell me our school is so pretty?"

"I guess it's alright," she brushed me off and went to sit with one of her friends.

When I got home Mama answered my questions. "Well," she said, "since getting off that Gilliam plantation in 1949, I've been busy finding places to live and a way to feed you. I haven't had time to talk to you about whether or not there were brick schools for you to attend. However," she continued, "it was rumored that the city fathers built Booker T. Washington High School in an attempt to get ahead of a court decision requiring Black and White children to study together. I don't know whether that's true or not." Then, she startled me, "Shreveport has a history of brick school buildings for Negroes. I knew before we left East Texas about Central. It was a high school for colored where students came from surrounding Louisiana parishes and nearby East Texas counties. They lived in boarding houses in Shreveport in order to attend the pioneering institution. Some of my teachers back in Smithland attended Central."

Years later I learned more about Central's history from Armanda who, after college, taught in the two-story red brick building. Her sources revealed the school was constructed as the city's first high school for African Americans back in 1917. For nearly thirty years, the institution fulfilled a mission of improving the social and economic condition of Blacks through education. Despite neglect during the two world wars, Central awarded hundreds of diplomas. After World War II, mounting complaints from the community about overcrowding and terrible learning conditions influenced Shreveport's participation in a national movement to improve schools. As a result, Booker T. Washington High School admitted its first students in the spring of 1950; and, Central Colored High School closed after the fall term of 1949.

Eventually, Central reopened, but as a junior high and then an elementary school. Armanda, a retired teacher who still lives in Shreveport, said last she heard the sturdy red brick building now houses within the African American community some services of the city's Board of Education as well as an archive of the school's rich history. In 1991, Central Colored High School was recorded in the National Register of Historical Places; and, in 2015, Booker T. Washington High School was added to the listing.

Amazing! In 1954 when I entered junior high, I knew nothing about the history of Central; nor did I anticipate high school years in a facility that would surpass the splendor of my beloved Union Street Junior High School.

B̰e somebody! Lift yourself! Lift the race!

"Make every child's potential a reality." A battle cry rooted in the ideas of Booker T. Washington and W. E. B. Dubois was my high school's motto. Early in the twentieth century, the educational philosophers debated whether equality for African Americans was best achieved through training in industrial trades—put forth by Washington; or, academic preparation leading to college degrees and professional careers—promoted by Dubois. When at the fork in the road carved by the two great thinkers, my high school chose both paths; and, in doing so, expanded options for students. However, we all rallied around the name, Booker T. Washington, and fondly referred to our school as BTW or simply Booker T.

Language Arts had been my favorite subject in junior high school; and, I arrived at Booker T in 1957 expecting another highly interactive class where words come alive. Unfortunately, my sophomore English teacher's passive style of instruction dulled the senses and dampened my enthusiasm for learning. My notebook rapidly filled with spelling and vocabulary words to be memorized and used in sentences. Even more dreadful were the two required compositions that year. In the fall term, the topic was, "What did you do on your summer vacation?" I wanted to scrawl across the blank page, *Nothing! Mama didn't have any money;* but I patched together scattered recollections of previous summers in

East Texas. My pointless writing never rose to the level of an essay, but I handed it in anyway.

The second assignment, "Write your autobiography," was even worse. Without any instruction on writing a composition, I jotted down what I considered the important facts of my life.

> *I, Bessie Lorene Waites, was born in 1943 to Edgar Eugene Waites and Tommie Martin Waites. I have two sisters and two brothers. They are named Thelma, Edgar, Honorene, and Stanford. I live on Clanton Street in Hollywood...*

On I rambled. The miserable draft was insufficient for a paragraph, not to mention an essay. It was promptly returned with spelling and grammar corrected in red. I left my sophomore English class feeling that words, my cherished friends since preschool, had betrayed me. I also pondered whether my elderly teacher had stayed too long in the classroom.

Lucky for me, skills in various trades were emphasized at Booker T. In an effort to increase graduates' chances of getting jobs that paid living wages, shop classes such as Woodworking, Auto Mechanics, and Dry Cleaning thrived alongside academic subjects like English, History, Mathematics and Science. Shop classes held my attention for a short period but my love of learning might have died had it not been for my mother's example.

Mama earned her diploma in night school at Booker T; and then enrolled in the first class of Black nurses in Shreveport. While completing her clinical rounds at the city's Confederate Memorial Hospital, she coped with my father's alcoholic outbursts; took in washing and ironing in order to feed and shelter our family; and, provided Christian counseling to patients on the polio ward where she was assigned as a student nurse.

I studied Mama as she studied her lessons. In the face of hardships, she encouraged herself: "Don't have a pity party." "Pick yourself up and keep moving." "Why linger here and rust? I'd rather wear out trying." Most impressive among her watchwords was, "Tomorrow is coming no matter what. If I don't give up and keep pressing, I'll be in a better place when tomorrow gets here."

Armed with words of encouragement and actions that spoke even louder, Mama's behavior commanded, *Focus! Discipline Yourself! Expect Success!* She earned the highest score in her class on the Louisiana State Boards for nursing. After graduation she went to work fulltime on the polio ward at the hospital. On a nurse's salary she purchased a home in the newly developed Hollywood Heights subdivision where our family finally settled after living in eleven locations over an eight-year period. What was the secret of my mother's success? She simply blocked out surrounding noise and concentrated on her goals.

In the 1950s, rising cases of polio created public panic. Like AIDs in the 1980s and the COVID19 pandemic of the 2020s, scientists knew little about the causes of the disease and its spread. People feared contact with polio patients, but not my mother. In a Christian gesture, she introduced Thelma and me to two teenage boys who spent most of the day in huge iron lungs that groaned and hissed each breath exhaled. James and Leon never had visitors and Mama appealed to her daughters for compassion. In her usual match-making fashion, she paired me with James, the younger of the two, and Thelma with Leon.

"You got the handsome one," Thelma said. Once she started visiting Leon she grumbled, "He don' think he's handicapped; always asking for a kiss."

"Did you kiss him," I asked.

"Naw, girl. How he gon' kiss somebody. The iron lung covers him up to his neck and he talks to me through the mirror over his head. Wait! Once I kissed him on the forehead 'cause he looked so sad. But, when he wears a chest respirator and starts talking about kissing, I tell him, 'I'm out of here!' "

James was the exact opposite of Leon. He was shy and timid. We barely communicated because I was bashful too. I sat in a chair near the crown of his head and, while watching television, we glanced at each other through the mirror. Finally, he mustered enough nerves to invite me on a date. At age fourteen, it was my first date.

"How will we do that?" I asked.

He answered, "The hospital will work it out."

James and I went to a football game at the Fair Grounds. Nurses and aides took him out of the iron lung, strapped a chest respirator on him and wheeled him into an ambulance along with a giant machine I thought was an oxygen tank. I climbed in and took a seat beside him. It was a smooth ride without sirens or any commotion. Once on the field, the ambulance parked near the end zone. I do not recall bands playing, teams squaring off or conversation between the two of us. All I remember is sitting with the back doors of the ambulance open; a cool evening breeze; and, the whistling rhythm of James' breathing. I wondered why he had not been protected against polio by the little sip of cool-aide tasting vaccine I had been given in elementary school.

Our date ended with the ambulance ride back to the hospital where I waited for Mama to finish her shift. Regular visits with James lasted throughout my sophomore year. Eventually we chatted about favorite school subjects. I shared interesting books and sometimes read to him; and his talks about sports always led to football.

Ours was a brief friendship with a lasting effect. With James, I learned to comfort people who face near-death situations. It is like I was given a gift. From my teens until now, friends, coworkers and people I barely know share the most heart-wrenching details of health conditions. The amazing thing is God always surrounds me with peace that surpasses understanding; directs the tone and tenor of interactions during difficulties; and sometimes uses me to ease the final transition.

A more immediate effect of friendship with James was the opportunity to watch my mother at work. Her enthusiasm for nursing and ministering to others inspired me to *make something of myself* so that I could help her. While the job at the hospital was a goal realized, the grueling work paid little and financial burdens still weighed heavy on my mother. If I made something of myself as teachers were always stressing, maybe Mama could work eight instead of sixteen hours a day. Following her lead, I decided to block out the noise and strive for a better future. The behavior of peers and the occasional lousy teacher faded in importance.

While the possibility of domestic and other blue collar jobs were not overlooked, teachers at Booker T drummed into students, "To be a professional, you have to be better than the children across town." I wanted to be a professional but the nagging question was, What *job?*

My most visible role models were nurses and teachers, but neither job was attractive. My knowledge of nursing consisted of observations of sixteen-hour shifts that left my mother with a sore back as she struggled to keep the family in our new home. *Not the job for me!* Teaching was a more likely choice but, no way could Mama pay for the required college education. Besides, I wanted a more glamorous job than teaching or nursing.

Like a typical teenage girl of the late 1950s, my career choice was all about fashion. During the second term of my sophomore year, I got an overnight job tending an elderly woman in a White neighborhood. Mornings, on my way to school, I boarded a bus of stylishly clad women headed to downtown office jobs. They wore high heels, tailored suits, flower-trimmed hats and carried cute little purses in gloved hands. I sat toward the rear of the bus, but heard their chatter about clerical tasks, break times around the coffee pot, and lunches at fancy restaurants. The more I listened, the more I imagined myself in Sunday best on my way to work as a secretary. Daydreams filled daily rides to school though deep down I knew the doors to downtown office jobs were closed to "Negro girls."

It was not an intentional act. It was the way she pranced onto the bus, ponytail bouncing from side to side and stood over me. I was sitting on the front seat lost in my *I-am-a-secretary* fantasy when my temperature shot up like mercury in a glass thermometer. *She's a teenager like me; why should I give up my seat? I'm not moving.* Dizzy with anger, I fumed.

The rousing horseplay of children returning home from school rumbled to dead silence. The driver closed the door but did not pull away from the bus stop. I stared straight ahead but caught sight from the corner of my eye of a blurry image of red and yellow as blood surged just beneath the skin up the girl's neck, over her face and disappeared beneath a carpet of blond hair. Nervously, she shifted her weight from one foot to the other as the driver turned in his seat to glare at me. I did not move.

"Nigggger!" he drawled. "Git yourself back yonder!" His beefy arm jutted toward the back of the bus.

A voice drifted up the aisle in a near whisper, "Girl, it's your sister."

In a split second, Thelma was wagging her finger under my nose and hurling threats. "Bessie, you better get out of that seat. Now!" she ordered with the authority of a big sister accustomed to obedience. I never lifted my eyes to meet hers.

I was a loner except when I was with my best friends, Armanda and Minnie V., who both travelled different bus routes to and from school. Thelma never sat with me. She was feisty, popular and mixed with the lively crowd. The minute we boarded the bus on Milam Street, she always headed for the long noisy rear seat in the very back. I sat alone on the seat just behind the driver.

On our way to and from Booker T, we crossed the Greenwood Road within blocks of Fair Park, a White high school. Yet, there was no concern about racial incidents. School-day "Specials" gave the false impression that Jim Crow bus laws had been temporarily suspended. Staggered citywide dismissal schedules were supposed to ensure a lack of contact between White and Black students. In a city the size of Shreveport, an hour difference in arrivals and dismissals was more than enough time to keep the two races separated. During those short heavenly commutes, the "Specials" belonged to Black students. Or, so I thought.

What is she doing here? She should have been gone! I sat motionless, in the motionless bus, with the fidgeting White girl waiting for my seat.

"You hear me Bessie? You better get up!" Thelma scolded, as fearful murmurs crept among the once merry bunch at the back of the bus. "You lost your mind?" she asked in complete frustration.

No, I was not crazy. Things had never been clearer. I was in the right place at the right time. The girl standing over me was wrong. At that hour of the day, I had more right to *my seat* than she did, *didn't I?*

"Sit down!" The driver ordered Thelma. "I'll git the police at Hollywood." He roared away from the curb with a lurch.

"You sho' gon' get it. Wait 'til I tell Mama," Thelma mumbled as she stumbled back to her seat.

My sister's threat and the bus driver's anger meant nothing. The do or die situation caused by my behavior did not enter my mind. A series of indignities were colliding in my head. There were laws that dictated where I sat, where I ate, and whether or not I took a sip of water from the nearest fountain when thirsty. The laws even required me to draw an outline of my foot on a piece of cardboard for the shoe size before I made a purchase.

Gripped by a sense of injustice, I sat glued to my seat clueless about the possibility of truly awful consequences. Had I been worried at all, it would have been about disobeying an adult. In 1958, the unwritten rule of most Black households in America was: *Children, respect your elders!* It did not matter whether the adult was right or wrong, Black or White. We obeyed and, if need be, grown-ups settled differences later. Determined to maintain the dignity afforded on daily rides to and from school, I was disobeying the basic rule that governed adult-child relationships.

Still, I had never felt more peaceful. In the middle of the commotion, I heard Grandma saying: *Right is right. Wrong is wrong, and right don't wrong nobody.* It was not right that I should give up my seat to someone my own age—especially since she had sauntered onto the bus late and laid claim to what was mine for only two hours of the day. It was wrong and I was not moving.

I never considered not making it home that day. There were no Black or women police officers within the city limits. White males—an officer and the bus driver, would decide how to teach me a lesson.

Being the *scare-de-cat* that I was, I should have been terrified but was unruffled. I wondered about the policeman who was a school-day fixture at the corner of Hollywood Avenue and Jewella Road. *What was his role?* Was he like a school crossing guard at the busy intersection? Or, did he keep the peace in Mooretown—the neighborhood I had once believed was a rough place? I had no idea what the policeman might do when he boarded the bus; but a vague notion that the response would not be good began to churn in my stomach.

The driver screeched to a halt at the intersection that he usually breezed right through. When he jerked the handle to open the front door, all eyes were on me. My eyes were glued to the front steps of the bus waiting for the policeman to climb aboard but there was a delay. I lifted my head and strained my neck to peer outside. The driver got out of his seat and he too scanned the intersection. The policeman was nowhere in sight. The bus driver was livid. He bounced back into his seat, yanked the door shut and waited for the green light. We were in for a ride!

The signal changed. The driver swerved left onto Hollywood Avenue. The bus zigzagged. I braced myself for skidding, scraping metal and breaking glass. It was a miracle the vehicle did not crash; but the wild ride was just beginning. Like a demon out of hell, the driver seemed bent on killing us all. He sped down a steep hill, through an under path, and barely missed the concrete wall that separated us from on-coming traffic. The Black students screamed to the tops of their lungs. I held onto my seat. Still standing, the girl was flung back and forth like a rag doll as she gripped the slippery metal pole nearest the front door. She would have been better off, had she taken the empty seat across from or even next to me.

After five minutes of reckless weaving and bobbing, the bus came to a halt to let the blonde off at her stop. Then, I pulled the cord. The next stop was mine. As I waited to cross the street, the other teen glared at me from a block away. When the light changed, we walked parallel lines into separate neighborhoods—hers White, mine Black. A concrete man-made ditch divided our two communities.

Thelma rushed ahead shouting angrily, "You could'a got us all killed!"

I ignored my sister. I did not even beg, *Pleeease don't tell Mama!* All my energy went to getting ready for the beating that waited. It was a slow walk the two blocks to the house.

Mama met me on the porch. "Girl what possessed you?" she asked.

"I don't nome." Fear had dredged up my deep Delta dialect.

After the longest pause, she chuckled, looked me straight in the eyes and said, "Well, don't do it again."

"Yas-sum." Again, I responded, in the dialect natural to field hands.

The magnitude of my mother's restraint was not wasted on me. A stern reprimand followed by a beating was in order. I had committed a major infraction of household and societal rules. In an era when racial oppression was suffered in near silence, I was expected to cooperate with the unfair practices of segregation. Fearful whisperings circulated in the community about loss of jobs, brutal beatings and even loss of life when eyes were cast in the wrong direction. People who spoke out on issues or who "sassed" a White person by talking back could mysteriously disappear. Caution was taken at church, at school, and at home if visitors were not the closest relatives. Angry words leaked from private dwellings could provoke the power of the state or arouse a hateful vigilante group. It was best to keep quiet and stay in line.

By refusing to give up my seat, I had stepped way out of line. The little chuckle from Mama as she said, "Well, don't do it again," spoke volumes about her quiet support of my behavior; but her tone said, *You lucky to be alive.*

Had I been dragged off that bus and taken to jail, it would have destroyed me. For purposes well beyond my understanding at the time, I survived the incident. By the grace of God, I emerged with a determination to break through the walls of segregation that separated me from a job of dignity. To succeed, I would have to study harder than ever.

Power Teacher

Miss Mae Etta Scott, pictured here with her American History class, also served as Senior Advisor for BTW class of 1960 (Photo: BTW Loin Yearbook, 1959).

$\mathcal{P}$*ower teachers* tackle the twin ills of poverty and racism that snare career goals in tangled roots.

In my junior year, such teachers revived my joy of learning. Ironically, renewed enthusiasm for academic subjects started with a loathing of history. It was not Mr. Webb's fault. The jovial little man who maintained a lively American History classroom was not boring; the required study material was boring. Endless reading assignments omitted African American contributions to the building of the country. Short passages on slavery with pin and ink sketches showed "coloreds" in shackles or in fields with their backs bent. The mockery of the readings was increased by used books sent to Booker T with the markings of White students scribbled throughout.

In an odd way, the distortions of history fanned my passion for reading. In order to get through homework, I pretended the assignments were short stories and fairy tales. In this manner, I waded through a version of the American past that could, in part, be described as "fictional." History textbooks had characterized my ancestors as dirty, stinking, lazy and dumb "primitives from the dark continent of Africa." It was hard to take lessons serious that were filled with such lies. How could you call a people lazy who labored in hot fields from sunup to sundown?

I had firsthand knowledge of my ancestor's brilliance. My grandfather, born twelve years after the end of slavery, was an avid reader. He told stories of how his parents learned to read while still in bondage. Under the brutal conditions of slavery my great grandfather learned to read and also had the ingenuity to teach my great grandmother. A person who is clever enough to learn and teach reading under the threat of death certainly is not dumb.

Sadly, distortions of the nation's history persist in textbooks today. I read Tanya Basu's 2015 article about a ninth grader who complained to his parents that African Americans were described in his textbook as immigrants who came to America seeking work. When I read the story, I bristled: *My great grandparents and their great grandparents were not immigrants. I am the proud descendant of Africans brought to these shores in chains; and who survived roughly two-hundred and fifty years of legal slavery in which they were considered property.* The textbook incident is a twenty-first century reminder that parents need to monitor the content and images projected in their children's schoolwork.

Thankfully, back in the fifties Mr. Webb balanced the version of history recorded in textbooks with brief profiles of Blacks who had left large footsteps in American history. In one digression from school board requirements, he distributed a mimeographed paper damp with purple ink. I held it to my nose and inhaled the cool mossy smell before reading, "Mary McLeod Bethune, an educator and activist for civil rights and child welfare from 1904 until her death in 1955." I paused and thought, *Oh! She died three years ago.* At that moment, a history close enough to touch sprang to life. My studies were no longer populated solely by people alien to my experience.

I was awestruck that a Black female born in 1875— barely a decade after slavery—had reached unimaginable heights in society. In 1904, Dr. Bethune founded the institute that became Bethune-Cookman College. She established and served as president of the National

Council of Negro Women. What astounded me, though, was her influence on national policy during the terms of several United States Presidents. She was a participant in Calvin Coolidge's conference on child welfare; a member of Herbert Hoover's Commission on Home Building and Home Ownership; and, as special advisor to Franklin D. Roosevelt, she was also Director of the Division of Negro Affairs as well as the Director of the National Youth Administration. Finally, she was a member of Harry Truman's committee on national security.

By handing out a one-page biographical sketch, Mr. Webb provided my first knowledge of an African American who had had a powerful effect on the history of our country. I doubted I could ever inhale the refined air of Dr. Bethune. Her achievements did motivate, however, an interest in reading more about the lives of Black people. I became an avid reader of *The Shreveport Sun*—the city's African American weekly newspaper.

While Mr. Webb kept me scrambling for historical facts about my heritage, the eleventh grade English teacher, Mrs. Geneva L. Smith, fed my literary appetite. Required readings included two Shakespeare plays, *Julius Caesar* and *Romeo and Juliet;* and two novels, *Up the Down Staircase* by Bel Kaufman and *Main Street* by Sinclair Lewis. The novels held my attention because they painted familiar scenes and modern situations; but I loved the works of Shakespeare. His plays stirred emotions previously aroused by the Romantic Poets I had read at age ten. Still, the most fascinating authors on the reading list were: James Weldon Johnson, who penned the Negro National Anthem, *Lift Every Voice and Sing*; and Phillis Wheatley, an enslaved African poet with whom I was especially taken.

Though I knew my people were smart, I had never heard of an enslaved or any other American woman who had written anything worthy of publishing. It was exciting to open my high school English textbook to a poem with the caption, "Phillis Wheatley, A Slave Girl."

Mrs. Smith did not tell students that Phillis Wheatley had toured England with her books back when George Washington was president; nor did our class discuss the historical significance of the poet's achievements during an era when our people were forbidden by law to read or write. Despite the absence of classroom discussions of the life and times of Phillis Wheatley, the simple inscription acknowledging the author's enslavement was enough to fan embers from Ms. Wheatley's flame that smoldered in my heart for a very long time.

Mrs. Smith was a stern instructor who left little room for dialogue. We students digested assigned readings and recalled the substance of texts in oral recitations, multiple choice exams or in occasional written summaries of passages to test our reading comprehension. The fun of her class was found in visits to the school library where we checked out books of our choosing and read for simple pleasure.

Joyful excursions to the library fed my hunger for the written word but I was unaware that a person could make a living from writing. As far as I knew, books were free, second hand or borrowed from school libraries. The only other familiar publications—comic books, romance magazines and newspapers—sold for five to twenty-five cents a copy. I thought, *Not exactly money-makers! Who can live off that?* I stuck with the more practical goal of becoming a secretary. Nevertheless, I left eleventh grade with a burning desire to write like the authors whose books I read in Mrs. Smith's English class.

*I*nstead of essay writing, sentence structure dominated my last year of high school. When it came to the almighty sentence, my senior year English teacher was a demolition expert. Miss Nelson would write a sentence on the blackboard and, laboring to understand its structure, we students tore it apart word for word. We toiled while she strutted around the room with busty chest jutted out, slim hips swaggering, and a yardstick in hand, ready to strike. With any failure to pay attention or give a correct answer, the ruler landed across the offending student's desk and the entire class jumped. Though she never hit anyone, all feared that she might. In an atmosphere of extreme tension, Miss Nelson taught Diagraming Sentences—a method of learning the parts of speech and how words in a sentence relate to one another.

The drills were relentless. Moving from simple to compound and then to complex and compound-complex sentences, we drew diagrams that identified how subjects, verbs and objects related to one another. Advanced drawings showed how adjectives, adverbs, preposition and conjunctions related to subjects, verbs and objects. By the end of my senior year, I had an in-depth understanding of the grammatical structure of the English language.

Ironically, my perfectly constructed sentences were never used in a single essay. Yet, Miss Nelson's gift was a precious one. She laid a strong foundation in grammar that has served me well in all sorts of situations. Whether at home or at school, whether with friends or family or job supervisors, today I am still sought after to proofread, edit and review the writings of others.

I emerged from Miss Nelson's class a more logical thinker. Matter of fact, while still in her class, I began to realize that effectively crafting words in relation to one another determines who governs the circumstances of life. For example, I took a closer look at the phrase "separate but equal" and saw how it was intended to put a positive spend on segregation. I understood, as well, how integration with "all deliberate speed" was double talk because the phrase literally meant *nothing but unhurried slow speed.*

My last semester of high school was in the first year of the turbulent 1960s. Later in the decade, I would ponder buzz words that reshaped the image of Blacks in society. By adding the noun, "power," to the racial designation, "Black," the image of a "helpless people" would be strengthened when Stokely Carmichael shouted, "Black power!" Likewise, by using a simple everyday conjunction, James Brown converted two simple sentences into the anthem, "I'm Black *and* I'm Proud."

Because of Miss Nelson, I also took note of how each generation in my family had attempted to gain greater control over their lives by shedding limiting societal labels. My great grandparents were branded "slaves" by their masters; my grandparents were called "field hands" on tenant farms; my parents were considered "colored" during World War II; and, I was called a Negro during the Korean War.

However, in 1960 I was beginning to embrace a self-determination movement in which I would be called "Black" though the term summoned an endless list of negative images. At the same time, a more positive identity was surfacing. By joining two words, "African" and "American," previously separated cultures seemed to unite. Until this day, I use "Black" and "African American" alternately. Who knows what will evolve as the search continues for the right combination of words to describe the African's experience in America? The impact of experience and learning on identity eventually produces new ways to describe oneself.

What I do know for certain is: my twelfth-year English class caused me to reflect on the power words have to determine one's standing in society. Though I would never have done so back then, I now salute Miss Nelson for the miserable year I spent diagraming sentences. In addition to introducing me to the structure of the English language and the power of words in the right combination, she proved that learning need not be fun. In a class where I was scared to death, I acquired a good eye for details and my overall grade point average spiked from C to B+.

If by chance you love words the way I do, Google, "diagramming sentences."

BTW teachers were a close nit group. When other instructors heard of my progress in English, they said I was a "late bloomer." Like the radiant colors of Chrysanthemums in late autumn, my steady academic progress blossomed in my senior year.

My Geometry teacher, Miss Theola B. Pryor, was a petite and shapely woman with a barbed haircut. The boys in the class would have drooled over her had she not been a strict no-nonsense disciplinarian. In Geometry there was no talking, no passing notes and no spit balls. I delighted in the use of musical sounding words like perpendicular that showed how lines intersect to form right angles; or in the knowledge that parallel lines stretched into infinity without ever intersecting. Analytical skills gained in Miss Nelson's English class were useful in sensing the logic of Geometry axioms such as, "Things which are equal to the same thing are equal to one another."

By the end of the fall term, I was seated at the table with Math whiz kids—all boys—and given work in Algebra. Though I have lost many of the specifics of mathematical axioms and equations, my aptitude for figures and budgets can be traced to the fundamentals taught by Miss Pryor.

My reputation as a smart student quickly reached church where Sister Anderson, the pastor's wife—herself a public school teacher, praised my academic achievements. In a teen-talk with young women on the value of a good education, she embarrassed me to no end. She dramatized her point by saying, "You fast little girls; you think you know something. You think it's what you got from here down." Then, in a quick gesture, her hand started at the waist and swept down toward the floor. "You ought to be like Bessie Waites," she continued but, this time, her hand swept upward from the waist to the head, "Bessie Waites got it from here up!"

Nooooo..., I groaned inwardly and wanted to scream, *Sister Anderson, Bessie Waites has it from here down,"* then zigzag my hand from my head to my toes. Church teens had already nicknamed me, "Grandma." In today's terms, they would have called me "a nerd."

I loved to read and I followed school rules to the letter—not because of piety, mind you. I simply thought differently about consequences. For my peers, the severity of the punishment determined whether or not they would cut classes, disobey teachers or miss homework assignments. In contrast, I considered the pain that such behaviors might cause my mother. I was horrified by the thought of my misconduct adding to her already stressful life.

Like any teenager, I yearned to be in with the in-crowd and I hated my skinny bare-chested frame. Girls with bulging blouses, big legs, rounded hips, and boys buzzing around them were the torment of my existence. Sister Anderson did not seem to know that smart was boring. I prayed she would stop holding me up as an example.

Yes, I excelled in academic subjects but the only place I felt included was in physical education classes. Our teacher, Mrs. D. M. Barnes, had a rigid dress code. Without failure every girl suited up in maroon shorts, white tees, white socks, and white tennis shoes. There was no lateness, no fooling around and no sitting on the bench. We all arrived at class ready to participate or else— it was rumored—suffer a paddling.

I never saw or spoke to a girl who had been paddled, but brothers, cousins and boyfriends reported legendary tales of dropping their pants and manning up to the stinging blows of "Little Sally Walker," the nickname for the paddle carved in the Woodwork shop. We girls never risked the possibility of such a fate. Everybody fell in line, dressed uniformly and was equally awkward in satisfying the physical demands of the class.

Though she was tough, the predictable routine maintained by Mrs. Barnes provided a stress-free oasis in my otherwise chaotic life. At the start of class, everyone warmed up with jumping jacks followed by laps around the gym. Then, we all clumsily shot air balls toward the hoops; played spirited games of volley ball; and learned to, waltz, stump the Virginia reel and to square dance.

The dance routines fostered an appreciation for music beyond the cultural tradition of gospel and blues. While television broadcasts of "hayride music" were often performed against the backdrop of a terrifying confederate flag, hillbilly songs took on a positive slant in Physical Education classes where country music struck relatable human chords of love and loss, joy and pain, hope and despair. I enjoyed the melodies that supported twangy lyrical narratives; and was captivated by the sound of the fiddle and the banjo decades before Rhiannon Giddens' amazing research on the African roots of the instruments. Her work also traces the influence of the African American experience on country music as a whole. Of course, I knew nothing about Rhiannon and her banjo back when family and friends were asking, "You like that redneck music?" Though they thought it strange, I nodded, "Yes," and kept on listening.

Like square dancing and country music, classical music entered my world through waltzing in Physical Education. As a follow up to classroom activities, Mrs. Barnes helped bring the Shreveport Symphony Orchestra to perform in the school auditorium. She also lightened the pace with occasional after school sock-hops. Never mind the strictly enforced no-shoes-on-the-floor policy, the gymnasium rocked to local teenage rhythm and blues bands. They performed soul stirring renditions of Sam's Cook's *You Send Me* and throbbing versions of Chuck Berry's *School Days.* Though I was too shy for dancing, I stood along the wall and tapped my feet. I left those socials humming: *Up in the morning and out to school/ The teacher is teaching the Golden Rule/ American history and practical math/ You studin' hard and hoping to pass.* The Chuck Berry tune stayed in my head through evening homework.

Mrs. Barnes and other teachers at Booker T strove to develop well-rounded young people. They had high expectations that required us to lift our sights to an unlimited horizon. Whether we liked it or not, we measured up. Theirs was a stern do-what-I-say-or-else approach to education. The "or else" options were never pleasant. Students, who misbehaved, were firmly reprimanded in front of their peers; paddled by one of the coaches; chided by pastors; or, worst of all, whipped a second time by parents. A network of strict discipline maintained between school, home and church resulted in the orderly pursuit of learning; and the vast majority of students benefitted from rich academic and cultural experiences.

$\mathcal{T}$he last semester at Booker T, I busily prepared for my secretarial job in the team taught classes of Mrs. Blanche H. Milloy and Mrs. J. S. Hall. Shorthand dictations from Mrs. Milloy were transcribed the next period in Mrs. Hall's typing class. In addition to team teaching, they had a special way of reaching beyond classroom boundaries to personally impact the lives of students. No doubt their husbands did the same with male students in Graphic Arts, taught by Mr. Courtland T. Milloy; and Brick Masonry, taught by Mr. Andrew Hall.

Though considered "vocational" teachers, Mrs. Hall and Mrs. Milloy did more than anyone to steer me toward a destiny of academic achievement. I was unfamiliar with the term at the time, but they had been mentors since I enrolled in their classes a year earlier. Back in my junior year, they had worked to secure a scholarship for me in a two-week sleep-away summer camp experience for "Negro girls." I wondered: *Why the special interest in me?* Many students were just as needy; and, though I did well in their classes, I did not consider myself a star pupil. Perhaps comments from teachers in my academic subjects made them aware of a budding potential they wanted to encourage. Or, maybe they had noticed my absence from all the school's extra-curricular activities.

Responsibilities at home and a part-time job left little room for anything other than studying. As much as I loved the idea of writing, I was not a member of *The Lion's* newspaper or yearbook staff; nor did I participate in Booker T's student councils and committees, sports teams, cheerleader and pep squads, or in the band, orchestra, glee club or choir. The debate, drama and 4-H clubs as well as uniform service groups such as the Junior Red Cross and the Student Safety Patrol Unit were also out of my reach. The lack of participation in the vast array of enrichment activities slanted my BTW years towards classroom instruction. I missed out on the carefree fun aspects of high school. Perhaps that was why Mrs. Hall and Mrs. Milloy sought a camp scholarship for me.

Sadly, their efforts were futile. The grants went to popular girls who dressed well, were club leaders and, in some cases, to the daughters and the friends of teachers, doctors and lawyers. Many of them could afford to pay for summer camp or had other opportunities to travel; but the experience would have been my first real vacation. I felt the sting of rejection and moped for weeks.

Sulking did not stop Mrs. Milloy and Mrs. Hall from moving to their next project. In my senior year, they got the bright idea that I should go to college. I had zero faith in their pipedream. First of all, my family had no money. Second, the only thing I knew about college was people returned from those schools to teach; and I had already decided to be a secretary. Third, I did not have the foggiest notion of how to get admitted to a college.

"You need to apply," Mrs. Hall said as she placed a double-sided form on my desk. The bold type across the top of the front page read, "Southern University - Baton Rouge, Louisiana."

"Put your name here," she helped me fill out the application line by line. "Tuition is affordable, fifteen dollars a semester, but room and board is more costly." She provided details that did not inform.

"What's tuition?" I asked.

"Well college is different from high school. You must pay for your classes. The fee is called, tuition."

"Oh. And board?"

"It's the rent paid for a room in the dormitory; and the cost of a meal ticket."

I started to ask, *What's a dormitory?* but the particulars about college were too bewildering.

While scribbling answers to the personal information requested on the application, I thought, *Mama can't afford any of this*; but Mrs. Hall was so eager. For fear of appearing ungrateful, I followed instructions, signed the application and gave it back to her.

"Mrs. Milloy and I have paid the fee for your CAT examination," she stated.

"What's a CAT?" I asked. It sounded like one of those medical exams Mama had taken in order to become a nurse.

"It's the standardized College Admission Test." Mrs. Hall answered.

I showed no visible sign of reluctance but fretted inwardly, *I don't want to take a test for something that's not going to happen. How can I stop them?* Since they had already spent their money, a week later I sat for the CAT exam while the two teachers took turns proctoring the test.

A very high test score! I have been admitted to Southern University! Upon getting the news, joy leaped in my heart, bubbled over, and then fizzled. I had no money for college. I lowered my gaze as hope crumbled. With lackluster, I told Mama, "I've been accepted to a college in south Louisiana."

"Praise the Lord!" she exclaimed; gave me a big hug; but poverty also wiped the grin off Mama's face. After a long pause she said, "Girl, I'm proud of you." Then, in her routine way of addressing problems, she added, "We gon' pray. God will make a way." With those faith-filled words, her attention returned to more immediate financial matters like getting the gas turned back on at our house and buying a white dress for my commencement.

Graduation from high school was a grand milestone. My mother had been determined that none of her children would return to night school for diplomas as she had. Her goal was accomplished. The prior year Thelma had finished high school back in East Texas and, I was poised to march with the BTW Class of 1960. Indeed, all five of her children would graduate from high school on schedule.

The flurry of my pre-commencement activities began with the junior-senior prom for which I had neither a ball gown nor a date. Luckily, I had attended the dance in my junior year and would treasure those memories. Highlights of that prom were captured in the 1959 edition of *The Lion*. The yearbook was published every two years; and though the class of 1960 was pictured as juniors in the volume, I happily passed it around for signatures of classmates and teachers. In the process, I noticed that the faculty section listed Mrs. Hall as a graduate of Southern University–Baton Rouge, Louisiana. I speculated, *That's why she wants me to go to college so far from home when Grambling is only a few miles down the highway.*

Formal commencement rituals began with a required baccalaureate service on the eve of graduation day. I do not recall attending but my good friend, Armanda, recently assured me, "Bessie, you know Mae Etta Scott wasn't going to let you miss that service." Referring to our senior sponsor and faculty advisor she continued, "Not a single graduate was allowed to miss the solemn event that featured a farewell address in the form of a sermon. Don't you remember? We marched into the school auditorium in our maroon caps and gowns. The baccalaureate sermon, entitled, 'Accept Nothing Less Than the Best,' was delivered by Dr. E. Edward Jones. Well, he was Mister Jones back then. He had not yet become The Reverend Dr. Edward Jones, pastor of Galilee Baptist Church and distinguished civil rights leader. Remember how he was dragged out of his pulpit on a Sunday morning and beaten for his civil rights activities?"

"No, I guess I had moved away by then," I answered.

"Anyway," Armanda continued, "he was a young man when he imparted wisdom to the BTW class of 1960. I'll never forget how he emphasized the importance of being the best no matter your job or station in life. He used one of the graduate's names. I don't remember whose; so I'll substitute my name. He said, 'If you are going to be a street sweeper, let everyone who passes say Armanda swept that street. Look how clean it is.' "

Dr. Jones must have been quite an orator. Armanda had latched onto his every word. If she said I attended the baccalaureate service, I was probably present at the event but plagued by doubts: *Will I be able to go to college? Will Mama be able to get off work for the graduation? Will I get dizzy while standing on line at commencement?* A sea of worries could have distracted me. I am thankful that my friend had paid attention. Because of Armanda's keen memory, I carry forward the message: *be the best, nothing less.*

The BTW class of 1960 did not stroll into the auditorium willy-nilly. For days, mandatory practice was required for lining up and marching to the same cadence. We also followed a strict dress code or we did not march. There were no sneakers and blue jeans. Boys wore polished black shoes and girls black pumps. Underneath our maroon robes we girls wore white dresses and the boys donned dark slacks with white shirts and black ties.

On graduation day Mama was all excitement and I was a bundle of nerves. I bombarded her with anxious concerns: "Do you know the way to the Shreveport

Municipal Auditorium?" "I hope the car doesn't break down." "What if I faint?" "Miss Scott said a hundred and ninety-four graduates will be present with their families. You know I get dizzy in crowds." "What if I'm out of step when we march into the auditorium?"

Mama finally put my fears to rest. "If that happens," she said, "I'ma point and shout really loud, 'Look! Everybody is out of step but my child!' " We laughed and, of course, I graduated without a mishap. Fear of being pulled out of line and embarrassed in front of parents and peers sent my classmates and me marching down the aisles swaying from side to side like tin soldiers.

The awesome power of teachers bolstered my first grand educational achievement. In classrooms, potential and reality had intersected in ways that made a difference. Indeed, teachers were guardians of my future. They exercised the fullness of their mission and sent my classmates and me into the world to chart paths that, perhaps, they had not and would never travel. In most cases, messengers would not return to tell of the success or failure of the voyagers they launched. Nevertheless, when the fanfare of ceremonies and celebrations ended, they courageously returned to classrooms to cultivate the next group of students. Truly, teachers are heroes. Daily, they marshal acts of faith and expect good results in an unknown future.

ॐ

Historically Black was not yet the awkward phrase used to describe African American colleges and universities.

In 1960, when Mama's old blue Chevy pulled up to the train station, it was simpler times and she happily sent me off to college. Spilling out of shiny Fords, Cadillacs, Studebakers, and two stretch limousines were Booker T. Washington graduates headed to Southern University in Baton Rouge, Louisiana. Some of my high school classmates had well-stitched suitcases and matching heavy trunks. I could not imagine what they carried in their grand sets of luggage.

Poor students like me dragged metal footlockers from the H. L. Greens Five and Dime Store. Packed in mine were two Sunday outfits, four skirt-and-blouse coordinates and three chemise dresses I had sewn from McCall patterns. Other items included towels, bedding and a red winter coat of cotton-rayon blend that warmed the body only when temperatures remained above forty degrees. Despite my sparse wardrobe, I was college bound.

Like Mama had predicted, "God had made a way." Income from a summer job of babysitting and housekeeping boosted my savings to around two-hundred dollars. In addition to clothing, I was able to purchase a one-way train ticket to Baton Rouge; to pay room and board for one semester; and to save a small fund for books and school supplies.

Mama helped carry the footlocker through the growing crowd outside of Shreveport's Central Station. Twenty students were ahead of us on line at the baggage counter. So, Mama said a hasty goodbye and rushed off to her nightshift job as a nurse.

The sign, "Colored," pointed me to the rear of the train. I brushed aside the indignity of a segregated compartment and delighted in my first trip more than forty miles from home. The overnight journey to Baton Rouge was a fantasy ride.

One minute I was under my mother's complete supervision; the next I inhabited a world of peers. A car had been reserved for the thirty or so Booker T. Washington graduates headed to Southern University. Enlivened by the rhythmic sounds of train wheels and transistor radios, *wanta-be* hip young men bounced from seat to seat flirting with the ladies. When an occasional guy sat on the arm of my seat, I recoiled. Never had I spent a night in the company of males other than family and relatives. I marveled at the girls who relaxed and curled up on the chests of boyfriends. Others propped their pillows against the windows and snuggled into easy slumber. After hours of horseplay, most everyone fell asleep. I remained wide awake. Through the night I watched as scenes outside the train window slid from open cotton fields to gigantic moss-laden Cypress trees.

At the Baton Rouge train depot, jitneys replaced the fine cars and limousines that had been at the Shreveport station. While the driver loaded luggage into the trunk and the front passenger seat of a fairly broken down car, I climbed into the back seat with two other female students. I dosed off but was jolted awake when the cab rumbled over train tracks and onto the main thoroughfare of the university.

Congested cafes, little night spots and small frame houses were left at the campus border. Scotlandville, a poor community of daily hardships, retreated as I entered a secluded environment intended to foster scholarly learning. Entrance into this brand new world was reminiscent of my mother's leaving-home experience. The first of her family to leave Texas and a member of the first class of Black nurses in Louisiana, Mama was a trailblazer. By going to college, I was following in her footsteps of family firsts. I intended to blaze a path worthy for future generations to tread.

Charted in 1880, Southern University was among the pioneering schools of higher education established a few decades after slavery. In 1914, Dr. Joseph Samuel Clark, founder and first president of the university, moved the school from New Orleans to Baton Rouge, Louisiana. His son, Dr. Felton Grandison Clark, was appointed president in 1939 and remained in the position during my time as a student.

My undergraduate studies began the decade before the awkward phrase, "historically Black," replaced the simpler description, Black colleges and universities. When I enrolled, Southern University was the largest African American institution of higher education in the country. The campus still rested on the original 512 acres of Scotts Bluff high above a bend in the Mississippi River. However, I joined a student body that had grown from 500 well on its way to a high of 10,000 under the leadership of Dr. Felton G. Clark.

Tucked among stately moss laden trees, dignified red brick buildings of the 1920s and 1930s housed offices of the president and the deans. Adjacent to the administrative building were a vesper chapel and a quaint little playhouse where I would later enjoy a student production of Tennessee William's, "A Streetcar Named Desire."

Sitting at the edge of "old campus," as I called it, was a poor relative without a rich history. "Cottage 5" was scrawled on a wooden plaque near the door of the lone frame house in the area. For an unexplainable odd reason, I paused in front of the building. Then, shaking off what felt like a premonition, I headed the few steps down the path to the freshmen cafeteria. Next door to the cafeteria sat an old gymnasium for women and just beyond was the infirmary. My brief tour of the Scotts Bluff area provided a sense of what college life must have been like in bygone eras.

I doubled back to the cafeteria for a light breakfast before heading around a sleepy lake and into the bustle of center campus. On their stone facades, ultra-modern buildings announced their purposes: Classroom, Science, Agricultural, Law School and School of Education. Lounging along the lake was a Student Union building that housed a cafeteria for upper class students and a cozy snack bar along with a barber shop, bowling alley, music rooms, and several small lounge areas.

My destination was the Men's Gymnasium—a spectacular new arena. Inside, winding lines led to tables organized alphabetically by students' last names. I proceeded to the "WXYZ" table for the "Waites, Bessie Lorene" packet before huddling with four of my high school friends to make decisions about course selections. Two hours later, we left the gymnasium proud Southern University Jaguars. Back on old campus, I ended my first full day as a college student dining with my pals.

The big mistake of my first semester began at the registration table. With thoughts of friendships rather than academic aims and goals, I tried to enroll in every course with my home-girls but only succeeded in registering in the same section of the math requirement. During the semester, we passed notes instead of paying attention to how to solve complex equations. Unlike with high school teachers, the professor ignored our immature behavior. At the end of the semester, his reprimand was stinging: I earned a "D" in College Algebra.

The grade marred my "B+" average and left a blemish on my transcript that could never be erased. I learned a costly lesson: Choosing a course of study is a serious undertaking that does not mix well with play. I pulled away from pals and made all future class selections alone.

In sharp contrast to the math disaster, Dr. H. D. Perkins' Introduction to Humanities course was the bright spot of my first semester. Head of the Music Department and master of many disciplines, Dr. Perkins was that rare instructor who blended command of subject matter with charisma. Much more than a talking head delivering stale lectures, he threw himself entirely into the teaching process.

With one hand dancing to soft notes, he instructed, "Listen to the oboe. See how the French horns come in. Now, the violins..." and his body began to sway to the mournful whine of the string section. Then both arm rose. As he conducted a little record player on a wooden table, he was swept up by a crescendo of powerful music. Eyes closed and shirt soaked with sweat, he went beyond telling the class about Leonard Bernstein; he channeled the New York Philharmonic conductor I had seen on televised broadcasts.

Dr. Perkins also had a talent for linking one field of study to the other. He moved the class out of enclosed towers of knowledge and illustrated how politics, philosophy, literature, music, architecture and the visual arts merge to form the culture of a specific people in an exact period of history. Classical music was used in the way today's cutting edge teachers employ rap to enliven the learning environment of urban youth. Rap music provides a backdrop for the exploration of a hip-hop culture that includes bold in-your-face poetry, break-dancing, and styles of dress that speak to the lives of youth at the dawn of the twenty-first century. In a similar manner, Dr. Perkins employed classical music as a gateway to various eras of European history.

I have no doubt that my humanities professor could have been one of the country's great conductors of symphony orchestras; but his genius was stifled by the insidious cruelty of racial discrimination. Irony is he was drafted from Southern University by LSU following the 1960s protests that ended legal segregation. It was my privilege, though, to bathe in the light of Dr. Perkins' brilliance in my first year at Southern University. He instilled an appreciation for classical music. Even more important, his interdisciplinary approach to learning sparked a lasting curiosity regarding the links between different fields of study.

*O*n the first day of my second semester, I was wandering the campus in a daze when, "Little Thelma, what's up?" wobbled into jumbles thoughts. It was Fats. He addressed me by my sister's name because they had been buddies back in high school and, once at Southern, their friendship extended to me.

"Where you going? What's up?" he asked again.

"I... I have to leave... school," I sputtered.

"Caaalm down, Little Thelma. Calm down so I can understand."

I took a deep breath, let it out slowly and explained, "I don't have enough money for the dormitory fee, a meal ticket for this semester or anything. I thought my work-study covered everything but it doesn't. I have no place to live."

Instantly, Fats took on the role of big brother. As a sophomore familiar with the bureaucratic red tape of college life, he marched me to the Dean of Women's office. Half an hour later, we left with a housing assignment at the odd little white building I had noticed my first day on campus. The premonition about the place turned out to be a good omen.

Cottage 5 was a student-run cooperative. Rooms were rent-free and each resident contributed fifteen dollars a month to a fund for food, cleaning supplies and other household items. Shopping fell to upper class women while cooking and cleaning duties rotated among all residents.

The co-op living arrangement that allowed me to continue my freshmen year was one of several critical impacts Fats would have on my life. In the spring semester of 1961, as study partners in Part II of Dr. Perkins' Introduction to Humanities class, we became friends. A cool cat with a spindly physique, Alex Willingham was anything but obese. Perhaps the nickname, "Fats," referred to his brilliant and hugely expansive mind. Not only was he book smart, he was streetwise. He knew how to purchase the cheapest used textbooks and where to get a fifty-cent bowl of red beans, sausage and rice without sneaking off-campus and risking suspension from school.

An ever so slight shift in social attitudes was an unanticipated result of my friendship with Fats. I hated heavy drinking because of my father's alcoholism but I made exceptions for my friend. Not only had he found Cottage 5, he helped me see the positive aspects of living in the most humble residence on campus. Often, he commented how lucky I was to live in a setting that would enhance any musical experience. During discussions of Humanities homework assignments our constant conversations about jazz enhanced my musical appetite. Because of Fats, the hidden joy of Cottage 5 became my prize spot in a bedroom overlooking the lake.

I shared the room with two girls—Mae Gladys Yates from Dallas, Texas and Hazel, a lanky six foot tall girl from south Louisiana. Lucky for me, my bed was pushed against the window. At night, I gazed upon serene waters where moon beams danced across the surface. On Mae Gladys' record player, Nancy Wilson crooned, "Guess Who I Saw Today." On misty nights when moss dipped curly tips into tranquil water, Ella Fitzgerald scatted, "A foggy day in London town." After the celebrated folk singer, Odette, performed at the college's Spring Lyceum series, my nightly great-ladies-of-song concerts included Nancy, Ella and Odette.

Oblivious to the summer of 1961 Freedom Rides, I settled in at Cottage 5 and turned my thoughts to choosing a major. I enrolled in a Sociology elective with the intent of making the subject my field of study. In the introductory course, my professor labored with statistics and trends that illustrated patterns of poverty. He aimed to raise student awareness of conditions that I already knew too well. Without the faintest hints regarding solutions, his descriptions of unemployment, hunger, and sub-standard housing were downright discouraging.

In selecting the course, I had confused Sociology with the helping profession of Social Work but it did not matter. Neither field of study appealed to me. I was not seeking broad solutions to social ills. My goal was to better my individual plight and that of my family. Like in high school, I wrestled once again with the question, "What job?" While deciding on a major, elective courses fanned my passion for literature; and personal dilemmas muted the rumbling of student unrest that would inflame the campus in the fall of 1961.

Choking under a cloud of tear gas, a small band of students crawled in the ditch alongside the Scotlandville roadway. Just above our heads, dogs growled, protesters shrieked and horses pounded the pavement. Barely visible through the eerie mist, mounted troopers were swinging Billy clubs. Sheer instinct carried my cohorts and me along the trench to the railroad crossing and back within the university's borders. Gusts of fresh air parted a path to the center of campus.

Driven by terror, students hurried to their dormitories; or, stumbled coughing and tearing to the infirmary. Like the majority seen in the medical unit, my red and burning eyes were rinsed with a solution and I was released. A less fortunate small group of injured young women were admitted for an overnight stay.

I dashed from the infirmary to Cottage 5. It was a night without calm waters, moon beams or soothing songs. I lay in bed shaken by images of the overwhelming force used to disrupt a peaceful demonstration. My mind drifted to thoughts of what might have happened had I been pulled off the front seat of a Shreveport bus in my sophomore year of high school.

Prior to the mayhem in Scotlandville, civil disobedience had resided in remote corners of my mind. At the beginning of the fall of 1961 semester, I had finally declared English as my major. Joyfully immersed in literary studies, sunny thoughts of a roving reporter for *The Baltimore Afro American* loomed large in my imagination. Near the end of the semester, I was sailing peacefully toward a career in journalism at the oldest

Black weekly in the nation when bolts of student unrest took me by surprise.

If signs of campus discontent had been evident all along, they had gone unnoticed for three semesters by students in my circle. Perhaps my personal struggles had created blind spots concerning civil rights. In any case, I was totally unaware that seventeen students had been arrested and subsequently expelled from the university the spring semester just prior to my admission to Southern. Had it not been for eyewitness accounts by two student leaders—Major Johns and Ronnie Moore, I might have never learned the details surrounding campus events that pre-dated my arrival. Luckily, the written student narratives were released in a Congress of Racial Equality (CORE) publication entitled, "It Happened in Baton Rouge."

On March 28, 1960—back when I was still preparing for graduation from Booker T. Washington High School, seven Southern University students sat in at the downtown Baton Rouge Kress lunch counter. This act of solidarity in support of the sit-ins in Greensboro, North Carolina quickly ballooned from seven to thousands of demonstrators in the downtown business district. When the university administration expelled student protestors and then had them arrested for trespassing, marches shifted to on-campus rallies. Prayer vigils and fiery speeches did not subside until students returned to their hometowns at the end the school year. Meanwhile, a court case, filed by CORE on behalf of arrested students, was working its way through appeals.

When I enrolled as a Southern University freshman in the fall of 1960, it was as if turbulent unrest in the previous spring had never happened. Though Jim Crow humiliation continued to assault anyone who stepped foot off campus, academic life advanced in apparent

90

tranquility. However, things changed toward the end of the fall semester of my sophomore year.

On December 11, 1961 the U.S. Supreme Court reversed the convictions of students arrested during the spring 1960 sit-ins. The ground breaking decision held that calmly asking for service at a lunch counter was not disorderly conduct. Despite the ruling, downtown lunch counters continued to refuse service to Blacks. The local chapter of CORE organized picketing in which twenty-three people were arrested; and another round of massive protests were planned.

Impassioned speeches summoned an indignation not felt since my frenzied high school ride on a Jim Crow bus. In spite of promises to Mama that I would never again disobey unfair segregation laws, I took a stand for justice and joined the ranks of thousands of Southern University students on a march to the county courthouse. It was a brief but violent experience in which a ruthless battalion of police herded marchers from Scotlandville back onto campus.

During two days of recurring visits to the infirmary, students gathered in small clusters where rumors circulated: "Fifty people were arrested at the demonstration!" "Yeah, the jailing continues." "The State Board of Education ordered the dismissal of any arrested students." "What did you expect? All the board members are White." "The president vowed to resign before he expels another student protester!"

It was a time of hearsay and half-truths. Actually, seventy-three students were arrested and the president did not resign. He continued to dismiss students. Then, before another march could organize, he shocked us all: "Did you hear? Felton G. closed the school!" "Whaaat?" "Yeah, we gotta be out of here by sundown."

We were young; hungry for change and only saw the good to be gained from student protests. We never considered possible losses. Hidden from our view were pressures put on Dr. Clark by an all-White power structure. We did not think about whether the president's decisions were weighed against the risk of a permanent closure that would deny college access to thousands. Certainly, the overarching context was beyond my comprehension.

The early December get-out-of-Dodge scramble was a big blow. School closure ahead of the scheduled Christmas vacation made it nearly impossible for me to leave because work-study checks had not been issued. Each of my trips home took careful planning. In order to have money for tuition and books, visits home were limited to the Christmas recess and the end of summer school. I would have stayed on campus year round if it had not been for those two periods of total shutdowns when dorms, classrooms, cafeterias, the library— everything was sealed tight. By the end of each semester, most of my savings were exhausted and I relied on the last work-study check to pay for the holiday trip home. The early dismissal meant raising enough money among friends to purchase a bus ticket. Thanks to their generosity, I exited the campus with droves of other students. It was a long and hungry ride to Shreveport.

When school reopened in the spring of 1962, news that several student protestors had spent the Christmas holidays in jail whizzed pass me. I was homeless. Without notice, Cottage 5 had closed for good.

Overwrought by the thought of going home in disgrace, I crossed the vine-laden ravine that separated the girls' dormitories from the rest of the campus. The footbridge, known as the "kissing bridge," seemed a peaceful place to pause and reflect, but I kept moving. I had heard too many spooky late evening tales of foggy nights when love-crazed young women leaped. Fear of ghost sightings had turned the rustic scene into a frightening abyss. Even in mid-afternoon, green foliage and ashen moss swayed in the breeze and taunted me with shadowy images of *haints*. I hated crossing the ravine alone but desperation pushed me forward.

The minute my home-girl, Lela Earl Smith, opened the door, I hit her with a barrage of disjointed facts: "The Dean of Women can't help. Fats isn't here. The library isn't open..."

"Slow down!" she said.

I continued, "Mrs. Jackson would take me in but I don't have her home number." The thought of getting in touch with the Assistant Head Librarian and my work-study supervisor, made me pause long enough to take a deep breath before asking, "Have you seen Fats? He always helps me in a jam."

"Well, we can't do anything about that now. It's too close to dark. Sleep here tonight," she offered and broke the dorm's strict no-doubling-up policy. "We're going to figure out something. You NOT going home!" were the last words I heard before slumping into a stupor on her bed.

At breakfast the next morning, Lela insisted I eat half of her plate of toast, eggs and bacon. I was forcing down small bites when I leaped to my feet and startled her. I had spotted Fats quietly having breakfast in a corner of the cafeteria.

I rushed over, "Fats! I have to drop out of school!"

"Come on, let's go out to the lounge," he patiently guided me to a quiet area of the Student Union. After hearing about my predicament, he instructed, "Wait in

Lela's room until noon and then meet me back in the cafeteria."

When we met at lunchtime, he announced, "I got a place for you. It's in Scotlandville." Worry overtook relief as my mind scanned the row of bars and cafes on the outskirts of the campus. Though frightened by forbidden places, I had no choice other than Scotlandville.

On the way to my mystery residence, Fats and I passed drab little stores that twinkled only in the dark. However, a few blocks beyond the cafes lay a quiet neighborhood that reminded me of home. We stopped at a little white house with a patch of green grass out front. The scene prompted memories of night walks to church with Mama that put me at ease. Wearing a seersucker duster, the middle age woman at the door led me through a tiny living room with lace dollies on the sofa and its matching arm chair. *A church woman,* I sized up my landlady as she ushered me into an immaculate kitchen that sparkled with shiny chrome. She opened a wooden door off to the right and said, "This is the room you'll share with another girl."

My eyes widened. The room barely held the double bed pushed against the window. Thoughts raced through my head: *I'ma sleep with a stranger? No dresser; I guess I'll be living out of my footlocker.* I pushed fear to the back of my mind; placed a small bag of belongings on the wooden chair just inside the room; and then dragged my footlocker to the end of the bed. Had it not been for the familiar feel of home and the fact that I completely trusted Fats, I would have bolted into the streets.

That night in a strange bed, I decided to tackle my studies with a fierce determination. Who knew how long my newest living arrangement would last? I needed to graduate as soon as possible. Thankfully, the little room turned out to be a peaceful place to study. The one night my roommate showed up to claim her half of the bed, she smelled of liquor. I decided to sleep in my clothes.

"You so gullible," Marjorie laughed and enough alcoholic fumes were released to make me high. "You some kind of country. Where you from?"

"Shreveport."

"I can't believe it. You my dumb home-girl?" she said with arms lifted as if appealing to the ceiling.

"You from Shreveport too?" I asked timidly.

"Don't worry home-girl, most of my time is spent with friends across the river," she responded to my being fully dressed and under the covers.

I relaxed and we talked into the night. It turned out Marjorie knew my first cousin, Tomprell. We ended our conversation around daybreak. She left before breakfast but not without a parting jab.

"You know what home-girl you not only dumb, you can't cook. I wouldn't feed a dog that stuff you fixing. I need to stop by sometime and bring you some food," she said before disappearing.

I assumed Marjorie was one of Fats drinking buddies and hoped she would stop by with food. She never returned. She was obviously a party girl but I later learned she was also a brilliant student. After graduating from Southern she eventually became a civil rights attorney. I think back now and wonder if she were involved in working with CORE to free jailed students whose education had been disrupted by sacrifices for freedom.

My studies progressed but poverty upended any student activism. I had moved off campus as the protests of the spring of 1962 moved onto campus. No longer was I surrounded by clusters of students buzzing with news of the latest developments. I regretted my inability to follow through with protests but appeased myself with the thought: Some are destined to tear down walls of injustice;

others are called to build a more equitable society. I did not know it at the time but God had, indeed, reserved a role for me in creating a more just society.

*W*ithout a roommate to worry about, I enrolled for eighteen credits each semester of the 1962-63 schoolyear. A rigid schedule of exhausting walks to campus, class attendance and work-study obligations barely left energy for the trek back to my room and a bed full of books. I had no social life and I even lost touch with my buddy, Fats.

Settings, plots, intriguing characters and philosophical ideas stimulated a passion for all things literary. An unintended and, at first, an unnoticed consequence of my intellectual fervor was the unraveling of long held beliefs. From earliest memory two values had shaped my identity: God is real and education is a must. At the core of my being, the church-girl and the student had always dwelt in harmony; but, what church people called *foreign ideas* were slowly separating those two essentials aspects of self.

A religious tradition of rousing praise and fiery damnation had left little defense against the logic of much of my coursework. One aunt wrote a letter warning, "Watch out for the devil. Don't let the demons in that school take you to hell." Otherwise, no alerts had been given that passing or failing a course might rest on whether I understood and agreed with points of view contrary to my faith.

Despite efforts to hold onto core values, important pieces of spiritual identity slipped away. Nietzsche and other nineteen century philosophers mounted logical arguments that suggested God is either passive or dead. Unable to respond with a rational defense in required essays, I chose questioning agnosticism (Does God exist?)

over definite atheism (God does not exist.). Straddling the fence of agnosticism seemed a safe place; but, not so. Doubt had entered my soul during a time when I most needed faith.

At the end of the summer term of 1963, students made a mass exodus out of the heat and the humidity rising from the Mississippi River. Poised to make my way in the world, I lingered on the nearly empty campus preparing to march in the August commencement exercises. While searching the bulletin board for English Department grade postings, my academic advisor, Miss Arthenia J. Bates, sent a work-study student with a note outlining where and when she wanted to see me. With graduation only days away, I puzzled over the request. It seemed odd to meet in a classroom instead of her office. Nevertheless, I was glad she was still on campus. I wanted to ask why the English Department grades had not been posted but had to wait overnight for answers.

Next morning, I entered a room set for drama. My legs went wobbly. Four to five English Department faculty members sat erect as statues behind a long table placed in front of the blackboard. The lone chair in the middle of the classroom was for an audience of one: me. The setting had a tribunal atmosphere.

What have I done? I searched grim faces for clues.

Miss Bates, the timid woman who dabbed beads of sweat from her upper lip and taught her classes in nervous whispers, had become lead prosecutor. "Miss Waites, we are concerned about your future," she spoke in loud somber tones.

I swallowed hard and nodded though I did not understand.

Then, Dr. Marshall, who taught Chaucer entirely in a Middle English dialect, found his modern voice with the stern declaration: "Very disappointing, very disappointing the way you squandered your time here at Southern!" I don't know what shocked me most: his regular way of speaking or his scathing criticism.

However, the gravity of the situation sank in when my Shakespeare professor sat mute and stoically stared me down. He was an energetic instructor, perpetually in motion, dancing around the classroom spouting: "All the world's a stage and all the men and women merely actors." Or, "If you cut me, do I not bleed." Shakespeare's dramas lived in his class. Yet, there he sat silently screaming volumes of displeasure.

While Miss Bates delivered her summation, I barely maintained my composure but no salty tears spilled from my eyes. I forced them back down my nasal passage into my mouth and swallowed them.

"Miss Waites," my advisor ended the meeting, "there is a slim chance that you can be saved. Be in my office at eight in the morning. I'm going to try to help you."

Oh, my God, I have failed. I staggered from the room, along empty corridors and into humid air with previously stifled tears flowing. From the Classroom Building, through the Student Union and across the ravine, I had no concern for occasional students who paused to watch the hysterical but voiceless girl who stumbled by them.

"Oh! Oh God!" Lela gasped.

I stood before her with a wet face and a mouth opening and closing like a fish out of water.

"Sit down," she said and rushed to the bathroom for the emergency roll of toilet tissue—the one used for boy trouble, homesickness, shortfalls of money and, on that day, for failure.

My grief was beyond words. Uncontrollable hiccups escaped in rapid succession until she finally gripped my shoulders and ordered, "Stop that! You better tell me something before I faint!"

"Wa-water!" I managed. She rinsed out a tea cup and brought water from the bathroom tap. With one sip, a fresh spring of tears flowed. Several small sips and I found raspy words: "I failed. I flunked everything. Mama is going to be so upset..." and then, I boohooed out loud.

"Now stop that! Don't you rattle my nerves one more second!" Lela rubbed her forehead as if she had a migraine. An eternity of silence engulfed us.

When I finally gathered my wits, I described the meeting with the English Department and abruptly returned to concerns about my mother.

"Mama couldn't afford her bus fare down here," I said. "She probably borrowed money from one of the church members; and she sure can't afford to lose pay for the days missed at work. She's making a big sacrifice to see me graduate from college. Her letter said she's arriving tomorrow. She's coming early 'cause she wants to be rested enough to enjoy every minute of the commencement ceremony."

I paused; tried to envision another outcome; but resigned myself to the sad conclusion: "Mama and I will spend the night at Mrs. Jackson's house and head back to Shreveport on graduation day. That way she won't lose another day's pay."

Lela patted me on the shoulder, "Didn't you say Miss Bates is going to try to help you. Wait and see what happens at the meeting in the morning. Come on, try to get some rest. My roommate already left for the summer. If things don't work out—but I'm sure they will—you and Miss Waites can ride back to Shreveport with us. My parents will be here tomorrow."

Lela's father was the Director of Winnfield Funeral Home in Shreveport. Previously, I had ridden home in one of her dad's limousines. At least, the ride with the Smith family would spare Mama the cost of a return bus fare and she would be comfortable.

Following a comatose sleep, I rose at sunrise, dressed, and followed Lela to the cafeteria but did not eat. At a quarter to eight, I headed across the street to the Classroom Building and nervously waited outside of Miss Bates' office. At eight o'clock sharp she opened the door and pointed me to the seat in front of her desk.

"You are going to need to sign some papers," she said and opened the thin folder in the center of an immaculate desk. She lifted out two documents and pushed them in front of me.

Flipping the pages, she instructed, "Sign here. Now there." I did as I was told.

After placing the papers back in the folder she said, "Miss Waites, I am going to put these in the mail for you."

What are those papers? I wondered but was afraid to ask.

As if reading my mind, she answered, "This packet contains the letter of acceptance for graduate study at North Carolina College and your approval of the terms of the fellowship you have been awarded."

Totally confused, I wondered, *Are they doing me a favor and letting me graduate? I might mess things up if I say something.* I kept quiet.

Miss Bates continued in a business manner. "You have no out-of-pocket costs for tuition or room and board. You will receive a monthly stipend of around two hundred dollars for books, supplies and incidental expenses. All you have to do is pay your fare to get there."

Then, she settled into cozy, informal, even poetic descriptions: "Louisiana flatlands are uninteresting terrains; but you'll love the mountainous beauty of North Carolina. Of course, the people are unsophisticated. They say *'bacca* for tobacco; and you'll have to adjust to nearby farms. The college is much smaller than the one here at Southern; but, magnificent scenery abounds."

As she droned on, visions of Beverly Hillbillies in Black skin popped into my head. I imagined myself at the bus depot and my suitcase being carried to a horse-drawn wagon by a man dressed in overalls with a straw hanging from the corner of his mouth. I left Miss Bates' office dazed.

Confusion turned to anger when the English grades were posted later that morning. I was graduating after all! I had earned an "A" in each of four summer term courses. What's more, the cumulative grade point average for my three years at Southern warranted the academic honor of Cum Laude. I should have shouted a *Thank-You-Lordy* for victory over the many challenges encountered in route to what should have been a glorious moment. Instead, I fumed: *They tricked me into signing a graduate school contract that I'm definitely going to break!*

I could not shake the anger but Lela was overjoyed to hear I was graduating. I said a sullen goodbye to my friend as sweet Mrs. Jackson picked me up for the drive to the bus depot to pick up Mama. All the way to the station, I railed against the English Department. Once my mother arrived, I barely stopped complaining long enough to introduce her to Mrs. Jackson.

Mama had to be tired from the trip from Shreveport. She had probably worked a double shift at the hospital before boarding a crowded bus to Baton Rouge. Without considering her fatigue the least bit, my tirade continued: "No way am I going off to North Carolina. I'm coming home, getting a job and helping you, Mama. The nerve of them! They are underhanded and I'm not bound by anything I signed."

The car was silent only a brief moment before I started up again, "You know what Mama? If you hadn't come all this way, I wouldn't even go to that graduation. In fact, I think I'll boycott..."

Mama had all she could take, "Oh yes, you're going to graduation," she said in a stern tone that overpowered my rage. "And you're going to North Carolina too. If I have to add shifts at the hospital to earn your fare, you are going to North Carolina!" No-nonsense Mama-anger took the wind out of my sails.

In dutiful obedience, my body showed up on graduation day but my spirit was not in it. I do not recall a single detail of caps and gowns swishing in the heat; of speeches dull or lively; of triumphant music; or, of jubilant student celebrations. The pride in Mama's eyes is the single image I retain.

It took months to appreciate the brighter future the faculty had plotted on my behalf. Like Mrs. Milloy and Mrs. Hall (my high school mentors), Miss Bates had seen in me a potential that overwhelming poverty had hidden from view. My college professor understood poverty and knew it would take a shakeup to alter my course. By organizing the unprecedented and painful intervention of English Department faculty, Miss Bates had steered me around a job that might have brought immediate monetary relief but would have stunted my overall development. With the wisdom of hindsight, I honor Miss Arthenia J. Bates and her colleagues for heaving me over a fence that separated me from a more fruitful life.

$\mathcal{C}$ *hurch-girl* meets city slicker. At least that is what it felt like.

"Heah," (*babee*) was unspoken but I heard it in his voice. "I'm Jimmy Blaake," he stretched his one-syllable last name for emphasis and ended the introduction with a drag of speech intended to be cool: "I'm from Jamaaica."

Jamaica? Oh he's a foreigner, I thought. I did not know he meant Jamaica, Queens in New York City.

He asked my name. I answered, "Lorene Waites." Looking to establish the use of my middle name, I offered it instead of Bessie which was a name assigned to old rifles, broken down cars or cows too old to give milk. No one at North Carolina College (now renamed North Carolina Central University) knew me. It was the perfect setting to make the switch to Lorene.

I answered Jimmy's series of questions in rapid fire order: "I'm a graduate student, not a freshman." "I don't know where I'm staying." "No, I don't have a phone number either."

He thought it was a brushoff but it was my first day on campus and everything was still in flux. He shifted his approach. With a slanted smile and a lazy voice, "Well Lorene," he said, "you ah FINE looking woman."

Ooooo! My heart quickened but my head revolted. His hip talk and ditty-bop walk sounded alarms that called up Mama-warnings: "*You a church-girl; those boys in the streets are too fast for you.*"

I have no intentions of speaking to him again, I squashed the internal debate forming with my mother.

Jimmy was twenty-one and a senior undergraduate who assumed I was a freshmen because I looked much younger than twenty. Despite concentrated efforts to avoid him, he popped up at every turn. I made it clear that I was at North Carolina College for one reason: to get my Master's degree. Besides, I was engaged. I was not looking for a boyfriend, friend-boy or whatever he wanted to call his relentless pursuit.

Jimmy smiled and gave a slight nod at every brief encounter. His daily but polite acknowledgements nurtured a friendly presence. In two weeks, we were eating nearly all our meals together. We debated civil rights issues; and, swapped stories about his girlfriend in New York and my fiancée in Louisiana.

Our closeness prompted a posse of girls to march into my room waving red flags: "Watch out." "Stay away from him." "You're a nice girl—a church-girl." "Yeah, and he's a dog."

I assured them, "I have absolutely no romantic interest in Jimmy Blake. He's just a friend."

With doubtful eyebrows raised one of them muttered, "We tried." Another shook her head as if she pitied me.

When I told Jimmy about my visitors, he laughed, "Oh, I know them girls. They're jealous because I used to hang around with some of them. You and I know we're just friends."

I laughed too and forgot about the girls with fire in their eyes. In spite of what they said, I liked Jimmy. He became my best buddy. We talked about books; listened to jazz and classical music; and he took me to Durham's foreign film theater to see *Tom Jones*—the film adaptation of the 975-page English novel I had read in Dr. Perkins' humanities class back at Southern University.

My friendship with Jimmy was flourishing by the time I responded to the letter from the head of the English Department stating that Dr. William J. Couch would supervise my work and sign off on the check for my fellowship stipend. *The same Couch?* I wondered and took a deep breath before tapping lightly on the closed door.

"Open," sounded like a muffled groan.

Oh my God; it's him! I could never forget that voice. He was the one professor who gave me the shakes during my undergraduate days at Southern University. His demeanor in the American Literature class was often one of sarcasm and he spoke to students as if he held us in contempt. My good-girl efforts had no effect.

One morning he bristled, "Students at LSU aren't reading newspapers in class. What the hell are you doing with that paper?"

"I... I was only..."

"You dreary..." He searched for the right word but failed. So, he bellowed, "You are not smart enough to read a newspaper at nine in the morning."

He sliced me to bits before I had a chance to explain that I was merely passing the paper along the row. When his rant had run its course, he droned through a boring lecture and left the room without a glance in my direction.

I struggled through the remainder of the term listening to criticisms heaped on other students. I vowed never to enroll in another one of his courses. My classmates must have felt the same way. For, without explanation, he disappeared from Southern University at the end of the semester. Perhaps low or lack of enrollment in his classes sent him on his way.

In the fall of 1963, an odd twist of fate placed me at the door of my most terrifying professor. Surely he had reviewed the fellowship paperwork; but, when I stepped into his office, he looked up without acknowledging that he and I had been at Southern at the same time.

Pointing to a stack of the *New York Times Book Review* piled high on the floor beneath the window, he said, "Organize those chronologically. Can you do that?"

I mouthed a meek, "Yes," and attempted to hand him my class schedule.

He responded, "I don't need that; my office door is always open."

I thought, *Not always; I had to knock to get in here.*

"You can start tomorrow," he said and shot a dismissive glance over the top rim of his wire classes.

I left Dr. Couch's office with dread of what was in store. The fellowship assignment made him faculty advisor and chair of my Master's thesis committee. I would have fallen to my knees and prayed, but studies of philosophy had set me adrift of "silly behavior" often described as, "illogical."

I was glad I had a friend in Jimmy. He encouraged me to be strong in the face of my professor's intimidating manner. Outings with my buddy kept my mind off the daily grind of work. We attended the Penn Relays in Raleigh; dinned on stewed beef at the Green Candle; and listened to jazz at the cozy Birdland night spot on Fayetteville Street. By October, Jimmy constantly teased about marrying me. Each time he did so, I reminded him that I was engaged. In November, he had the nerve to break up with me because he was "a man; and a man had certain needs."

Break up with me? I thought but responded, "I only have friendship to offer you, Jimmy."

"Well, when you see me tomorrow; just keep walking, okay?"

"Okay," I agreed but was thinking, *He has actually convinced himself that he's my boyfriend.*

He might have shooed other guys away with, "Hey man, stay away from my girl," but it did not mean that I was buying into his fantasy. I did not waste a smile on the silly boys who approached me, "I want to talk to you but you Blake's girl." I thought they were spineless.

Jimmy stood staring at me for so long that I repeated, "Okay, I won't speak to you tomorrow."

"Oh, before I go," he said, "let me play something for you" and he walked over to the piano in the lobby of the faculty residence where I lived while still waiting on permanent housing. To emphasize what I was losing, he played a jazzy rendition of *Misty*; and then threw in his own version of *Summertime* for good measure.

I was impressed. I did not know he played the piano; nor did I know those were the only two tunes he had memorized. *Wow, he's talented. I'm going to miss him,* I thought.

As it turned out, there was no chance of missing my best buddy. The next day on my way to an early morning class, I heard someone yelling across campus, "Bessieeee! Bessie!" It was Jimmy jumping up and down and flapping his hands. I gave a stiff-handed Queen Elizabeth wave and continued on my way. Later in the day, we got together for lunch.

Our friendship moved forward uninterrupted. Jimmy even escorted me to graduate school faculty-student socials that would have been awkward without him at my side. He was an old soul with a background of long suffering that made him wise beyond his years. Dr. Couch, an awful host, made snide remarks like, "I see we have our favorite undergraduate present tonight." His comments had little effect on my pal. With every remark hurled his way, Jimmy returned a well-crafted quip.

On the contrary, I matched wits with Dr. Couch only once. "Bethee," he mocked with a warped pronunciation of my name intended to get under my skin for being so bashful. While sipping a glass of wine, he mocked, "Bethee, I see two of you. Why is that?"

I wanted to say, *Because you're drunk*, but retorted, "Because you have two eyes."

"Ooooooh," he roared his approval.

Such were my social interactions with my faculty advisor. Daily trips to the office were just as bad. With a heavy heart, I reported to work. If he were present, I returned when he was in class. As long as I stayed out of his way, I did okay.

In spite of quirky ways, the work Dr. Couch assigned became increasingly satisfying. While organizing book review pullouts, interesting literary critiques kept me abreast of recent publications. Before long, reading the reviews became a weekly habit. If my advisor's subscription had lapsed, I would have rushed out on Sunday mornings and purchased the bulky *New York Times* in order to get the book review section.

My heart leaped the day I picked up an old edition of the College Language Association Journal that had been tossed on top of the book review pile. While flipping through the pages, my eyes fell on the face of a homely Black woman. The caption beneath the photo announced the release of *The Bean Eaters* by Pulitzer Prize winning poet, Gwendolyn Brooks. In fourteen years of schooling— elementary through undergraduate, I had never read a book authored by an African American writer. Dr. Couch baited the hook that snared me.

Captivated, I headed straight to the James E. Shepard Memorial Library to learn more about the unusual woman who dared to be Black, female and award-winning poet. My reading lists had been saturated with the history and literature of Europeans. While undergraduate studies of Shakespeare, Chaucer, and

Homer were especially fulfilling, I had longed to see the experience of my people in print.

Though four of the twenty volumes of poetry Gwendolyn Brooks was destined to write had already been published in 1963, my library search revealed few facts about the amazing poet. For further research, Dr. William Brown, the Graduate Dean drove me to the University of North Carolina at Chapel Hill. At the time UNC was segregated but extended research privileges to graduate students at North Carolina College.

Prior to enrolling at NCC, my Southern University adviser, Miss Arthenia J. Bates, had arranged for Dr. Brown to continue the mentoring process she had initiated. He was a grandfatherly figure in his seventies who shared Miss Bates' high hopes for my future. They both envisioned my study of English in a doctoral program at Ohio State University once I earned the Master's degree. Meanwhile, I was to report to Dr. Brown whenever I ran into academic roadblocks. Naturally, I turned to him with questions about Gwendolyn Brooks.

On the ride to Chapel Hill, spectacular scenery stretched for miles. I was surprised by a landscape more beautiful than the one at North Carolina College. The NCC campus had sweeping slopes of deep green hues dotted with fluffy clumps of snow resting in hilly nooks and crannies. However, the campus setting did not compare to the glorious North Carolina countryside. The terrain was every bit as breathtaking as Miss Bates had described. Narrow winding roads curved around ranches with white rail fences and branches of evergreens arched at the edge of roadways. It felt like riding through a Christmas scene pictured on the cover of a greeting card.

A couple of hours at the UNC library proved productive. Once the research was done, Dr. Brown treated me to lunch at a quaint antique shop that doubled as a restaurant. Tables were set in small old fashion rooms decked with embroidered linen, silverware and crystal. Thanks to my Home Economics class back in high school, I knew what forks and glasses to use and how to drape my napkin. An afternoon of fine dining followed. Clearly, the culinary excursion with Dr. Brown was intended as part of a refined education that would prepare me for "the better things in life."

The beautiful scenery and fine dining made me chuckle at the country bumpkin images that had formed in my mind when Miss Bates said, "The people...say *'bacca* for tobacco; and you'll have to adjust to farms on the outskirts of the college campus..." Just the opposite was true. North Carolina offered sophistication not previously experienced. Most of all, the research venture to Chapel Hill revealed fascinating details regarding the genius of Gwendolyn Brooks.

I learned that the Pulitzer Prize was established in 1917, the year Brooks was born. In 1949, she was the first African American writer to receive this highest of honors bestowed annually on an American author in a category of literature such as journalism, playwriting or, in her case, poetry. In addition, at the UNC library, I found her four published books of poetry: *A Street in Bronzeville* (1945); Annie Hall, the Pulitzer Prize winning 1949 volume; *Bronzeville Boys and Girls*, the 1956 book of poems for children; and *The Bean Eaters*, the 1960 publication that had sent me scurrying to the library.

While strumming universal chords of the human condition, the everyday language of Gwendolyn Brooks' poetry had tempos that roused my experience. Determined to understand why such a gifted writer was not included in my survey of American Literature textbooks, I decided to explore the artistry of *Gwendolyn Brooks* as a Master's thesis topic.

A flash of excitement crossed Dr. Couch's face when I shared the proposed subject for my research. It turned out he had befriended Gwendolyn Brooks in a writers group just after World War II. Perhaps he himself was a temperamental and frustrated artist. It certainly would account for his surly manner. The theory about his disgruntled nature aside, my goal was to compile knowledge supportive of the inclusion of Brook's poetry in required surveys of American Literature textbooks.

Dr. Couch guided the proposed thesis project through the English Department's approval process; and, in an unexpected act of kindness, loaned me his copy of *The Bean Eaters.* Musical tones of my people sang on every page. The poems echoed familiar expressions and portrayed neighborhood circumstances with which I was acquainted. At the same time, Brook's lyrical writing style reflected general human conditions of boredom, danger, pain and joy.

As the fall 1963 semester drew to a close, my thesis manuscript slowly took shape. I argued that Gwendolyn Brooks' poetry rested firmly in an American literary tradition that dated back to Walt Whitman's *Leaves of Grass.* In his 1855 publication, Whitman moved away from Victorian English verse to the rhythmic language of ordinary people. By World War II, the poetry of T. S. Eliot, Ezra Pound, Marianne Moore, William Carlos Williams, Robert Lowell and, yes, Gwendolyn Brooks followed in this pattern. Like her contemporaries, she plucked subjects from the lives of her people and was as unmistakably committed to illuminating the Black experience as other writers were in emphasizing their cultures.

A passion for Gwendolyn Brooks' poetry warmed chilly December days. I hit a rhythm in gathering information for my Master's thesis that was difficult to interrupt. So, I decided against taking the long bus trip home to Louisiana for the holidays. Since the library remained open except for Christmas Day, travel time would be better spent on cataloging and analyzing a growing mound of research data.

Jimmy left campus early for a holiday job back in New York but not before leaving a letter with one of "the boys" as he called his crew. At exactly noon on the day after his departure, an envelope was dropped into my lap while I dined in the graduate student cafeteria. I opened the letter and read, "Aha! Thought you weren't going to miss me, didn't you?" The tears flowed. Baffled by my behavior, I scolded, *Girl what's wrong with you? Jimmy thinks he's clever. He knew I would miss him around this time of day. He always peeks in and gives me a wave around noon. We've never missed a single... Stop it!* I caught myself, dried my eyes and redirected my thoughts to revising the outline for my thesis manuscript.

With all students gone home for the holidays, the campus was eerily quiet. Snow piled high and I felt alone in the world as I trooped down Fayetteville Street, pressed around corners of empty dormitories, and made my way to the library. Inside, not a person was studying. The lone librarian opened the stacks where faculty and graduate students had access to books restricted to others.

I pulled a faded Walt Whitman hardcover from the shelf; chose a window seat in the stacks that overlooked the deserted campus; and then settled into an afternoon of reading and notetaking on index cards. Later the cards would be helpful in citing specific passages used in the text of my manuscript.

Four days into the routine, my roommate, Matoka, showed up without warning. "What are you doing here?" She was incredulous and so was I.

"No," I said. "What are you doing here? I haven't seen you in a while." Ours was another of those off-campus housing arrangements common to Black colleges in the early 1960s. An assignment to a cramped room with a double bed for Matoka and me to share had ended our temporary housing in faculty quarters. She used the space to store her clothes but bunked with one of her friends for the semester.

"Oh, I just dropped by to pick up a few things. I'm on my way home," she responded. "You not going home for Christmas?" she asked. "Are you stranded because of the snow storms?"

"No, I wrote my mother letting her know I'm staying here to study."

"Nope! You coming home with me. No one should be alone on Christmas Day."

"I'll be fine here."

"I can't enjoy my Christmas with you cooped up in this tiny room."

"Matoka, I'm fine."

"Look, come home with me," she insisted. "My family cooks a huge holiday feast. I promise to have you back on campus the day after Christmas." I gave in and went to Rocky Mount, North Carolina.

On Christmas morning I insisted on giving Matoka's mom the five dollars I had saved to make a leisurely holiday call home.

"Merry Christmas," I chimed but Mama's attempts at hello were released in uncontrollable sobs.

My heart sank. *Had someone died?* "What's the matter, Mama?" I asked.

Once she caught half a breath, everything tumbled out at once: "We didn't know what happened to you. With all those buses sliding off icy roads, we didn't know whether you were dead or alive. You been getting strange

113

mail from New York; somebody named 'Pumpkin' it says here on the envelope. Then a guy calling himself, 'Love' showed up at the front door. He had a watch and an engagement ring. When I told him you didn't come home, he stood right there on the front step and cried. I didn't know..."

"Mama didn't you get my letter?" I interrupted.

"Oh, we got it this morning. We were so worried that Tomprell decided to search once more in the mailbox. Your letter was frozen to the back wall. I know we don't have much time before the call is cut off. What you want me to do with this Pumpkin mail?"

"Send it to me at the college. Mama, I'm sorry I made you worry. I love... *'Click'*...you." I held the receiver wandering if bad weather had interrupted the call. I hoped she had heard my expression of love.

What a Christmas! I went back to bed, pulled the covers over my head and cried myself back to sleep. Hours later, a study rap at the door woke me up.

"I'm not hungry," I called out.

"Foods not quite ready; you have a phone call," Matoka shouted through the closed door.

A phone call? I wondered who could be calling me in Rocky Mount. I did not leave the number with my mother. "You sure it's for me?"

"Yes. They asked to speak with Bessie Waites."

When I opened the door I was thinking it was probably one of the guys who tried to hit on me at the club she carried me to on Christmas Eve. I took the receiver and mumbled a dry, "Hello."

"Merry Christmas! This is your holiday Pumpkin."

"Jimmeee!" I squealed. "How did you find me here?" At the sound of his voice, glee replaced gloom.

"I got my ways," he answered and quickly added, "Come to New York."

"To New York? I don't have that kind of money."

"You have enough for a bus ticket, don't you?"

"Well, yes but only for a one-way; and what will I eat? Where will I sleep?"

"Don't worry about it. You'll stay with my family; we'll feed you; and I will buy your return ticket to North Carolina."

"I don't know Jimmy."

"Come on Bessie. It'll be fun seeing New York at Christmas time."

"Ummm, no. It's too risky. I'll see you back at school."

"Tell you what, two days from now I will be waiting for you at the Port Authority Bus Terminal. Tell Matoka to put you on a bus due to arrive around 6AM. Remember, Port Authority, two days from now, 6AM."

"Jimmy, I... Jimmy?" *Did he hang up on me?* Yes, he did.

When I told Matoka about the conversation, she got all excited. "Everyone should see New York at least once," she said.

Next thing I knew I was sitting on a Greyhound with fifteen cents in my pocket and the just-in-case phone number of Matoka's uncle in Brooklyn. *I must be in love*, I mused. *Why else would I be on this bus?* A lifetime of caution had been tossed aside; but I had the time of my life in the Big Apple. In the grandest fashion, my fall semester of graduate school ended.

In the spring semester I focused on writing my thesis. Of course, Dr. Couch was as brutal as ever in his criticism. He peppered his comments with sarcastic sneers like, "'Long and lovely lines,' who writes like that?" As I struggled through the drafting of the thesis, not once did he compliment my effort. He approved each chapter with a grunt. I finally handed in *The Artistry of Gwendolyn Brooks* with trepidation.

The defense of my work in front of the review committee was the next scary step. Once again, Dr. Couch surprised me. His ardent support during deliberations was amazing. Afterwards, he described my thesis as "the most in-depth analysis of Gwendolyn Brooks' poetry to date." Then, in a remarkably generous act, he scribbled her address on a slip of paper. "Here. Mail it to her," he said.

What was the contact with Gwendolyn Brooks like? I fretted over whether my thesis was worthy of mailing to such a distinguished writer. At twenty-one, I did not realized how fast dreams flee. While I procrastinated, romance diverted my attention. I failed to act.

*T*oward the end of graduate studies, Dr. Couch invited Jimmy and me to his home to celebrate the successful defense of *The Artistry of Gwendolyn Brooks*. When I attempted to express gratitude for his guidance through the thesis process, he responded with one of his weird riddles.

"Bethee," he said, "If Party A can't meet the needs of Party B then why does Party B need Party A?"

"I... I don't know Dr. Couch," I stuttered and was immediately annoyed with myself. "I just want to say thank you," I blurted and then sat moping while he and Jimmy listened to Bach and Chopin albums.

I wondered about my professor's riddle. What was he trying to tell me about my relationship with Jimmy? I wished he would come right out and say what was on his mind. I loved Jimmy; he was one of the impactful people in graduate school who provided new lenses through which to view the world. The other two were Dr. Couch and Gwendolyn Brooks. These three ushered in a season of profound change in my life.

Despite his testy ways, Dr. William J. Couch caused me to focus on the lack of diversity in American textbooks; and, he helped shape a keen eye for evaluating the content students consume in classrooms. It would be years before a Reed College article dispelled my limited definition of him. As an accomplished jazz musician in his teens, he eventually performed with Louis Armstrong, Nat King Cole, Cab Calloway and Ethel Waters. In addition to Gwendolyn Brooks, Ralph Ellison was a member of his literary circle, and was described as his best friend. My advisor may have been a disgruntled artist but one thing is certain: he was a genius.

I also discovered in the Reed article that Dr. Couch's role as my advisor was intentional. With a doctorate of philosophy from the University of Chicago and a distinguished musical background, he was highly sought after by White colleges and universities. Out of a passion for helping the neediest of students, he chose Black colleges and I became a beneficiary of his brilliance.

In addition to introducing me to Gwendolyn Brooks, Dr. William Couch set me on a lifelong path of reading the *New York Times Book Review* and guided my first fledging steps as a writer. Prior to producing a seventy-page Master's thesis under his tutelage, I had written nothing longer than a ten-page essay. Then, there was Dr. Couch's crazy "Party A, Party B" riddle that would haunt me for a very long time. It seems I also left an imprint on his mind. For, years later when I tracked him down for a reference letter, he answered the phone, "Hello Bethee," and wrote a glowing recommendation.

Gwendolyn Brooks—a truly powerful influence on my intellectual development—pulled my head out of the clouds and cultivated an appreciation for the poetry in my immediate surroundings. Her poems awakened an awareness of art in the life and language of everyday people. Because of her, I developed a keener sensitivity to ordinary events that enrich daily life.

As years flew by, I was blessed with a second chance to personally interact with the poet. While putting my mother on a train in Penn Station, I observed an elderly lady with luggage get up when Mama's train was announced. I made an attempt to assist the woman. She declined but extended her hand, "Hello, I'm Gwendolyn Brooks and I..."

Gwendolyn Brooks! She didn't have a chance to finish her thought. I was an instant bundle of nerves. One sentence tripped over the next as I explained: "I can't tell you how much you mean to me. *The Bean Eaters* changed my life. Because of you, the stories, the language, the idioms of our people are deemed worthy of academic discussion. When I finished my Master's thesis my advisor told me to send it to you. Dr. Couch said..."

"You know Bill Couch?" Up to that point she had nodded patiently to my dribbling adoration; but she perked up at the mention of his name.

"Yes. In 1964 he was my advisor at North Carolina College."

"How is he?"

"It has been a few years but, last time we spoke, he was teaching at the University of the District of Columbia in Washington."

"Oh, he was a dear friend. Here," she said while searching around in her bag, "this is my card. I would love to read your thesis. Send it to me."

I promised to do so; and then, she boarded the same sleeping car as my mother. The train eased into the dark tunnel at Penn Station. *Imagine Mama riding to Chicago with the Poet Laureate of Illinois!*

At the brink of the twenty first century, I was given another opportunity to share my work with the woman whose poetry had altered my life; but by then, I was wife, busy mother and career woman. I did not see the door closing. In December of 2000 when Gwendolyn Brooks died, the writer in me cried. My lament was this: Twice blessed with occasions to know her better, I squandered them. Could it be I already knew her in the best way possible? I savored the brilliance of her artistry as a graduate student at North Carolina College.

Of course, James Blake was the most influential of the three NCC figures. A number one supporter in every endeavor, he showed me how to navigate the world in a more spontaneous, less logical fashion. Jimmy silenced the voices of naysayers and won over the church-girl. With my Master's degree in hand, I headed to New York and married my best friend.

Bessie Waites weds James Blake
&
Moves to New York

Photo: The Blake Collection (TBC), 1964.

CREO

Another planet! The move to New York from lazy southern towns was a rocket ride to the country's most urban metropolis.

In June of 1964, the city was noisy, hot, sticky, and crowded with people who scurried about like robots. On my first venture to the corner candy store in Corona, Queens I was virtually sucker punched and left with tear-swollen eyes.

"A strawberry pop please," I requested with a broad smile.

A mid-sixties media image of a New York immigrant stood behind the counter. The tubby bald man with greying sideburns and the thick accent of many Corona merchants suggested he was a recent settler in the adjacent Italian community of Corona Heights.

"No. A strawberry pop," I said and gently pushed the frozen fruit flavored bar back to him.

He grabbed it, tossed it back into the freezer, slapped the countertop with his fat hand and shouted, "Next! Next!"

It was a crushing experience but Jimmy later explained, "'Pop' doesn't mean soda pop in New York; it means Popsicle."

I thought, *Oh, they speak a different language here.* Indeed, hundreds of languages and dialects from around the globe could be heard on the sidewalks of New York. Gradually, I came to love the sounds of the city but I never got used to the humiliating boldness of men on the streets.

I had been taught to look people in the eyes and greet them warmly. So, in the manner of my southern upbringing, I said hello to children, women, and men. It was common courtesy.

"Good morning," I chirped on my way to the grocer.

"Well, how you doing Fine Thing?" slid from the lips of the man standing just outside the store.

"Uh... I'm good," I said and pushed pass him.

On the way home, a curt, "Hi," to the next male did not stop his vulgarity. He responded, "Hi yourself. You sho' look good," and then kissy noises trailed just steps behind me. I was terrified.

Again, Jimmy schooled me, "Bessie, don't speak to anyone on the streets of New York. Don't even look at them—especially guys."

*Un*couth*!* I thought and stopped speaking to strangers but, unable to ease by without at least acknowledging people with a glance, I hid behind dark glasses and took sneak peeks at passersby.

Jimmy's friends teased, "Hey Hollywood." They thought I was trying to be cool like some movie star in sunshades.

Learning to navigate the streets was one of the most difficult tasks of settling in my new urban home. It took several months and many awkward blunders but, sadly, I learned to rush by my fellow human beings like a normal New Yorker.

I did not know the magnitude of the change until I returned to Shreveport and folks pointed, "Is that Sister Waites' daughter, Bessie? Been up there in New York; now she thinks she's too good to speak to anybody."

By the time I realized a breach was occurring, it was too late. One of the worst things about moving to New York was the absence of close extended family and friendship bonds. Each time I returned home, I had fewer connections with the people who meant the most to me. Thankfully, the friendships of Armanda and Minnie V remained intact.

*I*n marriage, I hungered most to fill the void left by the loss of friends and by the emotional crater my father had dug. I expected Jimmy to magically satisfy these yearnings but cultural differences challenged expectations.

My husband was from a fun-loving environment. While still newlyweds, he took me to a Bring-Your-Own-Brown-Bag dance where granny women and elderly aunties brought covered dishes of fried chicken and potato salad. Old men lined the table with Johnnie Walker Red, Bacardi, and Tanqueray; and then ordered set-ups of small buckets of ice and large bottles of coke, ginger ale and tunic water for chasers. After the first round of eating and boozing, a live band struck up the music and old women on canes, young women in tight skirts, old men with greying hair and jitterbugs with skinny neckties—everyone, except for me, hit the floor and shook it down to the ground. I stared in amazement.

Never had I seen elders dance alongside youth except in church and under the Holy Spirit. In the Delta South where I came from, if men drank in the presence of women other than at a honky-tonk, they had been caught by surprise. As common practice, they scrambled to get whiskey bottles from their lips, behind their backs and respectfully out of the sight of ladies.

I said to one of the hip party-goers at the BYOB dance that it was strange to see old and young dancing and drinking together. He responded, "It's a new world squirrel." His words rang with more truth than he realized.

The fast pace of the city was overwhelming. During the first five years of marriage, Jimmy insisted that I come along every time he went out to relax. After our first child, Kanari, was born I was forever searching for a babysitter. There were middle-of-the-week movie nights, occasional bowling dates and, in warm weather, weekend trips to Bear Mountain State Park or other New York sites. On cold winter evenings, the parade stretched through house parties, dinner clubs and dance halls.

The endless activity was utterly exhausting for a person whose outings had been limited to church, school and an occasional soda-and-potato-chips party at a friend's house. When I married, my idea of a fun evening was reading aloud Shakespeare sonnets and plays. Jimmy's idea of fun was party, party, and more party. He had boundless energy and was the life of every gathering. With chants, "Let's get this party started, right!" Or, "Party over here! Party over there!" He would get the place rocking.

Once everyone was swaying to the music, we lovebirds perched in a corner. Other couples teased, 'You two act like you just met." "What do you have to talk about after five years?" "Don't you get enough of each other at home?" The fact was, whether at home or out socially, there was never enough time. Jimmy talked non-stop about his childhood, his two jobs and his volunteer work. I was the attentive listener.

Lingering hurt from my husband's childhood consumed much of my emotional energy. Of course, I had brought to the relationship bruises from my own youth, but they paled in comparison to Jimmy's shattered family. When his mother was hospitalized back in the 1950s he and his siblings had been scattered among foster and children's homes. Since young adulthood, he had engaged in social activism to rectify injustices that contributed to the collapse of his family; and he pursued fun as a diversion from the unshakable pain of past experiences.

Constantly, Jimmy sought my sympathetic ear. From the beginning of the relationship, I probably should have been assertive in expressing my needs. Instead, I endured a five-year onslaught of words.

We were grabbing a bite to eat before heading to yet another party. I finally said across the restaurant table "STOP!"

He jumped. His head turned. His eyes searched the room for danger. Spotting no apparent threat, he gave me a puzzled look and started to speak but my hand flew up like a stop sign.

"Don't say another word!" I half whispered. "I'll tell you when to speak again."

Shocked to silence, he finished his meal while I enjoyed the relaxing clink-clink of forks against plates and the muted chatter of other patrons. After the check was settled, I walked to the car in blessed quiet. As we rolled across the Triborough Bridge to our Harlem house party, I delighted in the hum of the car engine and the twinkling New York City skyline. Jimmy must have been dumbfounded but I simply enjoyed the drive in peaceful solitude.

When the car stopped for the red light at the foot of the bridge on 125th Street, "You can speak now," I said.

He guardedly searched my face before asking, "What... what was that all about?"

In a perfectly cooled out manner, I responded, "I couldn't bear to hear you talk another second."

"You were bored with what I was saying?"

"No. What you were saying was interesting. I just couldn't bear the physical sound of your voice."

"The physical sound?" he asked perplexed.

"Yes. Don't get me wrong. You have a mellow tone. I just needed a rest from the sound. Now, I'm more refreshed."

"You weird; you know that? Being shut down like that was..." My mind drifted back to our college days when the dam erupted and unleashed his bottled up hurts and hopes. Expressions of long-held ambitions partnered with his entertaining gift for gab. In me, Jimmy had found a trusted friend and good listener and he had talked non-stop until I slammed the brakes at dinner.

"You are eccentric!" he declared and drew me back from my musings.

"No. You talk too much," I retorted.

He shook his head and, as usual, got the festivities started the minute we arrived at the party. For the rest of the evening, he shot questioning glances at me. In between dances, every comment was prefaced with sarcasm: "Is it okay if I speak?"

Next day, we fell into our old routine. Jimmy talked. I listened. With excitement, he planned the next party and, though tired, I tagged along happy to be by his side.

I tried to keep up the pace but did not have the stamina for evenings that started at eleven and ended at two or three in the morning. My biorhythm had an early-to-bed, early-to-rise beat. Until this day, friends rush to call in the early part of the evening because they know I unplug at eight o'clock—if not sooner.

On Friday nights, Jimmy would plead, "Bessie, don't go to sleep; we're going out."

"Just a short nap," I would say, but come eleven o'clock, he was unable to rouse me. I was worn out with mommy duties and household chores. Besides, I was not a party girl.

Over time, my husband started going out alone and I lived in virtual isolation in a city where it was difficult to get to know people. To further complicate matters, as his social calendar became bloated, he continued to work two jobs and to volunteer at a local youth center. I missed my best friend but his ship sailed distant seas while I stumbled along a barren shoreline.

Later, I complained to my sister about nights home alone, "doing nothing."

Thelma said, "Nothing is good. People around you doing their thing can be the wrong kind of something." I was not close to understanding the difference between loneliness and the solitude she described.

In our mid-twenties Jimmy and I saw ourselves as mature adults; but we were little more than adolescents making careless decisions. Without religious counseling, parental models or other guides to follow, our trial-and-error approach to marriage led to heated arguments. Each of us attempted to mold the other into preconceived notions of what love in action looks like. We lost sight of what most of our fights were about. The goal became winning battles in an undeclared war.

Without warning, small easily crossed mole hills loomed into mountains too high to climb. My mountain was overwhelming loneliness in a strange city with a preschooler, one new friend, Carole Wooten, and no relatives or casual acquaintances. Jimmy's challenge was learning to live in the intimate confines of a family household. After residing in huge multi-bed institutions since the age of nine, he was the most comfortable in larger social settings outside the home.

In the best of circumstances marital bliss is elusive. Influenced by a youthful 1960s movement to break with marriage customs of the previous generation, my husband and I became prey to one of the biggest myths. I felt homemaking tasks should be divided fifty-fifty. Despite my efforts to evenly distribute the workload, menial housekeeping duties fell mainly to me. Squabbles erupted; and, without spiritual wisdom, small spats ballooned into large disputes.

In a time of societal flux when traditional roles were examined and redefined, it was especially difficult for a young married couple. My situation was further complicated by a life that was no longer rooted in the certain knowledge of God's favor. Instead, happiness depended on Jimmy's deeds (or misdeeds) and on his thoughts about my behavior.

Attempts at reconciling hurtful clashes with the "happiness ever after" marriage myth underscored that Jimmy and I had made wedding vows wide-eyed and ill-informed. Like most couples, we promised "for better or worse," but each of us clung to separate desires while trying to remake one another into the ideal spouse. Without Christ at the center of our marriage, common aims were increasingly difficult to identify and even harder to satisfy. As the decade of the sixties reeled toward the seventies, the need for a peaceful, more purposeful life loomed large.

Clarity of Purpose occurs in unexpected seasons. In a time and manner least expected, my world turned on its axle. Almost all my statements about him had been hateful but on the 1967 Delta flight home for the funeral, I thought, *I'm glad I forgave Daddy.*

Jimmy had played a big role in softening my heart. With every negative comment made, he would leap to my father's defense: "Bessie, your daddy is a World War II veteran. You can't imagine his pain and suffering. It wasn't just fighting a war overseas; when he returned home, he was beat down by racism. He couldn't get a job in the South. You lived there. You know Black men were jailed, beaten, and lynched. Your father couldn't take care of his family. He was a broken man who turned to the bottle. That's why he wasn't there for you." Perhaps Jimmy identified so strongly with my father because of the battles he and other African American men were still waging to feed, clothe and shelter their families.

Like a farmer turning soil for future seeds, Jimmy countered my every complaint with a *your-daddy-was-a-wounded-soldier* talk. Over time, he readied a field for the planting season.

Usually Daddy was on a hiatus from his family. However, he had been at home and looking healthier than ever during my visit two years prior to his passing. He and I exchanged frosty hellos, but Kanari toddled over to climb into his lap the way she did with her father. I snatched her back like she was about to touch a blistering hot stove.

Daddy had never suffered children easily, but ordered, "Let the girl alone." Stunned by his response, I loosed my grip and Kanari ran into her grandfather's arms.

Again the next day, Kanari was at his heels when he started out the front door. I thought he turned to shoo her away. Instead, he picked her up, straddled her on his shoulder and off they went. Never had I seen him relax with a child before his first drink of the day.

Astounded by the grandfatherly affection he showered on my daughter, "Is she okay with him?" I asked Mama.

"Yes. He doesn't drink like he used to," she reassured me.

I was even more surprised a few days later when he approached me, "Hey girl, you wanta drive me to the store?"

"Me? You talking to me?"

He nodded.

"Okay," I said.

With the echo of one of Jimmy's wounded warrior sermons ringing in my head, I made a right turn off the Blanchard Road and zoomed alongside Caddo Lake. Occasional sloshes of water glimmered through the heavily wooded path. Just before we reached Milam Street, Daddy pointed, "Pull into the lot on the left there."

We parked in front of a hole-in-the-wall joint—the kind always forbidden to me. Had it not been for years in New York, I would have refused to enter the place.

I stepped into the square cinder-block building without windows and wondered, *What do people find in dives like these?* It was not quite noon and we were the only patrons. Dimly lit bulbs cast red hues that dredged up haunting sounds of Bessie Smith *Back-Water Blues*. Two tables were off in the corner to the left but Daddy headed straight to the no-frills bar. We climbed onto backless stools and he ordered a whiskey.

"What you want?" he asked.

"A coke," I answered.

He smiled, "Girl, you got some sense. You know better than ordering a drink in front of your father."

I smiled though he probably could not see me in the darkened room.

He took a sip of whiskey. "You know, I always wanted to sit and talk like this with your mother."

An awkward silence followed the comment. I had never had a real conversation with Daddy about anything—especially my mother.

"I don't mean I want to drink with her. I just want to sit and talk with her. She's a good woman. A righteous woman..."

A second pause: *What am I to say?*

Another sip and he continued, "She deserved better than me."

I remained quiet.

"I know I ain't no good, but I sho' miss her."

After a long silence, he shifted his attention to me. "Girl, you alright, you know that?"

My eyes had grown accustomed to the lighting and I studied his perfectly even teeth as he smiled. *I have his teeth,* I thought.

The smile faded and he spoke in earnest, "You a good listener. I want to thank you for that. Most people don't listen. No chance to say what's really in the heart. Yep, I want to thank you for listening." He drained his glass, set it down and put a couple of crumpled bills on the counter before resting his hand gently on my shoulder, "Come on let's go."

I stepped out the door into a blinding afternoon sun but a softer light glimmered in my soul. Inside a dive of a bar, the Daddy I always wanted had touched me. Compassion and forgiveness began to grow in soil Jimmy had prepared.

My whole life, I had seen only my mother's suffering while my father's sorrow had hidden behind angry outbursts and alcoholic stupors. The brief but genuine encounter over a whiskey and a coke had finally laid bare his humanity. With a budding knowledge of his anguish came the startling realization that I had placed my mother on a pedestal. Though she had never claimed to be perfect, I had made her so.

It took one earnest communication for me to see I had viewed my father through distorted lenses. Like most children trapped in a crumbling marriage, I chose sides. Mama—the parent with whom I spent the most time and the one who provided basic needs—was the one supported in every instance. Do not get me wrong; I had reasons to despise Daddy. His drinking, stormy outbursts and joblessness took a massive toll on the family; but, until two years shy of his death, I knew nothing about his pain.

My mother's every emotion had been communicated through church testimonies, the slump of her tired body, and stolen tears when she thought her children were not watching. The lack of such intimate knowledge of my father's suffering left me with a one-sided view of a complex marriage. Judgement about Daddy's character was best deferred because it required a balanced perspective rarely found in adolescents and young adults.

Mixed emotions of joy, sadness, relief and guilt overwhelmed me when I was finally matured enough to honestly consider my father's strengths alongside his frailties. The truth is he had greatly influenced my appreciation of arts, crafts, literary expressions and secular music. At his core, Daddy was a sensitive man who, as chief offender in the family, bore the heavy burden of harm inflicted. The brief chat at the bar exposed a self-accusing spirit that convicted him more completely than any charges made by others. He needed to forgive himself as much as I needed to forgive him.

With a gentle touch, Daddy had forgiven me for the scorn heaped on him. Of course, a glimpse at his vulnerable side did not instantly undo years of malice. When anger harbored since childhood was finally cut loose from its mooring, the world felt lopsided. Still, forgiving my father was the most liberating thing I had ever done. Once exonerated of guilt, I was freed to move forward. Two years later, I flew home without spite in my heart.

At the funeral, Sister Clara Bell's voice rang out, "God won't place a burden on his children that they can't bear."

"Amen," I whispered, thankful that I no longer bore a burden of anger that could not be rectified.

On his forty-fourth birthday, September 29, 1967, Edgar Eugene Waites, Sr. was eulogized at Bethlehem Baptist Church established by his great grandfather, Rev. Charlie Clark—a former enslaved African in America. Daddy was laid to rest in Gethsemane Cemetery in Smithland, Texas.

My father's funeral occasioned a life-altering exchange with my mother. On the night of his burial, she and I snuggled in her bed as if I were a little girl instead of a young married mother myself. In a cozy but vulnerable moment, a persistent question jarred Mama's memory.

"What can you tell me about my Grandma Bessie?" I asked.

Instead, of the usual, *I can't remember anything about her; I was too young when she died*, Mama surprised me by jumping into the scene at her own mother's deathbed:

"Deeeevil children! Deeeevil children! Look at these little devil children!" my mother groaned and continued, "I was three. My sisters, brothers and I were gathered around the bed with Papa when your Grandma Bessie started ranting 'Devil children!' Then, she grabbed me, clutched me tight and whispered, 'But you my little angel child.' A few days later she died."

The dramatic snippet about my grandmother ended as abruptly as it had begun. A depressing silence blanketed the dark room where Mama and I lay staring at the ceiling. She drifted to goodness-knows-where, while I scolded myself, *Bessie why didn't you just keep your mouth shut?*

The bittersweet morsel about my namesake had caused great pain on a night already filled with grief. Still, the account of Grandma Bessie Ross Martin's passing was a gift. I had spent years dodging negative stereotypes associated with the name, Bessie. That night I embraced the loving identity Mama had bestowed on me in memory of a mother she barely knew.

The deathbed tale marked a new beginning. I was determined to learn more about my grandmother. During the cluster of family reunions surrounding my father's funeral, I discovered that Grandma Bessie's father was a preacher and a freedman during slavery. As an only child, she lived in a sprawling house filled with finery imported from Europe; and she drew strength from her devout Christian parents. Though my namesake was from a privileged background, she was a humble woman who married a proud but respected dirt farmer—the beloved Grandpa who was god of my life until I was twelve.

Equally as important was my grandfather's retelling of tales told to me as a child about his own mother. My Great Grandma Hattie's story reminded me how the "first scholars" in my family, endured slavery and learned to read under the threat of death. Not only did my Great Grandpa Martin learn to read, he taught his wife, Hattie. While listening to family slave narratives, a sobering thought took hold: *Only two links—Mama and Grandpa—separate me from the long chain of slavery in America.*

Though knowledge gathered about my lineage was scant, information about Grandma Bessie added value to my name. In the sixties and early seventies, replacing European or "slave master" names with ancestral ones became a popular trend. The year Jimmy and I married, Cassius Clay changed his name to Muhammad Ali. When our daughter was born, my husband and I chose an African name, Kanari. A few years later, Lew Alcindor would become Kareem Abdul-Jabba. In such an environment, retaining the name I had just begun to love would be a battle.

When I returned to New York after Daddy's funeral, Jimmy pressed me to choose "a meaningful name; a good name." By that he meant an African or Muslim name. Instead, I searched through countless books of English names for the meaning of Bessie. I discovered that my name, along with Betsy, Beth, Rebecca and Becky, is derived from Elizabeth. It means, "House of God; a place where God dwells."

The next time Jimmy asked, "Have you chosen a good name?"

I answered, "I already have a good name." From that day forward, I wore the name, Bessie, with pride. Shakespeare was wrong. A rose by any other name does not smell as sweet. The spirituality and family history embedded in my name suggested that core meanings of life are found in the words we use to describe ourselves. Names issue mandates and mark starting points for goals to reach. My identity would be less distinctive with a name other than, Bessie.

Besides making peace with a name I had loathed, Daddy's death marked an entry point into a world filled with purpose. Stories of Grandma Bessie and Great Grandma Hattie re-ignited passions for teaching and for writing that had been dormant since childhood. I left my father's funeral determined to make the most of seemingly bleak career opportunities in New York.

Intermediate School 61 Queens

Me and my English as a Second Language class at I.S. 61 Queens, NY (Photo: Frank Brown, 1969).

The racial divide followed me north to a new kind of isolation.

My tiny cubicle in the paperback western division of Crown Publishing Company was at the end of a deserted hallway, hidden from any potential colleagues. No one passed my door. The job as Assistant to the Editor was dull; and the boss barely spoke to me. Getting John Lindsey elected Mayor of New York City consumed her attention. With no chance of building a social network, I ate lunch alone; and, at the end of each day, squeezed into a crowded subway car wondering: *Is this as far as a Master's degree in English will take me?*

I was proofreading yet another bad manuscript about the woes of Deadwood Harry the day my husband phoned at the publishing company to say, "You should leave that job. Enroll this summer in the Intensive Teacher Training Corp offered by the New York City Board of Education."

As a twenty-four-year-old desperate to belong to a community of New Yorkers, I leaped at the opportunity to become a teacher. Following Jimmy's advice, I completed the series of concentrated educational psychology and philosophy courses and was provisionally certified as an English teacher. In September of 1967 the Board of Education assigned me to a new Intermediate School in Rego Park, Queens.

Bigotry greeted me at the door of I.S.61Q. A hostile principal sarcastically announced, "Your highly credentialed qualifications are most needed in English as a Second Language," as he slapped a sheet of paper in my hand and walked away. I was stunned. I had no preparation for the class and the only information provided was a roster of student names with a room number printed at the top.

Later that morning, the orientation meeting for new faculty revealed that sought-after English classes had been assigned to young women of European background. Their limited work experience was similar to mine: but, unlike me, they had not completed the required Master's degree in English. It was disheartening. I had gone the extra mile and earned two degrees but did not reap the benefits of my accomplishments. I searched for reasons to remain hopeful and thought: *At least I am working in a school close to home.*

The afternoon of the first day, I discovered that my students and I would be pushed to the end of a second floor corridor eerily similar to the job I had just left at the publishing company. Inside the classroom things were labeled: "chair" "desk" "door" "window" "chalkboard" "coat closet..." After several minutes of near paralysis, I sat behind the teacher's desk and expanded the list of items: "floor" "ceiling" "wall..." Perhaps the vocabulary could be used to teach students to say and write simple sentences in English.

On the second day at I.S.61Q, an energetic bunch of multi-cultural adolescents overwhelmed me. They hailed from Italy, Puerto Rico and several South American countries but I spoke neither Spanish nor Italian. In anticipation of finding a job in Louisiana, I had chosen French to satisfy two years of college language requirements. A lot of good my rusty French would do in a city where Spanish was the native tongue of many residents.

Though the similarities between Italian and Spanish languages might have been small, it was enough for some student dialogue across cultures. I was left completely out of the loop and a classroom of angry teens ran the show. They knew an inexperienced teacher had been dumped on them. Even worse, they were excluded from the routine activities of the school. While their peers changed classes, English as Second Language students spent the entire day, except for lunchtime, in one room with one instructor who kept pointing to and calling out the names of various objects. Rebellion was inevitable.

Students walked around the room; tussled with one another, and hooted at me. Chaos reigned until I linked their plight as immigrants to my second class citizenship as African American. As a child in a strange new city, I too had experienced prejudice. Nevertheless, as early as elementary school, I had managed to land the role of teacher while at play or by assisting my classmates with difficult assignments. Memories of my youth re-ignited a fire for teaching; and I rose to meet the challenge of a new expression of racial discrimination.

My first breakthrough was with Adolfo. Roaming around the room was not enough for this nutmeg brown twelve-year-old from Ecuador. Blunt cut, straight black hair fell in bangs over a menacing brow as he bolted for the door. A portion of each day, he freely wandered around the building until the assistant principal brought him back without the slightest acknowledgment of the bedlam in our caged classroom.

With no help from the administration, it was up to me to address Adolfo's exhausting escape episodes. Finally, I pulled him to my desk, flattened his hand alongside mine and said, "We're the same."

He did not understand.

I pointed back and forth between his hand and mine, "Teacher! You! Teacher! You!"

After a while, he smiled his recognition of our common skin color and went quietly to his seat. Adolfo never dashed out of the room again. As a matter of fact, he helped me gain control of the class.

"Silencio!" he would shout at his peers and they quieted down for the boy who had been bold enough to leave the classroom whenever he pleased. Once his classmates were orderly, he extended his arms toward them in a grand gesture; said, "Silencio, teacher," and nodded as he handed the class over to me. I got it. Adolfo was teaching me how to tell the students to listen.

Angela was a tiny little Latino girl whose curly locks sparkled golden and whose personality channeled the spirit of Lucy in *Peanuts* cartoons. In her bossy fashion, Angela expanded my Spanish vocabulary to include, "*Cierra la boca* (Close your mouth! Shut up!)" and "*Siéntate!* (Sit down!). Sometimes I wondered if she were giving me curse words; but I did not fret because the commands produced order in the classroom.

Renee, a tall Italian boy, who knew more English than he let on, was by far the oldest and strongest youngster in my class of mixed grade levels. When he called for order, the noise ceased instantly. No one wanted to tangle with Renee, not even Adolfo.

What a wonder a little love brought about. By showing one student I cared, I reached them all. In a month's time, I had a disciplined, preppy group of students. However, theirs was an obedience reserved for me only. When other teachers covered the class while I attended required meetings, students sometimes put the instructors out of the room and barricaded the door. Even the dean was unable to get them to open up. However, the moment they heard my voice, scrambling for order could be heard from behind the closed door; and I entered a classroom of angels ready to resume the lesson where we had left off.

Drawing on their experiences, students slowly learned to speak English. Eager to tell about themselves, they stood proudly to address the entire class: "I am Renee. I am from Italy. I have one brother and two sisters." Their oral recitations sounded like my high school autobiography.

Next, they learned to write simple stories about their homelands. The assignment began the same for all students: "In my country...," and then blank spaces were left for them to complete the thought.

Adolfo wrote, "In my country, I angry. I run up to mountains." His story explained those flights from the classroom whenever he had been overwhelmed with frustration.

One day on my way home, I stopped at the ice cream shop beneath the elevated 7-Train Station at Roosevelt Avenue and 103rd Street.

"A pistachio cone," I ordered while digging in my purse for loose coins.

"No pay for my teacher," a familiar voice drifted to me. It was Renee beaming with the outstretched cone and repeating, "For my teacher."

It was the best ice cream ever. I took luxurious licks and drifted in wondrous thought: *I love my English-as-a-Second-Language students. We understand one another's situations. Ahhh, teaching, a magnificent calling!*

These many years later, I still have a heart for immigrant children. It is difficult to bear twenty-first century debates about the best educational approach for children whose second language is English. Though the pendulum swings back and forth between English only or bilingual approaches, I firmly support the bilingual method. In a torturous process like the one my students experienced, really bright children lose their native tongues and fall behind in their academic subjects. Why should any child be denied the very best education? There had to be a better way of teaching and learning for the neediest students.

$\mathscr{T}$he claim, "racially balanced school," was hypocrisy at the highest level. I.S.61Q lacked the diversity that ensures a well-rounded education for all students. On the teaching staff, there were no Latinos and only four African Americans—Mr. Frank Brown, Mr. William Patton, Mrs. Christine Sumpter and me. Not one of us was assigned to teach academic subjects. Adding to the pretense of a just system was the school's practice of fostering segregation by manipulating student programs based on race and ethnicity. White students were ranked as high achievers and placed in advanced and "special progress" classes; while Black, Latino and immigrant students were labeled "slow learners" and tracked into low-performing and remedial classes.

Destressed by the discrimination at I.S.61Q, I followed closely news reports of the stance of neighborhood parents and teachers in Brooklyn. A struggle for change escalated in the overwhelmingly Black district of Ocean Hill-Brownsville where more than ninety percent of the teachers were White; and parents had no voice in schools that were failing their children. When the United Federation of Teachers negotiated for a "disruptive child clause" in their contract that would give teachers the authority to reassign a child to a "special needs" class, tensions boiled over. Under the leadership of the African-American Association of Teachers the community demanded a greater role in rectifying the inequities at the heart of a dysfunctional system of education. A cry for community control of schools went up.

I watched with great interest the work of the Ford Foundation's Bundy Panel. In response to the committee's recommendation of trail decentralization of schools, Mayor John Lindsey decided to experiment with community control in three districts—one of which was Ocean Hill-Brownsville.

The African American teachers at I.S.61Q greeted the plan with excitement. We huddled at our cars after school and whispered praises of the mayor. The United Federation of Teachers' objections to the experimental school districts was no surprise to us; nor were we amazed when close to ninety-eight percent of New York City teachers went on strike and virtually shut down the entire system in May of 1968. A life of Jim Crow segregation and Up-North bigotry had prepared me for that moment.

Determined that Black and immigrant students would not miss much needed instruction during the strike, Mr. Brown, Mrs. Sumpter, and I caucused about re-opening the school. We reached out to parents in the Corona and East Elmhurst area where I lived; as well as to parents of Second Language students who lived in Corona Heights and Rego Park near where I.S.61Q was located. Apparently the hand full of teachers, clerical and other school staff, who were neighbors of immigrant parents, convinced them to stay clear of any attempt to open the school. Also, some parents were fearful that their immigration status might be questioned if they "went against teachers."

We moved forward with the support of a small group of Black parents. In the meeting at one of their homes, when a search for space was suggested as the first priority, one of the mothers protested, "Schools aren't officially closed. We are entitled to use the facilities paid for with our taxes." All agreed and she contacted her friend, Mr. Jervey Hamilton, a well-known community activist who lived on Ditmars Boulevard in East Elmhurst. For the longest I thought Mr. Jervey was an attorney because he was well-versed in Board of Education regulations. Actually, he was a New York City fireman.

At subsequent meetings at his home, Mr. Jervey provided sound advice about limiting the scope of instruction in order to conform to Board policies. Because no school administrators or support staff reported to work and no lunches were available, he suggested a half-day schedule. He also advised against shop classes or courses that required the use of machinery. In addition to adopting Mr. Jervey's recommendations, the group agreed that instructors should be qualified with an earned Masters to teach classes that would be offered.

Because Mrs. Sumpter and Mr. Patton's classes required the use of machinery, the group decided their involvement in teaching might raise questions about safety regulations that would hinder efforts to open the school. Therefore, Mr. Brown and I were chosen to implement the instructional plan called Freedom School.

Our Freedom School was reminiscent of the ones established in the early 1960s to instruct disenfranchised southern Blacks regarding strategies for voter registration. We shared with those schools the common goal of obtaining a voice in the institutions that determined the quality of lives in African American communities. In addition to addressing the academic needs of students, the I.S.61Q Freedom School aimed to provide support for working parents who were scrambling for adult supervision of their teens during the strike. We also wanted to demonstrate support for the citywide struggle for community controlled schools.

On the first day of Freedom School, Mr. Brown and I showed up with a group of thirty students and their parents and demanded access to the school building. To our surprise, there was no picket line. The custodian, obviously caught off guard, refused to admit us. However, after Mr. Jervey read him our right of access to the school for instructional purposes, we entered without incident.

Because her son, Edward, was a student at I.S.61Q, my sister-in-law joined two other parents in daily patrols of the corridors. With Gloria Blake Gordly on her post, I was confident that Mr. Brown and I would not be interrupted by heckling protesters. In an orderly fashion instruction was provided for the thirty students in attendance.

For obvious reasons, I taught English but added Social Studies because of a History minor in graduate school at North Carolina College. Mr. Brown was qualified to teach Reading and Art. He possessed a Master's degree and had authored several reading textbooks illustrated with his original artwork.

On the second day of Freedom School, we were met by a handful of strikers whose signs I did not read. Someone shouted, "Scab!" but the term was wasted on me. I was a native of Texas who had never witnessed a strike or heard the word, scab.

Upon arrival day three, a police car parked near the entrance to the school building and a small band of teachers jeered. The policeman remained for the duration of the thirty-six-day strike but the protesters never returned after the third morning.

Other than an article in a neighborhood newsletter that named me as a teacher who was splitting I.S.61Q along racial lines, the Queens effort in support of the Ocean Hill-Brownsville fight for community control of schools went unnoticed. There were no public rallies on our behalf. Mr. Brown and I were inspired by the dedication of parents and Mr. Jervey Hamilton, our

145

advocate. Until the strike ended, weekly parent-teacher meetings, held at his home, insured that Freedom School was functioning within Board of Education guidelines. At the last meeting, the group celebrated the power of cooperative team work. We had stood up for our rights; had instructed so-call low-performing students; and had modeled for them the scholarship of Black teachers.

Though encouraged by the achievements of Freedom School, I returned to an unbearably toxic work environment. On his first day back to work, the principal charged into my classroom. "Stay out of my office! I'm the principal of this school," he yelled as blood surged beneath his skin up to his grey hairline. I had never been in his office; so, I smiled inwardly and continued to work with my English as a Second Language students.

In the teacher's cafeteria, instructors who had never noticed me sneered openly and hissed, "Scab!" I did not care. They had barred me from their colleague circle long before the strike. As they tightened their little clicks, I continued to eat at a table by myself. The other African American teachers were sensible enough to avoid such insults.

On my daily ride to work with Mrs. Sumpter, she quietly suggested, "Why don't you bring your lunch and eat at your desk like the rest of us. Save yourself the hassle with those people."

I wanted to follow her advice but I was a rookie mom busy juggling household chores. It was all I could do to get Kanari off to pre-school before dashing around to Mrs. Sumpter's house for the much needed ride from East Elmhurst to work over in Rego Park.

Despite on-going frosty responses from teachers and the principal, my social circle dramatically increased because the Corona-East Elmhurst parents and community people embraced me. They were my first friendship network in New York City.

In the summer of 1968, Yeshiva University invited a group of teachers of immigrant children to share effective strategies and assignments. I enrolled in the series of Teaching English as a Second Language forums. While it was not yet a major field of study like English, Math or Science, I left the workshops armed with ideas for lesson plans and new ways of engaging students. In the fall term, hostilities persisted while the joy of teaching swelled in my heart.

Despite the stormy aftermath of the strike, African Americans made strides toward educational equity in the New York City school system. The cumbersome central Broad of Education relinquished some of its powers over teachers and instructional materials to newly formed local school boards. I was grateful for the small role I had played to improve the quality of education for under-resourced schools in my community.

By the fall of 1969, nearly six years after my arrival in the city, I began to feel like a real New Yorker. My husband and I purchased a home in Laurelton, Queens but I maintained close friendships in Corona-East Elmhurst. Teaching was increasingly rewarding but by the end of the semester, I was granted a maternity leave from I.S.61Q. In April of 1970 my son, Shango, a future educational innovator, was born.

For My Children

Clockwise from top left: Shango, Kanari, Takbir & RiShana (Photo, TBC, 1977).

☙❧

For my children, I went back to school; but thought, *I must be crazy.*

Deep down I knew returning to school had been a sound decision. Seven years after the Ocean Hill-Brownsville struggle, I enrolled in doctoral classes at Columbia University's Teachers College. It seemed a good way to enhance my children's learning experiences but I was growing weary.

In addition to school, pregnancy with our third child and a standoff with the New York City Board of Education consumed a great deal of energy. My husband and I were determined to secure the best schools for eleven-year-old daughter Kanari, and six-year-old son, Shango. Once we chose District 26 of Queens from the *New York Times* annual ratings of schools, the uphill battle for a transfer from our locally zoned district was underway. During the struggle for the desired placement, I taught Kanari and Shango at home.

The fight demanded a high tolerance for cat and mouse games. I argued with the bureaucrat on the other end of the phone line: "I do not want my child attending Intermediate School 59 where I recently taught. The social adjustments of adolescence are difficult enough without added pressures from students I have disciplined or an administrator with whom I have disagreed." I also explained to the paper-pusher that I had made home visits to meet with parents of disorderly I.S.59Q students; had organized parents when a shop teacher openly beat a teenage student with his fists; and in some cases was responsible for student suspensions. I felt these details

149

sufficiently laid out the case for my children's transfer from the district where I lived.

"Your request is denied," was the curt response.

"Well, I will teach them at home," I answered.

"The city will sue."

"I will counter-sue. I will not let you endanger the lives of my children!" I hung up and the stalemate between my family and the old New York City Board of Education ensued.

The same zeal brought to the Ocean Hill-Brownsville fight for educational empowerment of neglected neighborhoods, was tapped during the battled Jimmy and I waged for a quality education for our own children. Though local community school boards had been established following the 1968 strike, the remnant central Board of Education would decide on our 1975 request for Kanari and Shango's transfer from the neighborhood school to an adjacent district where they could learn in an environment free of old hostilities that persisted among a pre-dominantly White teaching staff who still targeted supporters of Ocean Hill-Brownsville as scabs.

Throughout several months of homeschooling, an anonymous female Board of Education official rang the house weekly to read various regulations that had been violated. Jimmy and I were not shaken. We had come of age at the peak of the Civil Rights Movement and felt it was our duty to challenge unjust laws and practices. We answered each call from the Board with statements regarding our responsibilities as parents to ensure for the children a quality education in an environment free of harassment. Over time, the calls ceased. I assumed the Board was working on its legal case. "We need to find a lawyer," I said to my husband.

Before the search for an attorney got underway, "Mrs. Blake," the dry voice on the other end of the line started without a hello or good morning.

Oops, here's the court date, I took a deep breath as the woman issued her order.

"Have Kanari report at eight o'clock promptly on Monday morning to Junior High School 67Q and take Shango, to P.S. 221Q." Then, *Click*, the call ended without a goodbye.

The steady drone of the dial tone had a hypnotic effect. A minute passed before I started jumping up and down. Fumbling with the phone, I called Jimmy at work, "We won! We won! The standoff is over. We got the schools we want! The children have been assigned to District 26 here in Queens."

In the absence of an explanation regarding the decision, I concluded that we had become small irritants, like steady specks of windblown sand in the eyes of Board members. It was easier for them to avert their gaze. In any case, they turned their attention elsewhere.

Everyone had said to us, "You can't fight City Hall," but we understood that small victories are won through persistence. Struggle had been marshalled against a seemingly unbeatable foe and we won because we did not give up. Jimmy and I relished the victory won for our children.

By the time Kanari and Shango re-entered the public school system, RiShana—the baby I was carrying when I enrolled in Columbia University—was six months old. I enjoyed mommy-baby bonding during the day but, two evenings a week, I rushed off to doctoral classes the minute Jimmy got home from work. The schedule flowed with ease until the morning I woke up groaning, "I'm sick."

"Sick?" Jimmy asked absent-mindedly and kept dressing for work.

"Pregnant," I answered over the gurgling sounds of a churning stomach.

"Pregnant!" He paused, walked over and sat on the side of the bed. "Did you say, 'pregnant'?"

"Yes. Pregnant again! Our other children are five years a part. RiShana is only six months and I am pregnant again. I have to drop out of school. You know I was sick the whole nine months with Kanari and RiShana..."

"Bessie," Jimmy patted my stomach with a silly little grin on his face. "This is good news. You're..."

"...going to throw up!" I ran to the bathroom heaving. He knew what to do. Downstairs he rushed and returned with a cup of cracked ice and fresh squeezed lemon juice.

"You don't have to quit school," he said as I sucked on a tangy chip of ice. "We are going to do this together. Remember, you weren't queasy the whole pregnancy with Shango. Maybe you'll have short bouts of morning sickness this time, huh?"

"Well, maybe." Though wobbly, I crawled out of bed to face a day of household chores leading to an evening of classes at Columbia.

By late summer 1976, during the heavy months of my fourth pregnancy, I waddled into the room ten minutes late but my classmates had grown accustomed to the routine. The seat nearest the door was left vacant for a hasty exit. The baby tightened into a ball as I squeezed my swollen belly between the back of the chair and its arm desk. Sips from the ever-present cup of crushed ice and fresh squeezed lemon juice slowed episodes of heaving.

I had finished my coursework and was finally at the dangerous ABD (All But Dissertation) stage in pursuit of a doctorate in education. The writing of the dissertation stalled many students and completely derailed others. The ABD challenge was two-prong: I had to conduct independent, self-directed research on a relevant and preferably unexplored topic in my field of study; and I had to produce a well written paper that contributed new knowledge to the field. If that were not grueling enough, the finished dissertation risked being ripped apart by a politically charged review committee. If such a dreadful event occurred, faculty members from different schools of thought would use my research to battle over opposing points of views regarding educational theory and practice. Scary thoughts of writing a doctoral dissertation troubled me.

On the last night of the dissertation seminar, I was still sipping the ever-present icy lemon water. I settled into my chair and waited for the lecture to resume. The instructor cleared his throat and in a lofty professorial tone announced, "I am pleased to inform you that an esteemed member of this class earned the highest score on this year's comprehensive examinations..."

He might as well have been a teacher at the head of a Charlie Brown classroom. The *wonk-wonk* of his voice barely registered in the middle of my swishing queasiness. Perhaps a flowery introduction had preceded the statement, but my head popped up when I heard, "Bessie Blake, you don't have to take a bow; but, class, let's give her a warm round of applause."

Me? The shock sent my mind scuttling over the tortuous months of preparation for the exam. Mounds of books and research studies had pushed Jimmy out of our bed. I studied day and night for the exam and diligence had paid off.

The morning session of the big test day had gone smoothly; I responded rapidly to questions. However, an unforeseen mishap occurred in the afternoon. On one of New York City's hot sticky July Fridays, the air conditioning unit automatically shut off for the weekend. My thinking slowed to a crawl. I spent much of the time pushing the baby from under my rib cage in order to take deep breaths of stagnant air. At the end of the ordeal, I stepped outside into overwhelming heat with a sense of disappointing failure. *I don't care anymore*, I had told myself.

In an amazing reversal of moods, three weeks later I delighted in the knowledge that I had earned the highest score on my comprehensive exams. It provided the pep needed to tackle the dissertation project.

In early November a baby boy was born and his father named him Takbir—meaning *God is the greatest*. He would be my last child. His birth also marked the last time I would enter a classroom seeking a degree. Most significant, however, was the departure of my beloved grandfather when Takbir was only months old.

With Grandpa's death, every step forward felt less steady. A once unending paved road to the horizon broke into shredded ribbons that floated backward and encircled me. A great portion of the wall buffering me against eternity had collapsed and left gaps through which chilly winds were blowing.

Focusing on my studies became painfully difficult. Thank God for the newborn and the toddler who motivated me to begin the dissertation research necessary to finish the doctorate. Because Takbir was delivered soon after I passed my exit exams and his fourteen-month-old sister, RiShana, had been born days after I completed the battery of admission tests for Columbia, I affectionately referred to them as "my little bookends" for doctoral coursework. Thoughts of them urged me to complete the educational journey I had begun.

Unfortunately, I was stalled at the ABD level. While pursuing the degree, the number of dependent children had doubled and household income had been slashed in half. I needed a job but had not worked outside of the home for three years. My skills were rusty and my confidence was shattered. Endless days of baby diapers, baby food and baby talk were taking their toll.

Once a week, I trudged up to Teachers College to meet with my dissertation advisor about possible research topics. On the subway home from one of the conferences, I grappled with my inability to move forward:

Girl you got to get out of this rut, I scolded.

My alter-ego responded, *I don't know how.*

Well, do something even if it's wrong, the practical Bessie countered.

The internal dispute was interrupted by a sparkly-eyed woman across the train aisle who grinned from a subway ad, "I got my job through *The New York Times.*"

It was as good a place as any to start. Next day, I popped into the candy store near home for *The Times.* The shortest ad in the employment section grabbed my attention: "Director of Language Arts wanted to supervise tutorial programs for adult students."

Jimmy was frustrated. He had been lobbying on my behalf for a big-sounding job with a fat salary in the Governor's Office. According to him, the position presented an opportunity to "address pressing issues affecting women."

"I have no experience as an administrator," I protested.

He argued, "More homemakers like you should take on leadership positions. You have excellent interpersonal skills. Your responsibility for running a household demonstrates abilities in planning, budgeting, problem-solving, and supervising projects. Those skills coupled with your advanced college degrees will transfer easily to a job as an executive administrator."

He sounded like a nice husband heaping compliments on his wife. I was not convinced. Low self-esteem tilted me toward a job far from the spotlight of the public arena. A lengthy stint as fulltime homemaker had left me feeling unworthy of lofty positions. Besides, after working for the New York City Board of Education, I detested the politics of self-interest and racism embedded in bureaucratic public systems.

Ignoring Jimmy, I phoned the number in the *New York Times* listing for a Director of Language Arts. After an intense interview and months of waiting for a decision, I was hired as "the second choice," one of the staff people informed me on the first day of the job. It did not matter. I was eager to develop reading and writing curricula for adults who were mostly mothers. Surely, helping this population of students earn college degrees would be counted as addressing "a pressing issue affecting women."

CREATURE

The School of New Resources at the College of New Rochelle was the perfect place to test fresh curriculum ideas.

I arrived at the Coop City Campus in the fall of 1977 fired up and ready to practice teaching strategies learned in doctoral coursework. As Director of Language Arts, I had leeway to innovate. Unfortunately, my enthusiasm was crushed in less than a month on the job.

Ted, I will call the young faculty member who strolled over to my desk wearing skin tight down-with-the-working-class overalls. Actually, he was a middle-class Black with a Harvard degree. I expected a welcome to the campus. Instead, he addressed me with contemptable familiarity. Leaning in close, he placed one elbow on my desk, peered over the top rim of wire granny glasses and asked, "You have children?"

"Yes," I replied warmly.

"How many?" he asked after a puzzling pause.

"How many what?" I wanted to know.

"How many children do you have?"

"Oh, I have four," I smiled proudly.

"Haven't you ever heard of abortion?" His sharp rebuke left my jaw ajar; and, before rage could find words, he swaggered away in a cloud of phony relevance.

Annie, the campus counselor overheard the exchange and rushed over to express disbelief. "Talk to Bob; he has three children," she said.

Bob was the Campus Director who hired me. I looked for him but it was the beginning of Christmas recess; and, in an attempt to get ahead of holiday traffic, he had left the office early.

I stormed into the frigid night, climbed into my car and struggled to harness my anger on the drive across the Throgs Neck Bridge, along the Cross Island Parkway, and onto the Belt Parkway into Southeast Queens.

The moment Jimmy opened the front door, I shouted, "I'm not going back!"

"Not going back?"

"No respect! No order!" I peeled off my coat and tossed it on the couch.

"Whoa! Whoa! Sit down, Bessie, and tell me what's going on."

"I was told tonight I shouldn't have had children. I should've had abortions."

"What jerk said that?" Jimmy exploded.

"Ted!"

"That..." He caught himself without letting the word fly. Growing up around endless cursing had caused my husband to detest profanity. So, we both stood panting in silent fury. He calmed and started in a measured tone, "What did Bob say?"

"He left early but it doesn't matter. I'm finished!" I continued to seethe. "I'm not going back. It's bad enough to be working in a basement. I'm not going to put up with insults and attacks. I... AM... FINISHED!"

I paused, waiting for Jimmy to fan the flames of outrage. He was known for speaking out against unfair treatment no matter how small. Well, this was a big deal. It was sexual harassment but I was unaware of any laws or regulations in 1977 that curbed such incidents in the workplace. I expected my husband to stand up for me.

He took an entirely different approach. "You have to go back," he said quietly.

Baffled by his composure I shrieked, "No-no! Ooooh no! I'm not going back! Didn't you hear me? I am NOT going back!"

"Listen to me, Bessie."

I shook my head, *no!*

"Calm down and listen!" he said with a sobering firmness.

I quieted.

"You have to go back. Don't give them the satisfaction of making you disappear in thin air. Go back. Give them a piece of your mind. Then, quit and walk out with your head held high." It was masterful psychology.

Yeah, I thought, *I'll tell them!*

The rest of the holiday season was spent rehearsing what to say and to whom to give notice. *I won't stoop to speak to Ted. I'll go straight to Bob,* I decided.

An adrenalin rush ushered in the New Year. Ready to get the unpleasant episode behind me, I arrived early on the first day back to school. The moment I got out of the car, I spotted Bob getting off the express bus from Manhattan.

At the curb of Coop City's Einstein Loop, with a cold wind whipping off the Long Island Sound, I started, "Bob. I want to talk to you!"

"Yes Bess, I came in early 'cause I want to talk to you too."

"I want to tell you…"

"No, let me go first."

"No, I'm going first!"

"Bess, I'm sorry."

He shocked me. How did he know? *Did Annie call him during the holidays?*

"That incident should never have happened," he continued. "I agonized over it the entire holiday and couldn't wait to tell you that no one should experience such behavior. I would have called but I didn't have your number at home with me and you're not listed in the phone book."

"Well, I came early because I'm disturbed people feel free to behave in that manner. I want to let you know that I won't work in such a setting."

"Please stay. It won't happen again. I already spoke to Ted and I'll keep on top of the situation."

"Well..."

"Please stay," he repeated.

Bob was so genuine in his appeal that I decided to stay; and I am glad I did.

In the Spring of 1978, the Coop City Campus of the College of New Rochelle (also referred to as CNR), was one of four campuses offering the adult degree program of the School of New Resources (alternately called SNR or simply New Resources). My campus mirrored the schoolwide student profile. The average age was thirty-seven. At ten percent, males were a clear minority. Among the women students roughly eighty-five percent were African Americans, ten percent Latinos and five percent Caucasians. The female population included housewives of Westchester County, working women of every economic level, welfare recipients and single mothers from low income neighborhoods of the Bronx, Manhattan and, to a lesser extent, from Brooklyn and Queens. Though of varied backgrounds, a common thread knitted the student body together. None had achieved their higher education goals at the traditional age set by society.

Because I decided to stay on at the Coop City Campus of SNR, my understanding of the mutually dependent nature of teaching and learning grew by leaps and bounds. Forever intrigued by words, I searched for the root meaning of "learn" and discovered the term comes from an Old English word, *leornian,* which means the same as "teach." In essence both "learn" and "teach" are about gaining knowledge through reading, studying and thinking. I was excited that SNR engaged in the classical pursuit of knowledge where teaching and learning is naturally blended in faculty-student partnerships. Had there been a school motto it would have been: To learn is to teach; to teach is to learn.

Bob's humility, coupled with his inquiring mind, made him particularly suited for a curriculum requiring faculty partnership with adult students. In a more traditional setting, he would have been addressed as Dr. Robert Mendelson but he insisted that students and staff call him by his first name. It was Bob's way of establishing a level playing field that supported mentoring rather than lecturing. Though the chief campus administrator, his commitment to a democratic learning environment caused him to sit eye-to-eye with individuals as well as small groups of students. His thought-provoking questions aided them in uncovering their inner skills and strengths. He frequently encouraged his students with comments like, "You already know more than you think. Your experience is valuable; keep examining it." Under Bob's tutelage, adults who had lost hope of earning a college degree began to take back the power to learn they had handed over to faculty lecturers.

Before working at SNR, my teaching mainly consisted of standing in front of a classroom and struggling to pour knowledge into students as if they were empty vessels. It was refreshing to walk into any classroom at the Coop City Campus and witness small seminars of ten to fifteen students gathered in a circle and involved in lively discussion.

"How does every teacher engage students at such a high level of participation?" I asked.

Bob answered, "Students are equal partners in the learning process. Teachers are masters of the content and theory of a given subject. Students bring with them knowledge and skills gained from life. They are parents; they are community workers; they are responsible members of society. In the seminar, their expertise is valued."

One of the unique aspects of the SNR seminar was the variety of structures that supported it. Rather than the traditional ten years spent in three-credit night school courses, SNR offered six-credit seminars that allowed adults to complete the bachelor's degree in roughly four years.

Also, unlike more traditional settings where a three-credit course required students to attend one-hour sessions on three separate days of the week, SNR's six-credit course responded to the busy lives of working students. The six-credit seminar was scheduled in a four-hour block of time once weekly; and was enriched by a two-credit independent study that students presented in class. To make courses even more available, classes were offered mostly in the evening and in locations convenient to the routines of adult students. This emphasis on access explained why the Coop City Campus was housed in the Einstein Community Center where adults congregated to conduct community affairs.

Once I understood the thinking that supported seemingly peculiar aspects of SNR, I knew I was in the right place. Not since kindergarten in my mother's cramped bedroom had I been so completely at home in an educational environment. If I had left SNR in a moment of highly charged emotions, the magnitude of the loss would have been too great to measure. Donna Tyler—a co-worker with whom I later became close—often quoted her father: "Don't let bad people push you out of a good job." Had I let Ted drive me away, I would have been robbed of a truly good job. Destiny won out and I settled into a joyfully invigorating learning process.

In his role as Campus Director, Bob hired faculty and staff with pioneering spirits. They were excited about innovative ways of teaching and were willing to work evening hours. Enthusiasm was evident in the confidence they placed in students' abilities to help shape and direct the learning process. I was fortunate to be a member of such a highly motivated team.

Urged on by the student-centered nature of learning at the Coop City Campus, I peppered Bob with questions about his techniques with adults. He began, "I am able to reach them because I understand that people who grow up poor resent people who take for granted the advantages of life as if they are entitled to the better things. Drawing on my own experience growing up as a poor kid of Irish-Jewish descent in the Bronx, I'm able to put students at ease because I share their skepticism about those who think that certain people cannot learn."

He ended with a statement of his educational philosophy: "Spend enough time with students who desire to learn and you can teach them; but," he said, "you don't teach them what you think they need to know. You find out about their interests and their experiences. Then, you say to them, 'This is what you already know. Here are some things you might need to know.' Once students plow through self-examination, they get good at setting learning goals for themselves." In other words, he encouraged partnership in the learning process between teachers and students.

From the beginning, Bob was a mentor and he continues to inspire my intellectual growth. In one of our recent conversations, he recommended as "a must see" Michael Moore's *Where to Invade Next*. The film highlights lessons America can learn from around the world. In the documentary, Moore includes interviews of Finnish educators, whose students freely explore independent learning opportunities. "It is an approach," says Bob, "in which learners get a real sense that they are smart and that they can do stuff. In other words, education becomes power in the hands of students. Learning is not just a matter of digesting a lecture or passing a test. Learning involves thinking through problems and applying what you know to real life situations."

Bob is an innovative educational thinker who came to SNR in the early 1970s during a period of major transition in his life. Like him, adult students and staff arrived at the school at points in our lives when dramatic, and sometimes traumatic, experiences dictated a need for change. Mine was a financial challenge; others dealt with illness, death of loved-ones, divorce or, as was the case with Bob, loss of a job. All of us were at vulnerable, teachable junctures. SNR's adult degree program offered a viable path forward. Race, gender, religion, social class and financial standing had previously separated us. At the Coop City Campus, a love of learning united us.

In the nation's largest neighborhood of high rise apartment dwellings, extremely motivated students were tucked in the basement of the Einstein Loop Community Center. At the end of tedious workdays, a passion for learning compelled class attendance. Many students rushed home to secure childcare arrangements before heading to campus. Once settled in classes, their stomachs growled at the gnawing aroma of Chinese food that drifted from a restaurant on the street level. There was no denying the academic outcomes of the fledging

Coop City Campus of SNR but the physical facility was grossly inadequate.

As Director of Language Arts, I was concerned about the lack of appropriate and sufficient tutorials for students who needed to improve their writing skills. Bob and I hired good tutors but skills development spaces were non-existent due to rapid increases in enrollment.

During an era of rising unemployment in the late seventies, students identified as "adult learners," "second chance," or "previously by-passed," flooded into colleges and universities across America. They wanted to re-tool for a job market that was rapidly shifting from manual labor to the use of technology. SNR students were no exception. At the Coop City Campus, expanding enrollment forced students with daytime obligations to seek help with skills development during evening hours when most classes were in session. Because of a lack of space, tutoring occurred at tables in the lounge area or at the end of hallways where distractions were inevitable.

"Come on Bob, this is unacceptable," I complained.

"You're right. You're right," he readily agreed. "Bottom line, we need a bigger place. I get it."

"Not just bigger, better! This place is like the hole of a slave ship," I declared.

Usually Bob had a political analysis for every situation but he promptly squeezed from a really tight budget the money to partition off sections of two classrooms for small tutorial enclaves. To his credit, he did not stop there. The two of us began to look for an appropriate campus facility. A move outside of the high-rise housing complex was likely to trigger a New York State Education Department audit; so, the search was limited to the boundaries of the Coop City community.

The localized search failed to identify a new home for the campus. However, there was an upside to scouting for space. Bob and I got better acquainted. Though it was the turbulent seventies—a time when most every conversation was political—candid dialogue rarely crossed cultural or racial lines. Not the case with Bob and I; we discussed difficult topics that Blacks and Whites usually avoided or whispered in silly indirect phrases like "inner city" when referring to African Americans and Latinos; or, "less fortunate" when describing poor people. In pursuit of better learning environments for adult students, honest dialogue bubbled up like spring water muddied only by the two of us wading into the stream.

He examined poverty, disease, crime and poor schools through the lens of a flawed capitalism. "It's all about class; about the haves and have-nots," he said.

"Yeah, and who are the haves and the have-nots?" I retorted. I took the position that racism is the fundamental sickness of American society and concluded, "Whether capitalist or socialist, you will find people of African descent at the bottom of government systems around the world."

Eventually, each of us recognized some validity in the other's point of view. Bob agreed racism was a factor but not the basic one; and I began to analyze the ways in which economic class drives disparities in resources allocated to Black and Brown people.

However, when I thought about the profile of students at New Resources, I was still prompted to ask, "What has driven us into the streets searching for decent learning environments?" The question was intended to provoke thought and I answered, "It is because ninety-five percent of students at the Coop City Campus are from African lineage. As you look around the College the quality of facilities improves in locations where the majority of student are of European background. The facts speak for themselves."

Despite our differences, a trusting relationship developed between Bob and me. Though he was my colleague for only one academic year, friendships born of honesty have lasted a lifetime between his family and mine. In the summer of 1979, he resigned as Campus Director to pursue private practice as a therapist. Before leaving, he recommended me as his successor. In doing so, he launched my career as an educational administrator. My promotion took effect in September of that year. As my husband had foreseen, skills learned as a homemaker were assets as I assumed leadership.

𝒫romotion to Campus Director meant automatic membership on SNR's Executive Committee. Among the five directors was Dr. Thomas Taaffe, the man whose thinking shaped the academic environment in which we worked. From him, I learned much about the beginnings of the school.

The college as a whole had not escaped the widespread campus unrest and Teach-Ins of the 1960s that pushed for social justice and curricula of inclusion. Indeed, CNR student activists were relentless in their attacks on the irrelevance of traditional educational models. In response to demands for different environments of teaching and learning, many single-sex institutions went coed but CNR remained true to its mission of educating women.

The new president of the college in 1972, Sister Dorothy Ann Kelly, rolled up her sleeves and worked with a bright young philosophy faculty member, Dr. Thomas Taaffe. Together, they mapped a brave new direction for the institution.

Believing that life experience is an essential element in any academic curriculum, Tom developed a pilot where students engaged in examination of their prior learning. Placing shared responsibility for instruction in the hands of students revolutionized his faculty role. A number of Westchester housewives audited his classes. As these adults examined their experiences, identified their existing skills and set goals for themselves, they began to develop and present course proposals for consideration. Tom's thinking expanded. As he watched the older students discover new resources within themselves, he realized adults are as capable of managing their own learning as they are other aspects of their lives. Tom named his pilot New Resources.

With administrative and political savvy Sister Dorothy Ann Kelly crafted the structural foundation for Tom's innovative approaches to learning. Driven by a larger vision than experimental classes embedded in a traditional arts and sciences curriculum, she pushed through changes in CNR's governing bodies and reshaped the college into a university model with three distinct schools. In the revamped institution, Tom's program became the School of New Resources in 1972. Two existing academic units became the School of Arts and Sciences (started at the founding of the college in 1904); and, The Graduate School (initially established as a program in 1969). The School of Arts and Science continued the college's original mission of providing a unique educational setting for women. The other two schools were coed. In 1976, the School of Nursing would be added as an additional coed unit.

With the new organizational structure in place, the college president spearheaded the New York State Education Department's rigorous quality review process. Along with the registration of a dramatically different CNR, SNR's undergraduate degree program designed for adults was certified. The new adult unit emphasized the social justice mission of the Ursuline nuns as Sister Dorothy Ann reached out to underserved communities in the New York City metropolitan area. Such dedication to education for empowerment of poor people mirrored the missions of "education for service" at Black colleges I had attended. It bonded me with CNR in a special way.

Access to learning in places where students lived and worked was one of many unique SNR features. In 1972, the New Rochelle Campus—located on the main grounds of the college—began serving the needs of surrounding residential neighborhoods. That same year, the first off-campus unit opened in Lower Manhattan. Sister Dorothy Ann Kelly, Tom Taaffe and labor leaders— Victor Gotbaum and Lillian Roberts—hammered out the contract establishing the District Council 37 Campus for union members that also had a retiree program. Tom was appointed Director of the first branch campus located at the union's headquarters.

When I joined the SNR Executive Committee in 1979, Dr. Thomas Taaffe was still director of the union campus and Sister Ruth Dowd administered the New Rochelle Campus. I took pride in the fact that the Coop City Campus had begun offering the same Bachelor of Arts degree in 1973, only a year after SNR opened. However, I was disappointed to learn that the program had remained in the cramped quarters of Einstein Community Center for nearly six years.

In January of 1979 the New York State Board of Regents certified one of two site locations being supervised by Coop City staff as the South Bronx Campus. Brother Edward Phelan was named Director of the new campus. Joining the Executive Committee around the same time as me was Dr. Louis de Salle, Director of the New York Theological Seminary Extension Center, opened in midtown Manhattan in 1977 but worked its way to full campus status by 1980.

A new breed of educational leaders developed learning opportunities for people without easy access to higher education. In local neighborhoods, increasing numbers of adults benefitted from quality academic programs run by SNR. At the same time, huge financial payoffs assisted units of the college experiencing declines in student enrollment. Along with SNR's growth, murmuring and complaints mounted regarding inequities in facilities between the branch campuses and the rest of CNR. The Coop City Campus basement quarters were constantly pointed to as an example but I was not discouraged. On the contrary, I was propelled forward by Zechariah's Biblical exhortation: "Do not despise small beginnings, for the Lord rejoices to see the work begin."

CREO

The Little Yellow Schoolhouse was on my mind when the president popped by my office.

Did she wink? I thought it strange behavior for such a formal Westchester nun. Do not get me wrong. Sister Dorothy Ann Kelly was a thoroughly modern woman. She drove herself to the Coop City Campus and appeared at my door dressed in a red blazer, white blouse and straight black skirt that fell just below the knees. Nothing about her said sister of the cloth.

Stunned, I jumped up from my desk, quickly gathered my wits and began an impromptu tour along the narrow basement corridors of the community center that housed the campus. *Is she here about the proposal?* I wondered.

As Campus Director, I had resumed the search Bob Mendelson had started for a new home for the Coop City Campus. An empty prefabricated building within the boundaries of the community of high rise apartment buildings had caught my eye. A closer inspection revealed what seemed like the perfect self-contained spot for adult learners. It had been used by elementary school children when residents first moved into Coop City; but had been vacant since the completion of the Truman High School complex—with its adjacent junior high and elementary schools.

I fell in love with the little yellow building while gazing from the sidewalk at the fenced-in yard. The possibilities seemed endless. It was a facility where adult learners could have a space solely dedicated to their use. I envisioned the beautification activities of a student run gardening club linked to the school's science offerings. For the first time the college's presence within the community would be displayed by a campus sign noticeable from the busy I-95 service road. Most of all, relocation within Coop City proper would forestall a name change and State Education Department audit.

Back at the office, I immediately drafted the proposal that became known as the Little Yellow School House Plan to Upgrade the Coop City Campus. Certainly, a visionary college president like Sister Dorothy Ann understood the connection between setting and academic success; but I followed channels and forwarded the proposal to my boss, the SNR Dean. Months passed without a response from him and I did not know whether the plan ever reached the president's desk. That is why her pop-up visit on a balmy fall afternoon was such a complete surprise. Bent on making the most of her presence, I showed the president every inch of cramped campus quarters at Einstein Loop.

As we exited one of the little tutorial rooms, I shared my vision of a skills development center at The Little Yellow Schoolhouse that would emphasize writing across the curriculum. Then, it happened again: *a definite wink.* I made a mental note but doggedly continued the tour intended to gain approval of the proposed campus upgrade.

Sister Dorothy Ann listened politely as she peered into overcrowded classrooms and staff offices with copy machines pressed against counselors' desks. In the middle of my pitch for more space ...*another wink? Nah, it seems more like a tic.* I ignored it and ended the tour.

The minute I stopped speaking, without one comment about the needs I had described or the reason for her visit, she asked, "Bessie, when will you finish your doctorate?"

"This May," I responded hesitantly.

She winked a fourth time and extended her hand, "Thank you for the tour," and then departed the campus as abruptly as she had arrived. I was astonished. That night I told Jimmy about the visit. He too was baffled.

It was not my first awkward encounter with CNR staff. As the only Black on SNR's Executive Committee, I was growing accustomed to the clumsiness of working in an all-White environment. I faced unending comments about my hairstyles; responded to requests to touch my hair; and ignored questioning stares when corn rolls turned to afros and then to straight hair. Sometimes, when nothing funny had occurred, deadpan stares were followed by quirky chuckles.

Early on, one of my new colleagues approached me and said, "Bessie, you work so hard; you're either a saint or a fool." The same day, a staff member from that campus expressed a similar feeling. "You work too hard. Oh my! You are a saint or maybe just foolish." It was obvious they had been gossiping about me. Both remarks also revealed a lack of dedication to helping overwhelmed first generation college students. With each comment, I smiled and thought: *I'm neither a saint nor a fool. I'm simply a Black woman doing what's necessary for my survival and for desperate students seeking success for their families.*

Such behavior on the part of my coworkers made it easy to receive Sister Dorothy Ann's visit and her winks as another in a series of missed messaging, where one person did not quite understand the cultural codes by which the other operated.

Several months passed without any action on The Little Yellow Schoolhouse. While anxiously waiting for a decision, I decided to teach the introductory composition course, entitled "Translating Experience into Essay."

*W*riting about oneself requires courage—especially on the part of adults returning to school after long absences. In the writer's workshop format of "Translating Experience into Essay," students painstakingly learned to trust their peers enough to share their writing. A breach of that trust sent me over the edge when a young woman, barely twenty-one, flounced into class late and disrupted an environment of easy communication that had been cultivated.

"Let's hear your essay," a classmate requested of the tardy student I will call Florence. Eager to enjoy the lively colors and ready wit usually woven into Florence's writing, ten students leaned forward anticipating a sure treat. Her essays were liked by budding writers; as well as by the author who had returned to school for his bachelor's degree though his book had been reviewed in the *New York Times Book Review.*

With all eyes on her, Florence unpacked her designer book bag; slowly pulled out a pen; then held it before the class. With obvious sarcasm, she began, "This is a pen. It's shaped like a wrench. I like my wrench pen. I write with..."

"Just who do you think you are?" flew from my mouth; and with a sullen undertone, I continued, "Flouncing in here late! Nobody cares about your darn pen. You got some nerves! Don't you..."

"Ugggh, pleeease stop," pitiful moans came from a fellow student who was a recovering addict unable to bear the sound of harsh words.

"Oh." His plea summoned memories of how small I felt when my undergraduate English professor had raked

174

me over the coals in front of the entire class. I took a deep breath; apologized to Florence; then, admitted to her and the class that my behavior was unprofessional.

My tone was overly friendly when I asked, "Now who would like to read next?" Some brave soul raised her hand and the class resumed a mellow flow. Unable to take her eyes off me, Florence never got into the rhythm of things that night. At the end of the evening, I reached out to her again. Both of us confessed immature behavior and laughed about the incident. Thankfully, the breach in student-teacher relationship was repaired. For the rest of the semester Florence came to class on time and earnestly participated. As she continued to wow the class with the clever twists of her narratives, I grew more comfortable working with assertive adult learners—some who were twice my age and others who were like baby sisters.

A blank page bullies the most skillful writer. The intent of "Translating Experience into Essay" was to reduce writing anxiety by allowing students to start the process with a subject they knew infinitely: their own experience. In order to minimize tensions caused by sharing their writing, several cautionary notes were outlined. First and foremost, respecting the integrity of one another's work was a must. Derision had no place in the seminar. Everyone's job was to assist the writer who was presenting by helping her to clarify what she wanted to say.

Second, unlike a private diary or journal, autobiography does not demand the disclosure of secrets or sensitive personal information. It is entirely up to the writer to decide which details to share in a narrative. A dramatic public event can be just as engaging as an intimate incident that occurred at home. In my class, students did not have to bear their souls for a grade.

Third, it was important to understand that the first draft of writing is almost never the final product. Writing is a process of discovery of ideas; of zeroing in on main ideas and providing supporting details; of rewriting and revising to clarify; and finally, of editing. It usually takes several drafts before an essay reads like it flowed from the writer's pen without effort.

Even when the process is clearly understood, writing remains an undertaking where editorial feedback is important. In the "Translating Experience into Essay" workshop format, students were subject matter experts as they wrote about themselves; and they were critics as they offered feedback regarding their classmates' work. My role as faculty was to foster an atmosphere that supported constructive criticism. I steered students away from comments like, *Fantastic! It's good.* Or, *I like it.* More helpful remarks or suggestions for improvement included: *"Your use of description is powerful." "I can see the bright colors and smell the odors."* Or, *"It's an interesting topic but I would better understand your point if you gave more examples and illustrations to support your opinions."* The latter kind of feedback assisted student writers in revising and rewriting their drafts.

Required textbooks aided in the writing process. Peter Elbow's *Writing Without Teachers*, guided student comments and questions as they critiqued one another's work. The book also provided freewriting exercises that stimulated the drafting of random ideas from which essay topics could be selected. As for me, Elbow's handy little paperback fast-tracked the shift in my teaching style from lecturer to facilitator of learning. The other two textbooks, William Strunk, Jr. and E. B. White's *The Elements of Style* and Daniel Pearlman and Paula R. Pearlman's *Guide to Rapid Revision* assisted in the editing of drafts. Both volumes remain desk references for my own writing.

As the semester progressed, "Narrate! Reflect! Connect!" became the class motto. Regardless of the topic or the length of an autobiographical essay, it is important to *narrate* fully—that is, share the details necessary to tell a really good story. Then, *reflect* on the personal meaning of the event. Finally, *connect* the experience to a significance that is larger than you, the individual. No writer wants to compose a great narrative and leave the reader thinking, *Interesting story, so what's the point?*

"Translating Experience into Essay" put fun into learning. The joyful sharing of autobiographies became springboards that moved students from storytelling to the expository compositions expected in college. By semester's end, they were ready for more analytical forms of writing; and I was hooked on reading and writing biographies. Indeed, we were all adult learners.

In rare moments, writing spills onto the page like waterfalls from well-travelled rivers; but, most of the time, for most of us, ideas seep from deep caves of foggy minds. Then, there are those, like my tutorial students, who are terrorized by the thought of writing. Though adults, they came to the writing process visibly shaken. Some squirmed in their seats and broke out in sweats. Distraught over her inability to put ideas on paper, one student screamed aloud, "Help! Help! Help!" Her cry fired a desire to better serve this neediest population of adult learners and led to my dissertation research topic.

I entitled the study, "Help for Adult Basic Writing Students" but my dissertation advisor said the topic was too broad. "Bessie, pinpoint the specific kind of help you want to provide and then connect your strategies to existing theories about writing," he said. Eventually, the project was approved as, "The Composing Process of Adult Basic Writing Students."

My research study on the composing process uncovered three important observations. One, basic writing students did not understand writing as a multi-step process that involves discovery of ideas, organizing ideas, and then correcting errors in grammar and mechanics like capitalization, punctuation and spelling. Two, their attempts to write perfect first drafts of essays revealed they were unaware of writing as a process that usually requires several drafts before the composition is a finished product. Finally, students in the study were unable to slow down the internal editor that climbs onto every writer's shoulder and picks apart what is written. In a panic to capture a thought on paper before losing it, these students chopped up ideas before they were fully formed.

To address challenges identified in the research, I engaged basic writing students in freewriting exercises where ideas were allowed to flow without attempts at correcting errors. If the student filled the blank page with one rambling thought without capitalization or punctuation, it was okay. At least they had gotten a series of ideas onto paper from which to choose main points for their essays. Then, in a process of review and elimination, students chose a topic; practiced writing main idea sentences; and then, they developed paragraphs with supporting details.

Throughout the writing process I encouraged, "Forget about what I want to hear. What do you want to say?" "Relax. Let the ideas flow and remember hold that editor back."

By intentionally breaking the writing process into smaller steps, basic writing students began to have success. In addressing the overall organization of their essays, they reviewed the sequence of sentences in each paragraph and chose the order of paragraphs that best supported the main idea they wished to communicate. Once paragraphs were arranged in the best sequence, their internal editors were released. Then, *Guide to Rapid Revision* became a useful resource for correcting grammar errors such as subject verb-agreement and sentence fragments. The pocket-sized book also helped them fix the mechanics of capitalization, spelling and punctuation.

While working with the neediest students, I completed my dissertation. In May of 1979, Columbia University awarded the Doctorate of Education with a concentration in the teaching of English composition and literature. Like so many difficult challenges, the value of the doctoral study experience was not realized until the last task was completed. Only then did previously closed doors begin to magically open.

I was eager to pack the Coop City Campus and relocate to The Little Yellow Schoolhouse. However, repeated queries to the Dean's Office revealed nothing about a planned move. Just when all hope vanished and I began a search for space outside the boundaries of Coop City, Sister Dorothy Ann forwarded the message that a lease had been signed.

A shout, "The Little Yellow Schoolhouse is my baby!" echoed along the basement corridors of Einstein Community Center and sent staff running to see if I were under attack. "It's ours! It's ours! A dream come true," I hailed students, staff, and anyone in earshot. All work ceased; we huddled in jubilation. In the midst of spontaneous celebration, I recalled Sister Dorothy Ann's awkward winks and thought: *That was it! She was trying to assure me of her support of the proposal.*

Because the Coop City high-rise development was a Mitchel-Lama Housing Program subsidized by federal, state and city funds, CNR's executive team unraveled a sea of tangled regulations in order to get the lease. Sister Dorothy Ann felt ongoing accounts of progress and setbacks would have dampened my enthusiasm; and she was right. Endless searches for space would have hindered direct involvement with teaching and tutoring; and maybe I would not have finished my doctorate on schedule. Thankfully, all things worked together for good.

In late fall of 1980, adult students streamed into a learning environment that matched the dignity of their maturity. I glowed with pride without the faintest notion that The Little Yellow School House merely scratched the surface of future endeavors.

CₛℬↃ

Jravel-Study, a popular School of New Resources learning option, contributed greatly to a well-rounded education.

For five years, students had returned from tours of Italy, France, Greece and Japan excited about cultural exchanges; explorations of their heritages, and, about budding global viewpoints that caused them to think about themselves as citizens of the world. Though SNR's predominantly African Americans student body had less knowledge of an ancestral homeland than almost any group, no such expedition had explored a single African country. Imagine my delight when Coop City students proposed study-tours of Senegal and Gambia, the land of Alex Haley's *Roots*. Now picture me as faculty-mentor!

At age thirty-six, I prepared for a voyage to the motherland. In the fall of 1980, the itinerary of the first study-trip to Africa was set for two weeks late July into August of 1981. News about travel to the continent generated waves of excitement throughout the school; and students from the five other SNR campuses met at The Little Yellow Schoolhouse to complete the required workshops. With the support of Carole Wooten-Hysmith (SNR staff assistant) and my husband, Jimmy (college counselor and African history scholar), the group set out on a pilgrimage to explore their roots.

At the airport in Dakar, a young man dressed like he was stepping off a street corner in Harlem walked right up to Jimmy, slapped him five and said, "Yo man, what's happening? My name is Guy. Can I help you?"

Startled and relieved that the brother knew several African American expressions, I welcomed his assistance. I did not realize that Guy knew far more than a few English terms; or, that his fluency in several languages was not unique. Most Senegalese spoke a minimum of three languages: Wolof, French and English. Awed by his command of English and conscious of my own ignorance, I gladly followed his directions.

He pointed Jimmy and me to a princely Senegalese man whose ebony skin glowed as he strolled toward us in a flowing powder blue robe. With effortless grace, the employee of the University of Dakar (the host institution for the African Travel-Study tour) assisted the bus driver in loading our luggage onto the vehicle's top rack. We thanked Guy; ushered our sizable SNR group into the bus; and zoomed into the heart of Dakar.

At the end of the sweaty open-air bus ride, I anticipated a sudsy shower but the vehicle veered off the street and into a bumpy cobblestone marketplace.

"Why are we stopping?" I asked.

"We are here," the driver answered with a broad smile.

"We are here? Here where?" I asked, thinking we had miscommunicated.

"We are here. Here!" he repeated with a trace of annoyance in his voice before bouncing down the bus steps and lifting his arms in a long stretch.

I stared in disbelief at the people in the teaming marketplace. Clad in a rainbow of purple, orange and yellow print dresses and galées, Senegalese women stood behind wooden tables stacked with equally colorful bolts of fabrics. The aromas of sliced mangos and of incense oils sold from side tables caused my nostrils to flare. Scattered on the ground were straw mats used as hair-braiding salons.

"Did we stop for a little shopping on the way?" I asked.

"We are here!" the driver said once more and began pulling luggage off the bus. He headed into a three-story cinder-block building smeared with burnt orange paint. Over the door, I read the faded lettering, *Hotel Clarice*. The place looked nothing like the glossy French chateau pictured in the travel brochure that had failed to mention the marketplace right outside the front door.

Horror must have been written on my face because the university host rushed over and assured me, "My sister, it's okay. It's okay."

While Jimmy assisted with the luggage, our host ushered me into a lobby not quite as large as my modest living room back home. He introduced me to the hotel manager, who looked more Arabic than African. With a broad smile, he began explaining that the one meal a day advertised in the brochure was a breakfast of hard rolls, jam and coffee served from eight to nine every morning.

Jimmy and the bewildered group of students tried to squeeze into the lobby with their luggage but were directed to form a line outside the front entrance. When the manager finished assigning rooms and issuing keys, he whispered to me, "I saved a very nice second floor suite with a view for you and the professor."

Bone tired and cotton-field sweaty, I trudged up upstairs for a shower and nap before searching for a place to have dinner. Jimmy carried the luggage and I unlocked the door.

"Suite!" I gasped. "He calls this a suite?" A faded red cloth separated the tiny little bedroom from the bathroom. The plumbing in the bathroom consisted of a commode and a shower that had no curtain. At least the fixtures were clean. However, one frayed and slightly stiff washcloth and a matching towel were provided for Jimmy and me to share.

"I have to buy towels," I groaned, "but at least these old wooden floors are beautiful. How old is this..." The squeak of a rusty wire bedspring stopped me mid-sentence. Jimmy sat bouncing gently on a two inch mattress that curled into a U under his weight.

I needed a moment to regain my balance. Intending to take in the view, I crossed the room, pulled back a tattered red curtain like the one at the bathroom door and lifted the old French window. "A room with a view," I muttered sarcastically. Our room overlooked the bustling marketplace I had just fled. The sing-song voices of African women selling their wares drifted upwards. At the moment, I was too exasperated to appreciate the beautiful lullabies that would put me to sleep at night for the next two weeks.

Never mind the scratchy towels; I stepped into the bathroom for the long awaited shower. Though determined to make the best of things, I wondered, *Are we Africans at the bottom rung everywhere even here in our homeland?* Just as I reached for the shower knob, a terrible banging shook our door. It was Carole. She was distraught for herself, distraught for the students.

"Do something!" she cried. "We have to move out of here!"

"Carole, it's not that simple," I tried to explain.

"No Bessie, these conditions are horrible and you have to get us out of here!"

She was understandably rattled. Unlike me, she did not have a "suite." In a more cramped room on the third floor, she was fielding a barrage of student complaints.

"Gather the group," I'll be up to meet with you," I said.

As soon as she closed the door, I turned to Jimmy, "That New Rochelle travel agent really botched it. They have to move us to the international section. What time is it back in the States?"

"Culture shock," Jimmy said.

"This is nothing like they made it seem. Let's see, It's around six here; so it must be…"

"Culture shock," he repeated.

I stopped calculating the time difference and asked, "What are you talking about?"

"Tell them they are experiencing culture shock. What's the point of coming all the way to Africa to duplicate the experience at home? This is a learning experience and we have just immersed ourselves in another culture. Let's have an open mind."

Of course I wanted to share with my husband the monumental occasion of my first trip to the continent, but I had invited him to join the tour for two primary reasons. His in-depth knowledge of African history would enhance the instructional experience; and, his job as a college counselor would be helpful in addressing student issues. Already, his presence was paying off. I wanted to kiss him.

I marched up to the third floor and delivered Jimmy's speech verbatim. Everybody relaxed and opened themselves to adventuresome learning. We were off to a good start after all.

*I*n a city the size of Dakar, it was impossible to hide the fact that a large group of African Americans had checked into the Hotel Clarice. Excited and perhaps a little shocked by our presence in lodging way past its glory days, half dozen men were waiting in the lobby the morning after our arrival. Among them were Amadou, an African American who had resided in Senegal for fifteen years; Malik, a native Senegalese home for the summer from graduate school studies at a mid-western American university; and Guy, the well-read Gambian who had greeted us at the airport and who had headed to the hotel to learn more about the descendants of Kunta Kinte. These three would enrich an already fascinating lineup of university lectures and tours.

Over the course of the stay in Senegal the richest learning experiences occurred outside of lecture halls. We journeyed to the country's oldest baobab tree; to fabric markets and fishing ports; and, to the slave dungeons of Goree Island from which my ancestors were most likely shipped off to America. At the House of Slaves, sometimes oddly referred to as The Slave Castle, I thought Jimmy was going to have a heart attack. He tried on wrists and ankle shackles; then crawled into cave-like chambers where the most rebellious Africans were confined until they were herded onto ships bound for "the New World." I left my husband jammed into his tight cell and headed upstairs.

Strolling along beautiful verandahs overlooking the sea, I surveyed scenes of my ancestral captors. Four-hundred years of violent history had conspired against my return but I was back walking in previously forbidden spaces. I celebrated an exhilarating victory. Goree Island proved the time-worn expression: One man's dungeon is another person's castle. Jimmy left The House of Slaves bound by depression and I walked away free of a hundred myths about my African heritage. The contrast between the caves and the verandahs of Goree Island left indelible lessons about man's savage inhumanity.

Though some events were just as moving, not all were as somber as the visit to Goree Island. Valuable learning experiences continued with informal interactions with ordinary citizens. As it turned out, the stay at the

Hotel Clarice made it possible for us to experience Senegalese life in an unscripted manner. In the international section where "locals" were allowed only as workers, the SNR group probably would not have met such a wide variety of people.

The adult students developed individual friendships with the Senegalese. Jimmy and I developed a relationship with Malik, a frequent visitor at the hotel. He invited us to dinner with his family. It was a touching intercultural and intergenerational exchange. Doors to various units of the family compound ringed a lush green courtyard. Knitted together by kinship, fathers and mothers, uncles and aunties, grandparents, great grandparents, grand uncles and a host of sisters, brothers and cousins lived as a community. The setting was much like the imaginary extended family group I had envisioned as a ten-year-old roaming free in the woods of East Texas.

Around the center of the compound vibrant African prints were scattered on the ground for seating. Steaming hot food was brought out on huge platters and placed on woven mats in front of us. The aroma of exotic spices floated from heaping mound of fish and rice laced with shreds of sautéed leafy greens and specks of red pepper. Following the lead of the couple seated next to me, I used my right hand (the customary and well washed hand used for eating). Gently fingering a serving-portion of the dish to the edge of the platter, I savored an explosion of flavors that sent me reeling back to a place and time when babies supped mashed food from their mothers' finger tips.

Jimmy shattered the hypnotic moment with a whisper, "I need a fork."

"Eat with your hands. It's the same as sopping up greens and pot licker with corn bread," I mumbled.

"I'm not from Texas like you. I'm from New York. I need a fork." His voice rose loud enough for anyone to hear.

Malik got up and brought a fork.

Jimmy dug in and, to the delight of the hosts, savored every bite with grunts and groans. Little giggles floated around the mat and we eased into relaxed dinner conversation. The scrumptious main course was followed by a dessert of sweet succulent mango halves, cubed on the skin and, for ease of eating, then turned inside-out like an upside-down bowl.

During after dinner chatter, Malik said when he first arrived on an American college campus, he thought African-American students spoke Wolof because they were always saying, "Yo! Yo!" Hearty laughter echoed around the compound at the thought that a people linked by blood and origin had grown to know so little about one another.

As light-hearted exchanges continued, Jimmy broke local tradition again. A seven-year-old boy inspected the umbrella hat my husband had been wearing as protection from the Senegalese sun. In an act of generosity, Jimmy said, "You can have it." Instantly, a tense silence fell over the gathering.

"Jimmy," Malik broke the silence, "You insult my family. We didn't bring you to our home to receive gifts. We brought you here to serve you."

"But, I have had such a good time. I want to show my appreciation."

"Jimmy, if you don't take the hat back, my family will be upset."

"I don't mean it as an insult. In America, we take a small token of appreciation when we are invited to someone's home for dinner."

Jimmy thought he was having a cross-cultural dialogue, but Malik ended the exchange with, "I'll get my uncle. He is the oldest member of our family and settles all disputes."

Two strong young men led an elder to the center of the compound. He had to be a hundred or maybe more, but he looked like royalty once seated in a high back chair with intricate carvings.

Jimmy and Malik sat on the ground before him. As Malik explained in Wolof, the elder made little chuckles.

Finally, the uncle cleared his throat and spoke rapidly in Wolof. The compound roared with laughter.

"Jimmy," Malik said, "My uncle says that you Americans have a saying: When in Rome do like the Romans do."

Jimmy quickly took back the umbrella hat; the elder quietly retreated to his dwelling; and family insult was averted. On the way back to the Hotel Clarice, Jimmy extolled the virtues of doing like the Romans.

"After all," he said, "we are guests in this country."

"Precisely," I responded.

However, his new understanding did not forestall future blunders. Two days later, we found ourselves on the verge of another cultural misstep. Cruising along in our air-conditioned tour bus, Jimmy pointed out the window, "Look, that's horrible! Flies crawling over children's faces and they don't swat them away."

I knew he spoke from a heart for young people and from a life devoted to serving children he thought were at risk. In an attempt at easing his anguish, I said, "Well, they are probably used to the flies. When I lived in the backwoods of East Texas, all sorts of insects were a natural part of the environment."

Unaware that the bus had stopped, Jimmy continued, "Nobody should have to adjust..." The door opened and swarms of flies rushed into the cool air. Screaming, swatting flies and pushing students aside, Jimmy bolted to the rear of the bus.

"Stop it Jimmy!" I mumbled through clenched teeth. "What happened to doing like the Romans?"

"Close that door! Close the door!" He shouted deep baritone orders. Half the students were trapped in the aisle staring at Jimmy and the others were outside when the driver jerked the door shut as ordered.

I gave my own order and I did not care who heard: "Jimmy, students are watching. If you don't get off this bus, there is going to be a riot!"

"Oh! Oh!" On wobbly legs he rose from the rear seat where he had collapsed, got off the bus, and ambled toward a long wooden table where fish dried in the sun. Flies were everywhere; and Jimmy waged a losing battle with them the entire time we were at the fishery.

On the ride back to the Hotel Clarice, flies darted throughout the bus. Thank God, they remained in the coolness of the vehicle once we exited. Relaxed in our room, I teased, "Jimmy, I don't know if I can take you out tomorrow. The culture shock might be too much for you."

By morning he had regained his swag and was in the marketplace attracting attention with his umbrella hat. Among the spectators was a young man with an infectious smile. When Jimmy smiled back, he bounced over and asked in broken English, "You Americana?"

"Yes. Are you Senegalese?" Jimmy asked.

"Yes," the young man answered.

"From here in Dakar?"

"No, I live in village. Ummm...Ah... ah, Grandfather say when I was a boy, Black people take from Africa, they eat by White man. I believe him first but I get old, I learn. I say 'Grandfather, not true, not true.' But he say, 'Is true.' He still believe it true."

Jimmy said, "Oh no, it's not true. Inside the Clarice are a whole bunch of us from America. BIG GROUP," he spoke loud the way people do when they are trying to bridge a language barrier.

Nodding with clasped hands, the young man pleaded "Come to my village. Then Grandfather see all Black not eat."

"Where is your village? How far?" Jimmy shouted.

"I take you there."

"How far?" Jimmy asked again.

"Ummm... Ah, we go; umm, we go one hour. You meet Grandfather. He famous in Senegal. He play kora. Very old now; not play anymore."

"Our group hasn't been to a village. Let me get back to you tomorrow," Jimmy ended the exchange.

Soon as he entered our room he started making his case: "We haven't been to the bush country. Students will get to see how the people lived before colonization."

I was reluctant but Jimmy did his research. Next day, he reported to me, "It's okay. It's fine. I checked it out with Malick and Amadou." Since both men were familiar with the African American experience, I yielded and secured transportation though I remained nervous.

SNR students piled into three vans and our convoy headed into bush country. My nervousness gave rise to a series of questions, "What's the name of this place?"

The young man was one of the few Senegalese I met, who had difficulty understanding English. Seeing the worry on my face he struggled, "Umm..., umm..." and then, unable to provide a direct response, he said, "Everything gon' be alright."

"How much longer before we get there?"

"Everything gon' be alright."

"What's the old man's name?"

"Everything gon' be alright," was the pat answer for every concern.

"Wow!" When we arrived at the village, bell shaped grass huts stood in sandy yards. In pens jammed between the huts, goats butted heads in play. Pretty little children stopped their games and raced with excitement to our vans. Students distributed sweet treats to outstretched hands; but the commotion swirled pass a boy about six and his sister who looked to be age eight. She pulled back her brother's hand. With the same reserve of the adults lingering near hut entrances, the girl stood erect like a regal little princess.

Jimmy was struck by her obvious dignity and asked her name. "Astou," she answered in a soft voice, never taking her bright fawn eyes off him.

"Is this your brother?" he asked.

"Yes," she nodded.

"A piece of candy," he offered.

"No," she shook her head.

He extended his hand to her. The delicate handshake of a young girl with dignity reminded Jimmy of his own youth. Whether hungry or not, his mother always told him, *"Little Jimmy don't you eat at anybody's house. We feed our own."* Probably Astou's mother was one of the women watching from a doorway. Her tiny handshake spoke volumes of family honor much sweeter than the candy being handed out.

Once all treats were dispensed, the host took us straight to his grandfather. Our group waited in front of a hut undistinguishable from the others in the village. Neighbors joined our circle to witness the unusual event of foreign visitors. The grandson went inside and re-appeared holding a frail old man by the hand. When he introduced the group from America, his grandfather studied us with a twinkle in the eye that slowly widened to a gleam. He murmured something in Wolof. The grandson dashed back into the house and returned with a kora.

Once comfortably seated on a stool with the instrument in his lap, the old man plucked several strings on the kora. The grandson happily announced, "Everybody know Grandfather, the whole country. Not pick up the kora for... ummm, ten years. He play for you. He happy you not eat by White man."

Against the backdrop of a flaming sunset, the Old Man struck a chord on the Kora and two girls around Astou's age ran to the center of the large circle that had formed. They were stunning beauties with skin of smooth black lacquer. As their grandfather strummed a soft tune, their bare feet tapped lightly in the dust while their white polka dot dresses swayed as if stirred by a gentle wind. I marveled at the rhythm of their young bodies and found myself rocking back and forth. From dusk well into the evening, The Old Man serenaded us under a star spangled sky. Moved by his loving gift, we honored him. Clasping hands with him and the entire village, we sang, "We Shall Overcome." It was a cultural exchange for the ages.

Little things seep into the spirit and leave lasting imprints. In addition to the unforgettable time at The Old Man's humble hut, the reassuring words, "Everything gon' be alright," still rebounds from a dark road with a young man whose name I never learned. Yet, forty years later, in mystifying and overwhelming moments, I console myself, "Everything gon' be alright."

Moved by the visit to the African bush village, the next evening my ear was inclined to praises drifting from a tent meeting that sounded like deep delta Christian worship back home. I had to go check it out. A young man near the entrance invited Jimmy and me under the tent. It was like a Pentecostal service. People were dancing in the aisles to blasting brass horns and thunderous drums. The service had hallmarks of a down-home, soul-saving sanctified revival.

"That was like the church I grew up in." I commented.

"That wasn't a church," Jimmy said. "It was a mosque. Didn't you see the Iman with the Qur'an?"

My husband and I were having distinctly different experiences. I had not noticed the Iman. I saw worshipers dancing like David danced. Like fire shut up in their bones, they gave their all to God. Despite being labelled as unsophisticated, this African cultural survival of lavish praise through music and dance had remained intact in many Black churches of America. Such worship was an embarrassment to those attempting to become dignified American citizens. However, in the churches of my childhood, drums, horns, tambourines, and holy dance were used in forthright praise of God. My husband's attempt to dissuade me fell on deaf ears. I was pleased to discover in Senegal the African roots of Deep Delta spiritual expressions back home.

Free days, when the SNR study group was not climbing into buses and vans for guided tours, Jimmy and I shopped in local marketplaces or took ten-minute walks to the international section of town.

On one excursion, the owner ran out to the sidewalk from a fancy shop, "I swear to God you are family. You are twin to my niece," he said. Beckoning a worker to confirm his observation, he spoke in Wolof; and then, repeated, "Honest to God you are the image of my niece. You and your husband must come home to lunch."

We chatted for a few minutes but declined the shopkeeper's invitation. I walked away feeling reconnected with African kin.

Three doors down I attempted to buy a small wooden carving.

"How much is this," I asked.

"How much you want to give?" the proprietor turned the question back to me.

I had grown weary of bartering. "Look," I said, "just tell me what it costs and I'll be happy to pay."

"Get out of my store!" he ordered flaying his arms as if he might strike me. "You want to be robbed, go to a European shop! Get out!"

Jimmy gently guided me back to the sidewalk whispering in my ear, "Remember, when in Rome..." I nodded but it took a minute to absorb the fact that the proprietor had been highly insulted by my disrespect of the way his culture conducted business.

As the Senegal tour was winding down, my husband and I were just settling into a predictable routine. Late afternoons, we searched out local restaurants for early dinners. I loved spicy Senegalese dishes full of heat. They reminded me of Louisiana cuisine drenched in hot sauce or spiked with cayenne pepper. Except for peanut sauces that were too rich for my blood, I stuffed myself with grilled fish, flavorful rice, sweet yams and fresh vegetables. Around sunset, after the marketplaces closed to break the Ramadan fast, we returned to our room.

Guy and Amadou, who had become fixtures in our lives, were always waiting in the hotel lobby. I played Gin Rummy 500 with Amadou, the African American macho fellow who had changed his name and resided in Senegal for fifteen years. Every time we played cards, I won. Determined to be the victor over a mere female just getting to know Africa, he trudged up to our "suite" for his daily whippings.

With each defeat, I goaded Amadou, "How many beatings can you take? Be a good sport, shake hands and say I'm the best."

"See you tomorrow," was his curt reply. Every evening he was back confident that he would win, but he lost night after night.

While Amadou and I talked trash over a deck of cards, Jimmy and Guy compared and contrasted the state of affairs for Blacks in America and Africa. Guy was surprisingly well versed about current events concerning African Americans but more interesting were his accounts of the history of Senegal and Gambia. He explained that in pre-colonial days the two countries had been one. During colonization the French took over what they called Senegal and the British seized Gambia.

"They weren't simply dividing territories," Guy lamented. "They were dividing families. I'm Gambian but I come often to Dakar to visit Senegalese first cousins, aunties and uncles."

When Jimmy told him that Gambia was on our itinerary, the two of them counted the days to the visit to Guy's home. Sadly, our group never made it to the land of Kunta Kinte. While the king of Gambia was in England for Prince Charles' marriage to Diana on July 29, 1981, there was an attempt to overthrow the Gambian government. The Senegalese army was sent to put down the rebellion; and Guy was distraught over the possibility of fighting his relatives. Wanting to give voice to his friend's grief, Jimmy carried his portable video camera to the lobby of the Clarice Hotel and began interviewing Guy and some of his buddies.

"Jimmy," I called him to the side. "Are you serious? You can't interview people about the war. You're a guest in this country. You could get all of us detained."

He immediately put the camera away and Guy left with his comrades. We never saw him again. Presumably, they returned to Gambia to fight against their cousins in the invading Senegalese army.

Not only was our itinerary altered by the attempted coup in Gambia, we encountered difficulty getting back to America. That August, President Ronald Reagan fired 11,345 air traffic controllers for striking. Our travel arrangements back to the United States were suspended for three anxiety-filled days. The labor dispute resulted in the decertification of the Professional Air Traffic Controllers Organization, but our group paid no attention to the dramatic shift occurring in employer-union relations in America. At the time we were consumed by thoughts of going home. I later learned it took six years before the National Air Traffic Controllers Association was certified (in 1987) as the labor union for those who work to keep the skies safe.

Never had I felt more American than the short period when I was stranded abroad trying to get back to my children who are descendants of seven generation of ancestors on American soil. When the airline called to confirm our return flight, I felt like dancing.

With the urge to dance, it hit me that I had been in Africa two weeks and, except on the evening of the trip to the Old Man's house, there had been no music. It was my good fortune, though, that Muslims ended their scared month of Ramadan fasting two days prior to the SNR group's departure. Suddenly, the city rocked to throbbing drum beats and rhythmic blasts of highlife music from brass horns.

In addition to the traditional feast, the 'Eid Festivities included battles of the bands from Nigeria, Ghana and Senegal. Along with massive crowds, SNR students flooded into the national stadium located, at that time, near the center of Dakar. With the first notes from the first band, Jimmy shouted, "Oh this is good!" He sprang to his feet and jogged down the stadium steps to loose railings that separated audience and musicians. When he vaulted himself over the barrier, a roar went up from the crowd; and, like a magic carpet, throngs of people slid over the fence behind him.

By the time I reached ground level, the stands were nearly empty and the fence had been flattened. I simply walked onto the field and danced the night away. What a rousing send off from the African homeland I had come to love.

On the day of departure, Amadou stopped by the Hotel Clarice. In the middle of my packing he pleaded, "One last game."

"No, Amadou, I don't want to end this way. Give me a goodbye hug."

"Oh, you scared, huh?"

"Nooo, I'm trying to pack."

"Just one..."

"Okay!" I stopped, beat him right quick and resumed my packing.

When the bus arrived to carry our study-group to the airport, Amadou climbed aboard. He assisted with luggage at the airport check-in. The waiting room soon filled with tearful farewells of students who had gained would-be lifelong friends but he started pestering me again.

"Don't do it," Jimmy cautioned. "By now, you got to know you are going to lose. Man she's just that good."

"Ah, let's have a little fun for old time sakes," Amadou taunted. I wanted to spend our last moments exchanging addresses in order to keep in touch but caved in to his wish for a showdown. It was a quick game; and I boarded the plane with regrets. When the flight took off my final image of Dakar was Amadou on his knees with hands pounding the tarmac over unavenged losses.

Travel-Study in Senegal was a transformative experience for students as well as for me. In journals, follow-up papers and seminar sessions, they told of how immersion in another culture fostered new strengths and uncovered hidden weaknesses. They recognized the limitations of English-only studies and set goals of learning at least one foreign language while in college. Students also returned from Senegal with a thirst for world history whether studied in classrooms or through travel. Indeed, several of them vowed to return to Dakar and to stay again at the Hotel Clarice.

As for me, the embracing kindness of the Senegalese people aroused a generosity to strangers suppressed since my arrival in New York City seventeen years earlier. I also returned from Africa declaring victory over a system that had severed all connections to my homeland. A newfound awareness of native tongues, foods, fashions and rhythms embedded in an ancient culture stirred emotions that would take decades to unpack. With each passing year, my understanding deepens regarding Africans' suffering on both sides of the Atlantic.

Dr. Bessie W. Blake, SNR Dean

I read the names of graduates as President Dorothy
Ann Kelly (center) presents degrees to adult learners
(Photo: TBC, circa 1983).

Gifted best describes the promotion. I did not seek the position. It sought me.

"No." "No." and "No," I said first to the outgoing dean; and then to two vice presidents who encouraged me to apply for the vacancy. At my core, I was still the girl at Hollywood Elementary School who preferred quiet corners off to the side of the playground. The Coop City Campus was the little corner of the School of New Resources where I made a difference for students. I had no desire to step into the floodlights of leadership.

While I was busy protesting change, the train to the Dean's Office was already barreling down the tracks. Hindsight revealed maneuvers had been underway since Sister Dorothy Ann's visit to the Coop City Campus with her perplexing winks. Actually, the Little Yellow Schoolhouse was a feather strategically placed in my bonnet. Likewise, the post-doctoral fellowship to Harvard during the summer of 1980 was another missed signal. I thought intensive training at the Institute for the Management of Lifelong Education was intended to strengthen my role as a young Campus Director. In fact, I was being groomed for the deanship all along, but was too involved in direct service to students to notice. I stubbornly refused to apply for the position.

On the way home from a holiday gathering of the Executive Committee, my husband abruptly began his case for my application. I assumed he had spoken to Sister Dorothy Ann at one of the several festivities of the season. The two of them were always caucusing around hot button political issues. I thought she had mentioned the upcoming vacancy in the dean's position. I was wrong. The outgoing dean had sat next to Jimmy at SNR's Executive Committee Christmas dinner. Motioning to the other end of the table where I sat, "Get her moving," he said. "Tell her to apply for the vacancy."

"Bessie," Jimmy argued, "you don't know what kind of boss you're going to get. You're likely to get a male who doesn't understand a student body that is predominantly female and African American."

"I don't think..."

"Hear me out," he interrupted and then he hit my soft spot. "You can better help students from the Office of the Dean than at the campus level."

I thought Jimmy had rested his case but it was only the opening volley of his daily efforts to get me to take on a greater leadership role. Finally, in order to test the waters in the central office, I accepted the position of assistant dean of the school. After several months, I followed up with my application for SNR Dean. News of my candidacy swept through the college. Murmuring took on the tenor of vulgar gossip. Most outrageous were speculations about sleeping partners who might have filled my head with the false notion that I was actually qualified for the role. "After all, there is a national search," loose lips comforted themselves.

Most painful, though, were the suspicious attitudes of my colleagues, the other SNR Campus Directors. The infamous Ted, who previously said abortions would have been better than my birthing four children, had transferred from the Coop City Campus to another SNR site and rose to the rank of Director. He was the newest member and the only other African American on the school's Executive Committee. As scornful as ever, he had the nerve to say, "If you are chosen, I can't work for you."

Lifted

As if that were not enough, on the eve of my interview deceit cozied up with dissent. A trusted member of the search committee called me at home to say: "When you come in tomorrow be inspirational. Today's candidate was dynamite." Of course, it was a person with a hidden motive but it would be years before I discovered the call had been driven by ambition.

In a panic I dialed Mama for prayer but could not reach her. Climbing into to bed fully clothed—shoes and all, I stuck my head under a pillow; pulled the covers around my shoulders; and curled into a tight ball. While frozen in a fetal position, a soft lullaby drifted from my mother's songbook:

Underneath a heavy load,
Doubt may come your way.
Lift your head up high,
Smile and say:
It is no time to faint;
I'll press my way...

Each word nudged, *Get up!* By the time the song ended, I was on my feet and at my desk scribbling notes about how to introduce myself to a group who already felt they knew me well. A sketch of my vision for SNR spilled onto the page.

Next morning, I rose early and dressed in a shirtwaist dress with tiny baby breath flowers splashed on a pale blue background. In white pumps, I headed to the kitchen with burgundy briefcase swinging at my side.

Shango was watching cartoons in the breakfast room. "Oh, Good morning," I said, poured a mug of decaf coffee and turned to face him.

He waved without looking up.

"Any advice for me today?" I asked recalling when he was nine and the only family member to read my dissertation. Weekly, he would measure the height of the stack of papers as the draft grew. Then, he would sit on the stairway leading to the second floor and read. "What does *composing* mean?" he would ask and then move on until he encountered another difficult word. Always he ended those sessions, "That's really good, Mom."

I was calm, even confident on the morning of the interview but for some reason I kept turning to my twelve-year-old son for encouragement. "Shango," I tried again, "get your head out of the television! Do you want to say anything to me? My interview is today."

"Yes. Have a good day," he managed a quick glance in my direction.

Silly boy!

I was half way through the dining room before he shouted, "Oh, Mom!" I returned to the breakfast room. "Are you wearing sure?"

"Sure?" I asked.

"Yes, the deodorant," he referred to the jingle in a television ad. "It makes you feel confident and secure."

"Yeah, right," I chuckled at his corny pre-teen joke and started to leave again but he stopped me.

"And Mom, don't be afraid to say nice things about yourself; even a dog wags his own tail," he ended with a thumb up.

Shango hit the nail on the head. My nagging uneasiness had come from a fear of sounding like I was bragging to colleagues when I shared accomplishments in the interview. Boosted by the wisdom of a twelve-year-old, I left the house relaxed and confident. With the search committee, the sharing of my achievements hit homeruns.

As news of my successful interview shook the college grapevine, enemies crawled from under moldy leaves. While the committee was still deliberating, hostility flared within SNR. Ironically, the Coop City Campus representative on the search committee, a Black male who called himself friend, declared to local campus staff that he did not support my candidacy because my responses to interview questions "were just too good." The betrayal was like a punch in the stomach. He sounded like the White employment agents who said back when I first arrived in New York, "Your Master's degree in English makes you over-qualified for our listings."

The possibility of my leadership was greeted with gloom by the SNR Executive Committee. Campus Directors openly expressed their dismay. I supposed they hated the idea of a junior colleague becoming the boss, but I could not rule out the likelihood that racism was also at work. Ted amplified his frank opposition and repeated, "I can't work for you if you get the job." His White counterparts were more subtle: "You should withdraw your candidacy." "I hear there are two strong front runners who have national prominence." "Save yourself the embarrassment of a decision against your application."

I left the Executive Committee meeting feeling like I had been through a buzz saw but I did not retreat. My refusal to turn and run was a testament to the power of perseverance instilled by my mother. She taught me from a child: *"Get some grit in your craw. Don't be a quitter." "Once you start a race, run on and see what the end's gon' be."* I stayed in the race and my tenure as SNR Dean began June 1, 1982.

Broken glass ceilings often lead Blacks and women across terrains strewn with jagged cutting edges. This was certainly true of my rise as the first African American Dean at CNR and the first female Dean of SNR. Once in the position, gossip increased. "She slept her way to the top," was the most guttural comment. "Ole Aunt Jemima got the job. Let's call her Aunt Bessie," had racial overtones that suggested I was the spouse of a foot-shuffling Uncle Tom. The seemingly well-meaning statement, "Oh, she rose through the ranks," dripped with sarcastic that implied I was a strident female who clawed her way to the top out of shear ambition.

Thank God, it is not the lies but truth that defines a person. The truth is I did not maneuver my way into the Dean's Office; nor was I promoted. Loving hands lifted me over a great many hurdles. My arrival in the Dean's Office was less a career move and more a calling. Purpose and preparation merged in my position as leader; and I knew exactly who I was and what I had to do.

From elementary through graduate school, I had been primed for the appointment by painful but rich experiences in segregated Black educational systems. Public school teachers, church tutors, college professors and a mother who was a great example of "breaking new ground" reinforced the clarion call: *Be somebody; and when you are lifted, reach back and pull others up behind you.* At the door of the Dean's Office, I intended to step down from broad shoulders that had hoisted me over a thousand barriers and secure the investments that had been made in me. I would say, "No!" to stereotypes plaguing Blacks and women who succeed. Mission not ambition motivated me.

Despite the swirling negativity of naysayers, I found a reason to smile. The appointment as head of one of CNR's four schools was worthy of note in *Jet Magazine.* The fact that the upward mobility of African Americans was still important enough to report signaled that my promotion represented an opportunity to make a difference beyond the lives of SNR students. Purpose and identity merged while studying my photo and reading the caption: "Dr. Bessie Blake, assistant dean of the School of New Resources, College of New Rochelle in New Rochelle, N.Y., has been appointed the new dean of the school."

I called and told my mother to buy a copy of *Jet*. Toward the end of our conversation, I vowed, "Mama, I'm not going to lose my soul in this job. Times are changing. Until now, SNR's mostly Black and female student body has had all Whites males in the leadership position. The college needs a Black and a woman dean and that's exactly what they're getting. I plan to honor my heritage as a descendant of enslaved Africans in America; to hold on to my experiences as daughter, sister, wife and mother; but most of all, I will hold fast to God's unchanging hand and reflect His love for all His children."

"Amen," Mama agreed with what must have sounded to her like an inaugural speech. "Don't change," she said. "Don't be an imitation. You are an original. Be the best YOU that you can be. Remember," she ended with a scripture, "Let every man or woman abide in the calling as he or she is called. You are called to be a servant?"

"Yes, I am a servant."

With that vow, a resolve took root in my soul to serve the needs of adult learners with fairness to women and men, so-called people of color, so-called disabled and other marginalized groups left behind because they are considered less deserving of opportunities. SNR's "second chance" mission fitted perfectly with an educational outlook anchored in my high school motto: "Let every child's—or adult's —potential become a reality."

At the start of my tenure of leadership at SNR, I received three solid pieces of advice. The out-going dean provided a practical tip, "Handle each communication once. Immediately jot a reply to correspondence or forward it to the appropriate person. Don't put off the required phone call; make it while the memo is still in your hand. Set appointments right away. Whatever action is needed, perform it instantly. Don't let the paper bury you."

My position as Director of the Coop City Campus did not begin to prepare me for the paperwork involved in managing SNR's individualized degree program. At seven locales, a combined enrollment of nearly 3,000 students was supported by roughly five hundred part-time faculty members and over a hundred full time instructional and support staff. Each semester, their personnel actions required my review and signature. The previous dean's practical administrative advice was put to use immediately.

The next pearl of wisdom was shared at the first educational conference I attended as dean. At a national gathering of historically Black college leaders in Washington, D. C., I approached Dr. Blake, not because we were related or because we had the same last name but because he had been an inspirational keynote speaker at the opening session. I asked, "What advice would you give me as I start my new position."

He answered, "You will receive all sorts of requests, but remember friends don't ask." His simple but wise statement would alert me to people's hidden agendas more frequently than I could have anticipated.

Finally, the CNR president's advice had two prongs. Her first counsel came in the form of a congratulatory note to my husband that began, "Jim, you and the children must be really proud of Bessie but remember it's lonely at the top." She ended with an invitation for him to become an active member of the college community. Then, though the Vice President for Academic Affairs was my immediate supervisor, Sister Dorothy Ann conducted a one-on-one orientation to my role as SNR Dean.

She perched on a powder blue loveseat in her office and I sat across from her in a sofa chair. Her first question, "Why would you be more successful than previous SNR Deans?" conveyed tinges of skepticism. In the moments of silence that followed, each of us sized up the other. Several of her agendas were obviously rooted in a historically Catholic culture while many of mine were historically Black in origin. We both knew my predecessors were White males, but I reached for the common base that could unite the two of us. I said, "Women, who make up ninety-five percent of the SNR student body, will have in me a dean who is keenly sensitive to issues faced as they seek an education." With my answer, undercurrents of tension eased from the room.

Next, the president inquired about my vision for SNR. Emphasizing initial priorities, I repeated much of what had been covered in the job interview.

"Well," she said, "don't jump right in; you should take a week's vacation first. It'll give you a fresh take on the challenges ahead." I started to protest but heard Mama saying, *Don't use the last ounce of energy; always save a spark to light the next flame.* So, I nodded my agreement.

"What do you plan to do about Ted?" The pointed question indicated his statements about an inability to work with me had been widely circulated.

I thought, *If only people controlled their tongues, they could minimize awkward and troublesome situations.* Unfortunately Ted had burned a bridge that could not be rebuilt. I answered, "I plan to fire him but I want you to know there will be a big fight."

"Yes, of course," she said, "but it is better to have the fight occur outside than to tear up everything inside the house."

"Right, when I return from vacation, I'll call him."

"No," she said, "Do it now, before you leave."

From my stint as Campus Director, I already knew firings were difficult tasks but I learned from Sister Dorothy Ann that delaying an inevitable confrontation makes things worse. I went back to the office and asked Diane Ross, my secretary from the Coop City Campus who had joined me on the dean's staff, to set an appointment with Ted for the following day. While at it, Diane arranged orientation meetings with Directors for my first week back from vacation.

With firings it is best to avoid wishy-washy language. I had learned to inform the person immediately regarding the reason they had been summoned. With a clear statement of the problem on the table, an honest conversation could follow. As my mother would say, *Do it and then talk about it.*

In Ted's case, there was no conversation. The minute I said, "Let's talk about reasons I shouldn't fire you."

"Fire me!" He flew into a rage, "You'll regret this," and then stormed out of the office. His explosive response was sad but not surprising.

With the Ted ordeal behind me, I flew to California for a wonderful week with my cousin, Tommie Whiteside. Tomprell (her family nickname) pampered me like a baby. "I got that," she would say when a piece of my clothing accidentally slipped to the floor. Tasty meals with fresh California fruit and vegetables were prepared at home; and after church, a fabulous Sunday brunch awaited at a quaint restaurant perched on a mountain ridge overlooking Pomona. The absolute best times of the visit were weekday drives into the foothills of Mount Baldy. On the edges of winding mountain roads, we drank flasks of tea and listened to trickling streams in the gorges below.

Birds sang their morning songs, rabbits scampered among the bramble and squirrels hurried up and down stunted little trees while Tomprell and I recalled our rural Texas roots.

I left California revitalized and arrived back at the office to a jumpy bunch of Campus Directors. In the wake of Ted's firing, they did not quite know what to expect. Apparently, my week away had allowed time for reflections about job commitment. Fruitful dialogues occurred regarding dean-director partnerships in service to student needs.

Still, there were roaring infernos and small brush fires that flared. In the small-fire category my predecessor was homesteading in the basement of the Dean's Office. He had a few months left on his contract and thought the lower level of Newman Hall was a good place to finish his term. His eviction was left to Sister Dorothy Ann.

Protests apparently organized by Ted flared at his former SNR site. A leaflet with a picture of Aunt Jemima dubbed me "Aunt Bessie." The text on the flyer opened with the claim that I was a suburban Westchester County woman who had never set foot in the Black community and ended with a call for a student rally on my front lawn. Of course, I lived in an African American community in Queens. When Jimmy heard about the threat, he said, "If they find their way to our house, an army of bats will be waiting for them."

A parallel effort was underway to bring busloads of students to New Rochelle to disrupt my first college-wide speech. Either the organizers did not know that I was married to Jimmy or they did not realize that his grassroots connections far exceeded Ted's. My husband's supporters infiltrated the organizing meetings and posed critical questions that redirected the dialogue away from protest and toward gathering more information on "the new sister in charge." The attempt to build a groundswell against me fizzled.

Simultaneous with protest plots, a lengthy memo landed on my desk from the chair of the SNR Coordinating Council—the governing body that linked the activities of all SNR campuses. The correspondence outlined a five-year plan for the school; was addressed to me; but was copied to the executive officers of the college, the SNR Executive Committee; members of the Dean's staff; and to the chairs of all SNR schoolwide committees.

Baffled about how to respond, I phoned Jimmy. "How can I reply to such a lengthy memo?" I asked and added, "They are trying to undermine my authority by setting the agenda for my tenure as Dean."

"Read it to me," he said. I painstakingly read the entire ten-page document.

"That's easy. Get a pen. I'll dictate a draft."

"Ooookay," I said with doubt about his ability to outline an effective response.

"Who wrote it again?"

"It's from the chair of the Coordinating Council."

"All right, address it to the author of the memo and copy all the people he copied. You got that?"

"Yes."

"You ready for the body of the memo."

"Yes." I sat poised to jot down every word.

"Inappropriate, exclamation mark," he said.

"Inappropriate!" I wrote and waited.

Silence.

"And, what's next, Jimmy?"

"That's it."

"That's it?"

"Yep, that's it."

I paused before breaking into uncontrollable laughter.

"That's superb," I said, hung up, typed the response and sent it out. That day Jimmy taught me how to avert paper wars that waste time better used addressing real problems.

Perhaps the most awkward moment of those early days of leadership occurred at the home of a member of the Dean's staff. Throughout an evening of dinner with her friends from Louisiana, she kept repeating in different ways: "Bessie is the first Black dean at CNR." "She was noted in *Jet Magazine*." "The college is committed to diversity and has appointed her as dean." "As the first Black dean, the job must be difficult for you, Bessie."

"There are challenges," I said and remained pleasant. Actually, I was more surprised by the really nice meal she had served than I was by her nonsensical prattle. At the office she was the classic absent minded professor who burned heated leftovers; set off the fire alarm; and walked around eating her lunch out of a charred pot. At her home, a delightful main course was served at a well-dressed table before she put on a pot of coffee. While it percolated, she asked out of the blue, "Bessie, as a Black, what difference do you find between living in the South and living in New York?"

The minute the question left her mouth, my husband started kicking me under the table. It was his signal to be nice.

"Ummmmm," I responded as if in deep thought. "Let me see. The difference? Oh, when I was growing up in East Texas, our nearest neighbor was a White family. Mama used to send me to Miss Ola to borrow a cup of sugar; and Miss Ola would send Joe-boy to our house to get a cup of flour whenever she ran short..."

The listeners hung on every word of the idyllic tale I was spinning. The story would have grown into a saga about the happy Negro in the Old South where everybody got along; but, just when I was about to sing *Zip-a-dee-doo-dah,* Jimmy gave me a hard kick under the table.

I ended quickly, "...but, since I moved to New York, I've never lived close enough to a White person to borrow a cup of sugar."

The host broke the deafening silence that followed, "Let me check on that coffee," jumped up and left my husband and me to entertain her nervous guests from Louisiana.

Jimmy broke the ice with small-talk questions, "Hey man, where are you from in Louisiana?" "What kind of work do you do down there?" In this fashion, we sipped coffee and made it through the dessert course.

Why did I do it? At work, the staff member had signaled on several occasions that she was the academic leader of the school and I was there to take care of administrative details. I felt she had invited me to her home and onto her turf in an attempt to put me in my place as SNR's figurehead. My response was a way of putting her on notice that I planned to exercise the full measure of my responsibilities. That night at dinner, I was not about to entertain *I-have-made-it-to-the-promised-land* myths designed to make me squirm. Besides, everyone at the table lived in a segregated neighborhood whether in a Louisiana town or a New York City suburb.

On the way home, I wondered about the shallow dinner questions. Did my skin color prompt her misbehavior? Could it have been a case of one woman's inability to accept another woman in a power position? Or, was the assistant dean just plain socially inept?

Two decades later I moved to Long Island City, New York in an upscale predominantly White neighborhood. Unpretentious Jason from North Carolina knocked on my apartment door. He asked to borrow a cup of flour.

Without knowing it, he had crossed a racial divide and carved a permanent place of affection in my heart.

$\mathscr{R}$oughly a month after my appointment as dean, I faced one of the greatest challenges of educational leadership. A visit from the Middle States Association of Colleges and Schools was imminent. The organization monitors the quality of programs offered by colleges and universities in the mid-Atlantic region of the United States. Comprehensive reviews occur in ten-year cycles. Since its previous ten-year evaluation, the size of the CNR student body had doubled due to SNR's highly successful adult degree program. Such growth in enrollment usually raises red flags about whether the new program is a "diploma mill" that simply passes out degrees to boost income. The impending Middle States visit was sure to demand justification for SNR's bold new teaching methodologies. A negative review would lead to fundamental changes in the educational model. At worst, the school could be closed. My job as SNR's chief academic officer was to forestall such disasters.

Amid questions of whether or not I could do the job, the Vice President for Academic Affairs handed me a draft document reflecting the self-study that all colleges undergo prior to the arrival of a team of external evaluators. "Read it and tell me what you think," the VP said.

The self-study report had been developed consistent with the *Middle States Commission on Higher Education Self-Study Guide.* The SNR section of the draft satisfied requirements outlined in the manual. It was accurate in its descriptions of the school's academic programs; candid in describing the strengths and weaknesses of student support services; transparent about plans for future

215

improvement of facilities; and glowing in detailing impressive statistical data on student and alumni achievements. Yet, the tone of the draft was bothersome. It had the defensive ring common to pioneering programs that blaze uncharted paths.

The evaluation team member's first impressions of the school would be formed by the self-study report forwarded to them prior to their arrival at the college. Except for one individual with expertise regarding adult learning, the team was composed of faculty and staff from traditional colleges and universities where courses were delivered in lecture formats. An experience-based academic model that relied heavily on discussion formats was sure to raise questions.

As Dean and editor of the SNR's section of the self-study report, my challenge was to translate statements about educational innovations into language readily understood by traditional academics. For instance, the first draft of the school's section on curriculum stated "grants credits for life experience" without elaborating. The revised version began with the claim, "Educators—whether traditional or non-traditional—can agree that all college level learning need not take place in classrooms." Once common ground was established, the case was made for a learning model built on the educational philosophy of Thomas E. Dewey in his book, *Experience and Education.* The revisions explained how SNR used Dewey's emphasis on interactive and experiential learning in every aspect of the program. A short, paraphrased version of the statement read as follows:

> *For adults, who have a wealth of knowledge and skills gained from involvement with jobs, family and community, the objective is not preparation for*

life. Rather, the goal is to help the mature student enhance and advance their circumstances.

To avoid the unnecessary study of material already learned, SNR has set up a number of ways to evaluate the prior learning of adult students. Some choose to compile a Life Experience Portfolio where knowledge and abilities gained from life experience are matched with skills learned and objectives achieved in college courses.

The Life Arts Projects is another means of valuing student experience. This two-credit independent study is essential to SNR's six-credit seminar and is completed by all students. The assignment requires students to conduct independent research on topics covered in the course; to apply the knowledge and skills learned to their own circumstances; and to present the finished work in class. Not only is the Life Arts Project a source of new learning for the individual student, peer reactions to the presentations intensify the learning process within the six-credit seminar and charges the course with a vitality that makes learning exciting.

In-depth descriptions of the integration of experiential learning into the curriculum, such as the one above, introduced the incoming evaluation team to new approaches to teaching and learning employed by SNR.

Once the revised self-study report was submitted, the attention turned to assuring that practices at all branch campuses were consistent with policies and procedures published in the schoolwide catalog. A series of meetings, named The Dean's Forum, were established. Audits were done by the dean's staff preceding each campus forum. Associate Dean, Donna Tyler, conducted reviews of academic records such as Life Arts Projects, Life

Experience Portfolios along with curriculum files, and faculty qualifications; while Assistant Dean, Patricia Furman, audited records of enrollment data, attendance and financial aid disbursements. Their reports contributed to agendas for three meetings on the day of the Dean's campus visit: one with the Campus Director; another with the Director and campus staff; and the third, where students voiced concerns and raised questions, was attended by the entire campus community.

As the newly appointed dean I needed a quick learn. Detailed knowledge of each campus was essential to a successful team visit. Forums were the easiest way to obtain a bird's eye view. The information gather would enhance my ability to advocate on behalf of the unique aspects of an individual unit while highlighting its vital place in the fabric of the whole school.

As it turned out, the Dean's Forum proved to be a valuable way of assessing and improving the school's delivery of services to students. Eventually, once a semester each campus hosted a Dean's Forum.

In the original forum leading up to the accreditation visit, I explored with staff the need to consider the audience of the self-story report in the choice of language used to describe the SNR degree program. "Come on," I said, "we know we're wonderful but we want others to experience what we feel about our program and our students. Some of the visitors are going to see six-credit seminar in the report and think that we are giving away credits. When they arrive, it's up to us to show them otherwise. How do we do that? We speak in a language that they understand."

At each campus, there were those eager to bridge gaps in understanding between traditional and innovative educational thinkers; and those who felt any use of "the customary language of higher education" would change the character of the school. I must add that most staff did not know the gravity of the Middle States visit and what we risked losing. Rather than pushing the panic button, I chose to persuade them to my way of thinking.

"Well," I responded, "we already use many of the mechanics of traditional academics. We evaluate student work by assigning grades; we count hours for which we assign credits. Just like any college we measure the aims and goals of our program. Why don't we just say so? Do we really want to face continuous Middle States visits because of the tone sat by the language we choose? When we refuse to use more than one dialect to describe honestly what we are doing, we risk losing vibrant, effective learning models proven to work with adults. We must be open to constructive criticism. A less than perfect evaluation can help us achieve even greater success." With majority agreement on the last point, the school moved forward with one voice.

The Middle States team arrived at CNR on my fortieth birthday. Dr. George Pruitt, President of Thomas Edison College (now Thomas Edison State University) in Princeton, New Jersey was the team Chair. He was a friendly man, knowledgeable about adult learners. His amiable manner put me at ease and freed me to speak with passion about access to quality higher education for communities with few to no such resources.

During the several days spent combing over every aspect of the school's functioning, Dr. Pruitt's diligence in evaluating unique aspects of SNR's academic program was evident in his candor as he provided constructive criticism and suggested areas of school improvement. He also shared leadership strategies that stimulated my development as a newly appointed dean. One such tip was: Establish a clear line of communication with branch campuses; connect it to on-going evaluation; and then build it into the school's organizational structure.

Indeed, those initial conversations with Dr. Pruitt regarding my vision for SNR were the beginning of a mentorship in educational leadership that led to my six-year membership on the Board of Director of the Council for Adult and Experiential Learning. CAEL is a national organization serving the needs of colleges, universities, unions, corporations and government entities seeking to help adult learners as they "navigate on-and-off ramps between education and employment."

Of course the long term impact of leadership strategies was far from my thoughts while the Middle States team was on campus. The unnerving week the entire school spent on its toes consumed all my mental energy; but the rigorous review was well worth it. The team evaluation resulted in positive declarations of SNR's highly innovative instructional programs. In the spring of 1983, the school and its five branch campuses were fully accredited by the Middle States Association of Colleges and Universities.

Along with the need to increase branch campus library services, suggestions were made regarding the use of emerging tools in the assessment of experiential learning. I did not care that the recommendations meant another five years of rigorous evaluations. I was excited about the visiting team's strong endorsement of the school's plan to develop the Brooklyn and Harlem Centers into full branch campuses.

As a result of SNR's accreditation, I served on a number of Middle States teams evaluating other cutting edge degree programs. Also, my membership on several boards of directors and advisory committees to educational institutions provided a cross pollination of knowledge that helped move Brooklyn (by 1985) and Harlem (by 1987) to fully accredited branch campuses.

The new campuses inspired SNR staff to greater innovations. One program enhancement was called Adult Career Counseling and Education Support Services. ACCESS formalized student advisement as a primary instructional activity. In three advisement courses— Experience Learning and Identity, Career Interest Review and Designing the Future—students were aided in setting personal goals; mapping detailed plans for the completion of their degrees; and for developing career strategies after graduation.

The implementation of ACCESS coincided with the economic downsizing and layoffs in the 1980s American economy. Due to the flexible and adaptable nature of the advisement courses, SNR staff was drafted as "expert" members on corporate, union and university design teams seeking to retool large segments of the workforce. As consultants, the staff obtained a national reputation for the school as a whole. Some colleges adopted the entire ACCESS model and others utilized the single course that best supported its curriculum.

The ACCESS advisement model created an opportunity for SNR to participate in a national study aimed at establishing standards for measuring the quality of adult learner programs. Elza Dinwiddie-Boyd, Louis deSalle, Kristine Southard, Patricia Spradley, Robert Tate and Donna Tyler joined me in a comprehensive examination of SNR's delivery of instruction and services to students. The report submitted to the benchmarking team was followed by site visits to our seven campuses. Study of programs across the country resulted in the identification of SNR as one of five "best practice" schools in the nation. Co-authored by the Council for Adult and Experiential Learning and the American Productivity &

Quality Center, the book entitled, *Best Practices in Adult Learning* acclaimed the school's overall approach to the education of adults. The publication gives in-depth attention to the ACCESS, curriculum and faculty models; to the effective examination of prior learning; and to opportunities for student participation in a course proposal process each semester. With the best practices publication SNR became a beacon for struggling adult degree programs worldwide.

Regardless of the school's notoriety, the greatest reward remained in the overwhelming achievements of students. Not only did so-called "bypassed" adults complete long-delayed baccalaureate studies, they attained advanced degrees in prestigious Ivy League institutions and in local colleges and universities. Link by link, chains of mental and financial bondage were broken as SNR alumni returned to their communities as social workers, teachers, pastors, lawyers and as civic and business leaders. Accolades flowed to the school all because courageous adult learners entered partnerships with a group of forward-thinking educators who reached beyond the restrictive lines drawn around the learning process and dared do something new.

Added Resources of prayer, godly counsel and sound advice armed me with "can-do" boldness in small and seemingly insurmountable situations.

The first month on the job as SNR Dean, I complained to my mother, "I'm sitting here in a glass bowl. An entire wall of my office is constructed of floor-to-ceiling windows with glass sliding doors along a busy hallway. The previous dean liked to keep his eye on staff every minute of the day. I delegate tasks; trust people to do their jobs; and then follow up at crucial intervals."

Though Mama was in Louisiana and I in New York, we chatted daily. "This office layout doesn't work for me," I said on another occasion. "It's like living inside a Nikki Giovanni poem. Oh, that's right, you don't know her. Well, she wrote a poem about dirty windows that kept her from seeing out and tracking what people were doing; but they couldn't see in and watch her either. I think she was making a statement about the need for privacy. Anyway, that's the way I feel; I need some privacy."

Conversations had detoured into the land of poetry since I was ten and Mama always listened patiently. When my flight of poetic reverie ended, she said, "Bessie, you have not, because you ask not. Ask for what you want."

"Oh!" I had expected a more sympathetic response but the simplicity of her bold statement spurred action. I hung up the phone and called Fred Sullo, the college's Director of Facilities Management.

"How can I help you, Dean Blake?" he asked.

"I'd like to order a wall," I said as if requesting a pizza delivery.

His belly-laugh shook the phone wire but next morning a construction crew was at my office. By day's end, the glass wall had been replaced with sheetrock painted the ocean blue I had chosen. The foamy color was framed by white wooden baseboard and ceiling moldings. A heavy walnut door opened to the busy hallway. Through its tiny stained-glass window, I saw only blurred figures moving along the corridor. No one could see in and I could not have been happier.

The wall was the first of many audacious requests. Amazing upgrades of SNR facilities started with the advice, "Ask for what you want," from my unflappable mother. On the slew of construction projects that followed, Fred and I developed a close working relationship. We huddled with architects and shopped with interior designers to modernize SNR facilities in the South Bronx, Brooklyn and Harlem. To my great delight, we moved the Coop City Campus from the Little Yellow Schoolhouse to a renovated high-tech brick building within the local community.

Mama was a good listener; gave sound counsel based on scripture; and was instant in prayer over unending challenges I faced as dean. When she finally visited CNR in 1986 for Kanari's graduation from the college's School of Arts and Sciences, her spirituality was evident to staff and students alike. It could have been the way she dressed—a long hemline, no make-up, and no jewelry. I am convinced, though, that it was her quiet spirit that caused people to seek her prayers without verbal prompting. After all, I wore no makeup and followed the fashion trend of the maxi dress but no one sought my prayers. In Mama's case, the matriarch of a New York State drugstore chain, whose daughter was also graduating from CNR, asked for prayer. At the graduation dinner my mother quietly sought God's blessings for the woman and her family.

A few years later, a similar incident occurred at the Coop City Campus. While in town for Thanksgiving, Mama attended a Dean-Student Forum. The meeting involved fiery exchanges regarding issues of financial aid, grading policies and the request for a childcare center. At the conclusion of the session, I could not believe my eyes. Instead of the usual battery of follow-up questions by students who did not speak up in the forum, a spontaneous prayer line formed in front of my mother. Because I had made no reference to her being a minister when acknowledging her at the beginning of the meeting, I watched in awe as she accommodated students and staff. I longed for such spiritual anointing but felt I would never have the faith my mother possessed. I too relied on her prayers; believed in her supplications; and, when alone with her, submitted requests for my problems.

$\mathcal{M}$ama's light guided many of my on-the-job decisions but my husband did the day-to-day heavy lifting. Whether it was planning, budgeting, supervising the operations of seven academic units or networking to raise friends and funds for SNR, Jimmy provided ready critiques and encouragement.

Sister Dorothy Ann Kelly recognized his importance in subtle winks; but she also publicly declared, "Bessie and Jim are a team. People shouldn't underestimate his role." She was right. The Office of Dean was a politically charged arena where every request had to be weighed for hidden agendas. My husband's insights and honest feedback were endless.

Jimmy's work in higher education and, more importantly, his involvement in community organizing and politics were vital to the inner city campuses of SNR. From the unit on the main campus in New Rochelle to four branch campuses in the Bronx and Manhattan and to the fledging sites in Brooklyn and Harlem, my husband knew movers and shakers in the locales. He used his connections to advocate for SNR at community events. Frequently, he met one-on-one with religious, political and civic leaders. Jimmy even dressed in tuxedos (which at first he hated but learned to enjoy) and escorted me to countless dinners and fundraisers where we both networked on behalf of adult learners. To spare me from lonely drives, when his work schedule permitted, my husband also accompanied me on short out-of-town speaking engagements in the northeast region of the country.

His supportive role exposed him to many indignities. Intellectual snobs singled him out. At a national conference of distinguished educators assembled at Rutgers University, the moderator introduced me as one of the panelist, "Dr. Blake holds her doctorate from Columbia University and has done post-doctoral work at Harvard." She should have stopped there but for some odd reason she continued, "Her husband also joins us today. He is on the faculty of Borough of Manhattan Community College and he, he, he..." she stuttered, lapsed into an awkward pause and then blurted, "Sir, do you have a doctorate?" Jimmy rose and answered, "No, but can I stay?" Laughter rolled around the room and cleared the tension.

About a year later, the question of his credentials surfaced at a Black college where I was keynote speaker for the faculty convocation. The inevitable moment was not as obvious as the previous blunder. After a split second hesitation, the moderator simply bestowed the doctorate on Jimmy by stating, "Well, he's a full professor;

so you know everything is in order." She spoke the truth. Everything was in order but not in the way she assumed. Jimmy had not been formally awarded the title Dr. Blake, but the Master's degree from Columbia University's School of Social Work was recognized by City University of New York as equivalent to the requirement for a doctorate. Based on the most advanced degree in his field at the time, he had been granted tenure and promoted to full professor. Despite his academic accomplishments, he endured with good humor the arrogance encountered while on the road with me.

It is baffling how people, especially in academic circles, get hung up on titles and degrees. Conceit and ambition often overshadow knowledge, skills and service to students. Even at CNR—an institution with a solid reputation of education for service and the place where Jimmy provided relentless support of college endeavors, I constantly received calls with the question: "Dean Blake, we are sending an invitation to you and your husband, how should we address it?"

At first, I toyed with the caller: "Isn't my address in the college directory?"

"No-no," was followed by clumsy pauses and the query, "What title should we use for your husband."

"Address him as Professor James Blake," I said; but apparently they never noted the title in their records. The very next week, my phone rang with the same frivolous question.

Over the twenty-year period of my deanship, Jimmy's service to the college was enough to award him an honorary doctorate. Then, I would have said to CNR staff, *address him as Dr. Blake,* and the problem would have been solved. Though he was never fazed by it, the unending pursuit of my husband's status got under my skin.

Thankfully, Jimmy has a special way of putting people at ease despite their flaws. He enjoys the lighter moments of life but is bold enough to stand and fight in the most difficult situations. What I like most about him, though, is his self-confidence and the manly strength to take a professional back seat to his wife.

I had no peers at CNR. No other dean faced the challenges of running a multi-campus school with student-designed individualized courses of study. Adding to the burdens of school responsibilities was the racial gap between SNR and the rest of CNR. As the only Black in bi-monthly dean's meetings, I constantly faced culturally insensitive situations. A prime example surfaced each semester when the four deans provided overviews of their respective schools for the college's newest staff. At the orientations my colleagues were introduced as *Dr. Whomever* and I was introduced as Dean Bessie Blake. I ignored the slight and delivered an enthusiastic presentation on behalf of my beloved school.

It was obvious to incoming New Resources staff that I was treated differently and a slew of questions usually surfaced about why I was not called Dr. Blake After several semesters, I raised the issue in a dean's meeting; and, to a person, the vice president, the assistant to the vice president and the three other deans protested: "Oh, that's petty." "Nothing is meant by it." "We have more important matters to address." Finally the assistant to the vice president attempted to end the conversation with a dismissive statement: "Well everybody knows that the title of Dean is a more prestigious title than Doctor."

I responded, "Well, why discriminate? Why not honor the four of us equally by merely using the title, Dean, for everyone?" The exchange ended and, thereafter,

I was introduced as Dr. Bessie Blake. Unfortunately, subtle forms of racial insensitivity continued.

"Bessie," the Dean of Arts and Science chimed at one meeting, "if I ever say anything racially insensitive I wish you would carry a water gun and squirt me."

Well, I did not have a water gun but I cocked my thumb pistol, aimed it at her and said, "Pow." She looked utterly confused.

Ultimately, to relieve the pressure of isolation, I sought other cutting edge college and university programs and gained a group of sorely needed colleagues who understood the effects of discrimination and were in tune with the needs of adult learner programs. These emerging practitioners and advocacy organizations for adult students provided opportunities to examine issues I faced as an academic administrator. As a group their critical resources boosted my career onto a national stage and into international arenas.

During the years of Reagan's trickle-down economics, corporate layoffs of blue collar workers spiraled. As dean of a successful degree program specifically designed for adults, I served in an advisory capacity on a number of retooling-the-workforce ventures. In addition to CAEL endeavors, there was a term on the Board of the National League of Nursing's Baccalaureate and Degree Initiative intended to address a shortage of nurses. In Detroit, UAW-Ford drew, in part, on the experience of SNR's D.C. 37 union campus in crafting re-training modules for auto workers. At Cambridge College, I had the good fortunate to serve on the design team for a Master's degree program for inner city working adults in the Boston area. Perhaps most impactful in shaping my vision of future SNR innovations was the year of service on the design team of The University of Phoenix's on-line degree program. On these and other projects, I discovered colleagues with leadership challenges similar to mine.

I returned from the University of Phoenix excited about the enhancement of learning through the use of technology. Contributing to my understanding of the potential of distance learning in individualized degree programs was Fred Sullo, head of CNR's physical plant and Herb Boyd, SNR adjunct faculty and award-winning journalist and columnist for the *Amsterdam News*. Fred advised about the wiring of administrative offices and campus classrooms. Herb delivered an intensive tutorial on computer-assisted learning.

At first I was skeptical. "But you can't doddle on a computer." I glibly responded to Herb's instructions.

His quick rebuttal was, "Yes you can," and with fast motions of the computer mouse, brilliant hues of squiggly images appeared on the screen. The drawings reminded me of an early learning experience in Mama's bedroom where the alphabet I colored became art hanging on the wall. That moment of recollection put to rest my cynicism; and I delved into meaningful discussions with Herb about the possibilities of computer-assisted instruction.

In an era that predates Zoom, Eventbrite or Webinar, Fred suggested connecting computers with video cameras to allow teleconferencing between branch campuses. With the installation of the needed wiring, fledging remote-learning techniques reduced the need for SNR students to troop throughout the city for inter-campus registrations.

Work done with Herb and Fred expanded my thinking regarding technology-assisted instruction across the curriculum. I drafted a fifteen-year strategic plan for SNR that had as its goal the development of an Adult Learner Institute where educators would receive training in distance learning techniques. Unfortunately, the plan was too futuristic for SNR's staunchest critics within CNR. Today, in the middle of a pandemic when educators (elementary to college) are forced into crash courses on remote learning, I shake my head and think about missed opportunities to train hundreds of teachers and school administrators in the uses of remote-learning formats. Nevertheless, I am thankful for individuals and educational organizations that served as resources for my professional development in the1980s.

CAEL, a far-reaching advocate on behalf of adult learners, had the most powerful influence on my growth as an educational leader. The six-year tenure on the organization's Board of Directors kept me informed of national and international trends in adult education; and, in the process, a respected group of colleagues emerged. Morris Keaton, George Pruitt, Pamela Tate, Ike Trebble and other visionary thinkers influenced my career. Through the CAEL network, my role as evaluator and lecturer carried me to major cities and small towns across the United States as well as to Mexico, Puerto Rico, England and Scotland.

On my first trip to the United Kingdom, I had been warned of an upsurge of racial incidents in England. Sure enough, upon arrival at my hotel in London, the frosty question, "Are you sure you're in the right place?" was asked. Following a superficial search of the guest register, the pretentious clerk at the check-in desk suggested, "Perhaps you have the wrong hotel."

I was in the right hotel but I did not fly to England to wage a fight against racism; so, I found a comfortable seat in the lobby while my colleague, Dr. Louis deSalle, graciously registered both of us. The check-in incident was one of several negative encounters brushed aside in order to focus on the mission of expanding services to adult learners.

Norman Evans—head of England's Learning from Experience Trust (LET—the British counterpart to CAEL), had put together an itinerary of United Kingdom colleges and community based educational programs. Among colleagues exhilarating conversations were held in hospitable settings. In one such forum I addressed a group of educator's about the needs of adult students in urban settings. Sightseeing in London was limited to a glimpse from the conference of the changing of the guard next door at Buckingham Palace. Then, Louis and I traveled to the Community Based Resource Unit of Liverpool University.

At the Merseyside Writers Workshop, I browsed several publications. One student author simply penned her name, "Bessie." Her poem opened: *"Sitting behind the desk was one/of those men in clean grey suits/* and ended *"the man in the clean suit...did the dirty job/of firing [me]."* Half a world away from SNR, I marveled at a namesake who, like my students back home, also wrote from slices of life experience. I left Liverpool with a handful of pamphlets and chapbooks to share with students in the United States. After a heartwarming day at Merseyside Louis and I returned to the hotel and packed.

Early the next morning, we boarded a train to Scotland. The excursion through pastoral scenes was the closest I would come to fulfilling a childhood dream of walking through Shakespeare's England. Though the itinerary left no room for touring, spectacular vistas and Gaelic sites of Scotland's were enjoyed from train, auto and hotel windows. In the highlands, golden sunsets shimmered on the River Ness from dusk to dawn without night ever falling. Edinburg's night skyline sparkled like encrusted gems on a finger ring. Before heading to

Glasgow, I declined a hearty breakfast of eggs, potatoes and haggis—a sausage made of chopped lamb's heart, lungs and liver mixed with oats. In Glasgow, the Royal Scottish Automobile Club was perched on a cliff above the raging North Atlantic Sea. The sight conjured images of World War II warships my father had described. The first evening in the city, I devoured the best plate of salmon ever.

Lining the motorway in route to a Glasgow community experiential learning project, rows of grey high-rise apartments reminded me of the slums of urban America. I assumed people of African descent lived in those buildings of sharp angles unembellished by shrubbery. Once gathered with a group of locals in the community room of one of the structures, I realized I was the only Black in the circle.

In the workshop, a young woman who looked to be thirty sat next to me. She was voiceless during an animated roundtable discussion about how integrating experience with learning is a powerful molder of identity. At the end of the session, she pushed through lively chatter and whispered in my ear, "I'm an alcoholic."

It was a vulnerable moment of disclosure—like a confessional. The anguish on her face said it was easier to divulge her secret to a stranger she would never see again than in an open discussion with classmates. Though stunned, I gave her hand a gentle squeeze and said, "You're going to be alright."

"But, I'm fifteen and I'm an alcoholic," she muttered again.

"You're young and you're here trying to turn your life around. You're going to be okay," I repeated and then paused before opening my arms. We shared a brief but tender embrace. She managed a faint smile and left the room. The best I could do was shoulder her pain for a fleeting moment. Though I shared our exchange with the workshop host for follow-up, the teen alcoholic with lifeless eyes still haunts me. The agony of a young Scottish girl confirmed that poverty and suffering are blind to skin color.

The Scottish people were warm and gracious. My send off from the first visit to their country was filled with friendly goodbyes. They invited me back for return engagements; and, ultimately, we established a summer cultural exchange program between SNR and Glasgow students who traveled to the South Bronx Campus. I benefited personally from the exchange of ideas as much as SNR students. Their sharing of common experiences and goals caused me to muse: *We're all God's children. Focus on skin color and other superficial differences are divisive ploys used to separate and exploit people.*

Enriching national and international cultural understandings would not have been possible without sturdy anchors fondly remembered as *added resources.* My success as dean rested on a host of willing contributors: mother, husband, colleagues in a variety of educational settings; a talented staff; and, on my largest group of supporters, SNR students. Their service as resources to their children, co-workers and communities inspired me daily. As a fellow adult learner, I grew strong watching the tenacity of students; as well as from the wisdom they brought to bear on my multiple roles.

The student impact was never more evident than at SNR Dean-Student Forums. For instance, The New York Theological Seminary Campus meetings never ended without a minister blessing me from the crown of my head to the soles of my feet. When on the D.C. 37 Campus, students who were also union leaders liberally offered unsolicited but useful information on labor regulations. In addition, women at all campuses rallied around me.

Working mothers offered helpful hints on how to balance work and family time; or, they pulled me aside with quick dinner recipes for a woman on the move. Others acknowledged me as a strong female role model who encouraged them to overcome obstacles standing between them and their goals. I was motivated by the knowledge that my sacrifices were making a difference in the lives of students.

The most inspiring event on the SNR annual calendar was student-centered. A keynote speaker from among the graduates of each campus rose at the schoolwide commencement dinner to recall the challenges and joys of achieving their learning goals. I still resonate with the words of one student orator who declared, "Life is a marvelous mystery to be live." His speech elaborated on how expecting the unexpected minimizes missteps that can throw people off balance at every turn.

On the occasion of SNR's twenty-fifth anniversary, other speeches were highlighted in a special edition of *The Quarterly* (CNR's alumni newspaper). Their testimonies spoke to the impact of New Resources' diverse learning options. Eva Foster, of the New York Theological Seminary campus, applauded the teacher-student partnership model and concluded, "...we are not lost in a bureaucratic system but are instead part of an adult academic community."

Charles Green's comments spoke to the mission of the school when he stated, "I entered college for the sole purpose of obtaining a B. A. degree. Somewhere between then and now, I developed an appreciation for the enhancement of human life and spiritual growth. "Education," he said, "changes our perspective on social and human values." Charles is now a teacher in the New York City School system.

Gloria Abad said, "Faculty members have been so supportive and instrumental in helping me find my own voice...and fellow students have imparted the same encouragement, support and warmth." The examination of personal experience in a Life Arts Project opened a door to a career in the social services; and Gloria studied for a Master's degree in social work at Hunter College.

During two decades of graduation dinners, students repeatedly referred to the core course, Experience, Learning and Identity where they read Plato's Allegory of the Cave. Because of the reading they began to see philosophy as a means of unraveling the complex realities of urban environments. Then, there were the inevitable impassioned speeches of mothers regarding the positive effects their academic successes had on the study habits of their children.

Student speakers confirmed again and again positive outcomes of the SNR adult learner degree program. Following an hour and a half of electrifying speeches, graduates, their guests and well-wishers enjoyed a delicious meal served by an army of traditional age student waitresses. In an elegant setting of candle lights, sparkling crystal, and dazzling floral centerpieces, proud members of the SNR family celebrated achievement in its many forms. Each year, I left the SNR commencement dinner inspired. As partners in the learning venture SNR students were a source of continual renewal of my commitment to fulfill the institutional mission of "education for service."

Family matters! Balancing job and home-front duties became a juggling act during my tenure as dean.

In cases where the line between career and personal life blurred, decisions usually favored family entering my work space rather than work infringing on my private life. Linda Ebinger, a trusted aide and only staffer with my home phone number, knew when it was absolutely necessary to contact me. As a working mother herself, she had a keen sense of which calls from my children to handle herself and when to pull me out of a meeting. Not only was she a topnotch office manager, she was incredibly skillful in helping me maintain a seamless line between job activities and family responsibilities. Whenever Linda was out of the office, all staff was instructed to interrupt me without fail when my husband or children called. Most times, I stepped into an outer office for unrushed conversations.

A working mother needs a big bag of tricks. At home, I constantly tried new strategies. In simpler times when RiShana and Takbir were pre-k, I adopted an end-of-the-day cuddle time that smoothed the transition from work to household duties. The minute the babysitter opened the front door, "Cuddle time! Cuddle time!" the little ones shouted with glee, grabbed my hands, and pulled me upstairs to bed. Glad to snuggle together, the three of us rested quietly. Sometimes one or all of us fell sound asleep but, usually, fifteen minutes of power napping was sufficient. I roused the two of them and we spent quality time together while I prepared dinner.

By the mid-eighties Kanari was off to college. The younger children were in middle school and Shango was in high school. Yet, magnets clung to the refrigerator door holding a slew of papers detailing chores, dance lessons, Wednesday pizza nights, Friday movie titles, Saturday morning band rehearsals, and Sunday swim lessons at Queens College. The daunting process of drafting, revising and implementing schedules revealed a desperate need for *me-time!*

The morning walk became a daily journey to the significance of small things. Loose heavy clothes hung from my shoulders with an easy freedom. The front door slammed and Jimmy stumbled along on safety patrol. My body slowly unwound in the freshest part of each new day. On the path to Springfield Gardens High School, sleepy eyes locked with mine offering genuine greetings in fleeting glances. Delicate crocuses poked through frozen ground. Flecks of red sunrise filtered false hopes of warmth through the boney fingers of winter trees. Once on the track, I fell in step with the rotating rhythm of the earth. Walking—a holistic exercise—drew me closer to nature; elevated my spirit; strengthened my body; and ordered my thinking for the day ahead.

Involving the family in my professional life also helped me cope with a pressurized career. While my husband and three of the children accompanied me on short out-of-town business trips, at age eleven RiShana was too busy pursuing her artistic interests to tag along with me. I chauffeured her and her friends to dance classes, flute lessons and choir rehearsals. Payoffs for the constant grind in New York City traffic ended in joyful concerts and recitals in public school auditoriums; and, in the dazzling evening she along with her best friend, Colette, performed at Carnegie Hall as members of the citywide school orchestra.

On the most treasured trips with RiShana, we chirped about Toni Morrison novels and Maya Angelou autobiographies while in route to the local high school track field for the morning walk.

RiShana was an inquisitive young woman always digging beneath the surface of what appeared to be ordinary circumstances.

"Ma, why don't we own anything?" she asked and brought our high-stepping walk to a halt.

"We own things." I said

"What?" RiShana demanded to know.

"We are homeowners...wellll..." I paused, "...the bank owns it but we will own it someday. The car is... or, it will be ours in a year. It's almost paid off."

"I'm not talking about houses and cars; I'm talking about real things, like department stores. Why don't we own department stores?" It was one of those awkward moments when a child posed a question that the parent should have been raising.

Having no ready answer, I shifted the question back to her. "Why do you want a department store?" I asked.

"Because I like Black dolls and there are no Black dolls in the department stores."

"Well, maybe you will be the one who builds stores that sell Black dolls," I said. A disquieting silence followed my response and the zest for walking was lost that morning.

Thank God for the resilience of children and new mercies every day for parents who do not have all the answers. Next morning we returned to walking and talking about favorite children's books like Mark Twain's *Huckleberry Finn*, Bebe Moore Campbell's *Sweet Summers* and Mildred D. Taylor's *Roll of Thunder, Hear My Cry*.

Shango was also a deep thinker but he was never too busy for a short out-of-town trip. On a January trip to evaluate an adult learner program in Florida, I gave my son an all-day pass to Disney World. At age seventeen, he was old enough to spend the day on his own. Besides, within months, he would be in college at Hampton University. My general but firm instruction was, "Be back at the hotel by four o'clock!"

At the end of an exhausting day of meetings, I returned to the room around dusk. No Shango. I turned on the television to a devastating forecast of frost that was sure to ruin the orange crops. No news of injured or lost teens aired. Where was I to start the search? I slid the balcony door open and walked into the frigid night trying to clear my head. From twenty stories up, I spotted a brown arrow shooting across turquoise water.

Who's crazy enough to swim in this weather? I thought and let out a scream, "Shango!" Of course the sound of my voice disintegrated before reaching ground level; and, so did my desire to reprimand him. I was simply relieved that my son was safe. I was also happy that Shango had not bungled his first step toward independence.

My ten-year-old son was more dramatic than his older brother. He took literally his father's instruction, "Take care of your mother while y'all gone." In route to a CAEL Board of Director's meeting in Chicago, Takbir held me hostage in a sleeper compartment on Amtrak. He cancelled the dinner reservation in the dining car and had the attendant bring trays to our roomette but I could not eat a bite. I feared he might fall from the top bunk bed where he dangled upside down.

Things got choppier on the streets of Chicago. When two big dudes with do-rags glanced at me as they passed, "Stop looking at my Mama," Takbir ordered.

They spun around, "What you say?"

"I said stop looking at my Mama!"

"You don't know who you messing with," one said as both started advancing on us.

Takbir squared his shoulders readying for the fight but I started pleading, "Don't hurt us; he doesn't know what he's doing."

"Yes I do. I'll...,"

I collared my son, "If you say another word, I will break your neck." He was not afraid of those guys but the Mama smack-down cooled him out while I continued, "Please! Please!"

"Yeah, you better check him!" one guy grumbled.

"Right, rein him in!" the other echoed as they strolled away with danger fading with each step.

Did Takbir actually challenge their manhood? Or, were they just messing with us? I did not know; nor did I want to find out. The encounter was stressful at that moment but today the incident is a treasured childhood memory to laugh about.

As a junior at CNR's School of Arts and Sciences, Kanari went on several short east coast trips. Following the evaluation of a new academic initiative for adults at Spellman College, my daughter and I enjoyed a great holiday shopping spree in Atlanta before attending the annual Spellman-Morehouse Christmas Concert. Mournful renditions of Negro spirituals lifted our aching hearts from the depths of slavery to a triumphant heaven. Both of us returned to New York more closely tied to our roots.

Such were the misadventures and delights of traveling with my children as I sought ways to engage them in my professional life. Still, power walks, cuddle times, family meetings, schedules galore and out-of- town trips were not enough to reconcile the demands of family and work. I yearned for more quality time with my children and looked to neighbors and friends to help fill the gaps.

$\mathcal{F}$amily Day, a holiday centered on children, was rooted in fond childhood memories of my mother, two sisters, two brothers and a humongous extended family of four grandparents, two great grandparents, seventeen aunts and uncles and their spouses along with sixty-nine first cousins.

Against a background of strumming guitars, thumping pianos and stirring hymns, gatherings of the Martin-Waites clan had unfolded like country bake-offs. Homemade cakes and pies covered yard tables draped with blue-and-white checked oilcloths. Inside an unpainted frame house, turnip greens and peas pulled from fields at sunrise bubbled in iron pots on a wood-burning stove. The kitchen table was covered with platters of fried fish that "slept in the lake last night," or fried chicken whose necks had been snapped at daybreak. Savory aromas of pickled peaches blended with whiffs of Texas green onions; and large slices of sweet beefsteak tomatoes that rested on white plates. Nostrils flared in anticipation of the feast.

People grabbed plates of food and wedged into informal spaces. Children sat on the porch and its steps. Men leaned against fence railings with loaded plates in their hands and laughter on their lips. Women served their prized dishes, but barely nibbled at the food as they perched on straight-back cane-bottom chairs that dotted the kitchen and trailed into the two bedrooms of a three-room house. Though my kin were considered dirt poor field hands, the East Texas clan was rich in ways that did not meet the eye. Love was our family's currency. It was the engulfing type of affection that I wanted for my children.

In the late 1980s while my New York family blossomed, beloved Southern relatives quietly crossed eternity's border. On visits home to Shreveport, the mortality in Mama's sagging body was obvious in our lingering hugs. In East Texas, precious pillars of the family structure had already collapsed. Grandpa was dead. Mama's dear sisters, Aunt Too-Too and Aunt Minnie, were gone. Grandma was old. A whole era was slipping away; and my heart ached for people, places and good times of yesteryear.

In an attempt to recapture the vibrancy of an extended family, a call went out to friends and neighbors. I wanted to establish a new sense of family that reached beyond blood ties. A holiday named Family Day was born.

In addition to filling a void left by departing kin, Family Day encouraged children to share their talents—no matter how small. In doing so, the holiday plugged some of the cultural gaps in public school curricula that generally omit the African American experience. Coming so close after Christmas, the new holiday minimized commercialism and illustrated the value of thrifty spending.

A couple of years prior to the 1986 passing of the national Dr. Martin Luther King, Jr. holiday, the Blake household honored the "drum major for justice." The celebration of an expanded definition of family was scheduled on the January Saturday closest to Dr. King's birthday.

The stage was set for an evening of feasting and entertainment. Adults brought covered dishes and a gift costing ten dollars or less to insure every child would leave the event with a present. Each child arrived prepared to share a talent or a loving expression. Nearly twenty of them blanketed the living room floor waiting their turn to perform for an enthusiastic audience of parents and friends.

Jimmy emceed the parade of youthful talent. Presentations were as simple as a preschooler who overcame her shyness and said, "Hello." They were as rousing as a ten-year-old (now famous rapper, Talib Kweli) who dramatically recited Dr. King's entire *I Have a Dream* speech. With a full heart and tearful eyes, a teenage girl sang, "learning to love myself is the greatest love of all." The living room rocked when Shango, Takbir and RiShana dubbed themselves *The Disco-ettes* and lip-sank hits by Michael Jackson. To round out the Blake performances, RiShana wore her favorite pink tutu and did encores of ballet dances she choreographed; while Shango and Takbir teamed up with our next door neighbors, Sheldon and Eric Booker and popped-and-locked to hip-hop beats. The entertainment ended with a magnificent duet by Cheryl Coleman and her daughter, Cherohn who, at age two, echoed piercing notes of Minnie Riperton. The wonderment of children discovering their voices moved all who attended Family Day.

Kanari, a sophomore in college, joined my best friend, Carole Rivers Hysmith in distributing gifts. Though Carole's children were young adults making their way in the world, she donated shopping bags of presents that children gleefully ripped open. Then Carole worked alongside Joanne Booker and other women who served sumptuous homemade dishes of peas and rice, mac and cheese, sweet plantains, potatoes salad, collard greens, string beans, steamed cabbage, tossed salads, salmon cakes, baked bluefish and every style of chicken imaginable. In the background, Piano Man, a fixture at future Family Days, played dance and sing-along tunes that tickled the fancy of the child in us all.

By eight in the evening, satisfied bellies poked toward the ceiling and tots gathered in a circle on the floor. My sister-friend, Michele Khaldun, brought with her to the celebration Clarice Taylor, of *The Cosby Show* and *Sesame Street* fame. The children beamed with excitement as the *Aunt Reese* character came to life in the middle of the living room.

The night ended with comments from the Family Day founder. "We organized this celebration because we want to concretize the meaning..." I was interrupted by vigorous tugging at my shirt tale.

"Bessie, they are preschoolers," Jimmy whispered.

"Oh! Oh! Are you having a good time?" I shouted.

"Yeaaaaa!" the children cheered in unison.

"We made a party so you can see the real big family that loves you." I pointed to parents, preteens and teenagers ringing the walls of the living room and spilling through the arch into the dining room. "Isn't your family beautiful? Stand and clap for them!"

Excited tots jumped up and down screaming to the tops of their lungs. Family Day ended in their triumph yells.

The January jubilation continued for ten years. My phone would ring as early as October. The Khalduns—Michelle, George and their three children Fanon, Zuhirah and Furqan—gave updates regarding song and dance rehearsals. Mothers pressured by excited children called with descriptions of art projects, skits and speeches that would culminate in nervous but breath-taking performances on the next Family Day. I attempted to pass the baton to a new generation of young parents, but no one took hold of it. When asked to host the event at their homes, excuses were plentiful: "Your place is bigger." "You are the warmest hostess." "Jimmy is the best emcee; no one can match him." Quietly, the tradition faded, but abiding memories of love, sharing and commitment to community remain from a very special holiday for children.

*V*ictories at work were often overshadowed by crises in marriage. While Jimmy remained the number one supporter of my professional endeavors, his bloated schedule of volunteer projects left little room for family.

"Jimmy you have ten trains running; one is bound to derail," I complained; but, most days I was the one on the verge of hopping the tracks.

In our mid-forties, Jimmy had replaced partying with politics. He was almost always out of the house running for elected office or engaging in noble causes. Much too often, I was home pondering Dr. Couch's cynical riddle: *If Party A can't satisfy the needs of Party B, then why does Party B need Party A?*

Endless schedules, family meetings, and once-a-year Family Day events did not bring the sought after peace. Financial stability, rewarding work or positive interaction with the children did not define the quality of my life. It all boiled down to the relationship between my husband and me. After nearly a quarter of a century addressing Jimmy's interests on his turf, with his family and friends, I wanted to be near my mother during her elderly years. Every time the subject of relocating to the South was broached, I heard the same cliché: "If you can't do it in New York, you can't do it anywhere."

I took Bible verses out of context to justify my anger. "...a man shall leave his mother and father and cleave to his wife..." I quoted a phrase from Genesis 2:24 to Jimmy; and then, interpreted the word, "man," as applying only to males. Not once did I read the verse to mean *spouses* should leave their homes and cling to one another.

Two institutions—one in Georgia and the other in Minnesota—sought me for college president. Both schools were ideally located for frequent visits to Mama in Louisiana and easy access to New York for Jimmy. When he refused to meet me halfway, a smoldering resentment flared: *Really! How long can I flop around like a fish out of water?*

"Jimmy, I can't breathe; you're sucking in all the air," was a constant complaint. Divorce seemed the only solution but a grief similar to the death of a loved one foiled every attempt to leave. At points of complete marital desperation, I longed to talk to my best friend, my husband, but he and I were estranged. In a torturously slow decision making process, I realized the need for godly counsel. An honest face-to-face mother-daughter session was best. I wrote to Mama frequently with lighthearted stories about the children; but the state of my marriage was not the sort of thing to worry her about in a letter. I went home.

Mama was a seasoned evangelist in her sixties and a good listener. At the end of sorrowful tales of one marital dilemma after the other, I confessed I no longer knew how to pray.

"You pray all the time," she said. "Just talk to God. Tell him what's in your heart."

"It's that simple, is it?" I had come to think of prayer as eloquent speechifying.

"Yes, it's that simple. Talk to God the way you are talking to me right now. If you expect an answer, He'll answer. In other words, 'Have faith in God,'" she quoted her favorite scripture. "He'll supply your needs." Mama spoke about prayer in such a natural easy manner that I vowed to try it no matter how awkward.

In addition to advising me to resume my prayer life, she encouraged me to stay with my husband. "Girl, get some grit in your craw! You got to persevere! Stick to it! Learn to endure hardness like a good soldier of Jesus Christ. You say you want what's best for your children. Well, the children need their father. Isn't Jimmy a good father? Doesn't he have a loving relationship with the children?"

"Yes I have to admit the children adore their dad."

"Then, be strong for your children. Don't dump pain into their young laps that you can barely handle."

During the short visit home, Mama showered me with tidbits of mother wisdom: "Let's not have a pity party." "Don't feel sorry for yourself like some little weakling without a God." "True love is long suffering." "Have some backbone. Be strong!" She even repeated what she had said when I became Dean back in 1982: "Ask God for what you want. You have not because you ask not."

On the last day of the visit, she concluded, "Bessie always put God first in your life. With Him at the center of your marriage, you'll be fine." Holding up a Bible limp from use, she added, "This book is a mirror. Read! It will show you if you are dressed right for the journey."

Armed for spiritual warfare, I returned to New York and prayed for Jimmy to change but he did not. Improvement came only after I prayed for a change in myself. I asked God for peace of mind. He responded, *Forgive!* This inaudible unction in my soul caused a seismic shift in my marriage. Conversations with God replaced squabbles between my husband and me. At first, prayer time meant talking about all my troubles. Eventually, quiet meditation left room for God to speak; and I listened.

Jimmy continued to work several jobs and refused to leave New York. I could have continued the rant about the unfairness of it all. Instead, I waged an internal struggle to forgive rather than criticize his behavior. Oh, sporadically, I let loose; but most times I whispered, "Study to be quiet." Mama had scribbled 1 Thessalonians 4:11 on a piece of paper and mailed it to me. Quiet recitation of the verse got results.

Jimmy interpreted my silence as sulky resentment, "Bessie, you know you're angry; why don't you just admit it?"

"Really, I'm not angry with you, Jimmy."

"Yeah, you are. You have *held resentment.*" He threw one of his social worker terms at me.

Bouncing the "resentment" ball back and forth would have led to a dispute. I kept my mouth shut. Gradually, peace replaced strife; and my husband's absence became precious periods of solitude. Along with morning walks and reading good books, writing for pleasure was added to my daily routine. Most of all, I studied the Bible as I had done as a child.

The Bible—the book that demands self-reflection— cast the spotlight on my faults. As I examined my own heart, I read beyond my mother's favorite scripture Mark 11:22: "Have Faith in God," and found in Mark 11:25 the key to my emotional healing:

> *And when you stand praying, if you hold anything against anyone forgive them so that your Father in heaven may forgive you your sins.*

I realized that mercy for my inadequacies required merciful responses to my husband's shortcomings. Bitterness is a form of arrogance. In effect, every time I forgave my husband, I humbled myself before God and His infinite wisdom.

Compassion fashioned a better marriage. I stopped playing the blame game with Jimmy; tore up my scorecard; and no longer tried to sort out who was at fault for how many penalties. In short, there was a ceasefire. The war for the upper hand in my spousal relationship ended. Whether or not I was right in the eyes of God became the important score to monitor.

When I stopped complaining about every little mistake, I realized how much Jimmy showered me with compliments that made me feel perfect. As if were entitled, I had placed the burden of my happiness on my husband's shoulders. He had become the family I missed, the friends not yet cultivated and the very joy sought from life.

Though I had not confided in her about marriage woes, my usually quiet sister-in law's unsolicited comment helped in the battle against slipping back into a pattern of self-pity. "Happiness is a decision; and I choose to be happy," Hellen had said on my visit home. Up to that point I had viewed happiness as a state of being, an emotion imposed by the circumstances of life. Sister Hellen's Bible-based wisdom activated a freedom of choice rooted in scripture: "*...and whosoever will may come...and take the water of life freely.* (Rev. 22:17)." With an understanding that God is the source of true happiness, I chose to enjoy Jimmy's compassionate nature, his devotion to family, and his lively, fun-loving ways.

Daily acts of forgiving caused a spiritual awakening that shed light on the persistent riddle that logic could not solve: *If Party A can't satisfy the needs of Party B, then why does Party B need Party A?* The answer was clear; Party A can never satisfy or complete the needs of Party B. The deepest yearnings of the heart can only be satisfied by God. My mistake had been fashioning Jimmy into an idol, a little god, capable of fulfilling my every need. In the marital relationship, I had over-emphasized, *What's in it for me?* If Party A can't satisfy the needs of Party B, perhaps the higher calling is for Party B to address the needs of Party A. Life is never perfectly balanced. Some people are placed in our lives so that we can care for them.

Once I realized judging is for God, the cloud of resentment lifted; and I saw my husband's sincere desire to change. Hope dislodged anger. Living in the warmth of Jimmy's love rather than the suffocating smugness of self-righteousness put sparkle back into the marriage.

Thank God, I took my mother's advice and stayed with my husband. Like many couples, I had thought divorce was in the best interest of my children. Truth is: saving the marriage was in the best interest of our children. I did not saddle them with pain too heavy for their slender shoulders. The mess of the marriage had been created by Jimmy and me and the clean-up was ours not the children's job. Whenever we felt tension building, we began to sit and examine shifting needs in the relationship. Our children benefitted from witnessing our struggles to live in harmony. They learned to tackle difficulties in a variety of social situations; and, at the same time, they continued to enjoy an unbroken relationship with a really good father. To this day each of them has a special closeness with their dad.

Had I left Jimmy in my forties, I would have missed the mellow years. Fresh understandings and up-dated agreements renewed our wedding vows in ways that exceed milestone celebratory rituals. We have negotiated nine distinctly different marriages and are working on our tenth contract. The nice thing is I get to be a bride over and over again.

"The Renaissance Man"
&
his Princess

Gordon Parks and his daughter Toni Parks Parson
at the opening reception for her debut photo exhibit,
I-Sight (Photo: TBC, 1991).

Among royalty is what Mama meant when she spoke of celebrity for my husband and me.

"Oooo, Brother Blake people are going to read about you," she said to him.

"God, you are going to elevate Bessie. Ummmm, you're going to lift her from the dunghill and set her among princes," was foretold for me.

"Bless Bessie and Brother Blake's going out and their coming in," she ended the customary prayer before travel.

On the flight from Shreveport back to New York, I pouted in silence: *Dunghill? I'm a college dean. Why is my life a dunghill?* Vanity tilted the focus toward past achievements and away from a divine foreshadowing of greater things ahead. I was not the slightest bit curious about the royalty—that is, the leading figures—destined to enter my life. Gender bias in mass media had made me jaded. Coverage usually cast the spotlight on men and left women in the shadows of important events. As a result, I sulked about what my mother had said about Jimmy and dismissed the possibility of bright lights in my future.

True to Mama's prophesy, less than a month after our arrival back in New York, news reporters began running up to my husband with their camera men and interviewing him on topics about which he was remotely familiar. Those brief seconds of fame were followed by a series of print articles; and then television appearances profiled his family, his work with youth, his community activism, and his runs for political office.

With each instance of press coverage, I mimicked, "Ooooo, Brother Blake people gon' read about you." Though said in jest, the frequent digs slowly confirmed that God works through prayer and prophesy even though things were not working that way in my case.

Parallel to Jimmy's rapid ride into the spotlight was my slow crawl in the background. Consumed by motherhood, job, wife, and devotion to my aging widowed mother, I forgot about the blessings that had been spoken over me. When two amazing people bridged the gap between my passion for the arts and my role as SNR Dean, I was totally surprised.

Nearly five years after the "set among princes" vision, the "Renaissance Man" and his daughter entered my life. Gordon Parks and Toni Parks Parson provided my first close encounter with an iconic African American family. Almost immediately, my career, family and personal aspirations merged. Father and daughter spent time and talents enriching learning opportunities for SNR students and I was the incidental beneficiary of their generosity.

Until the airing of a Gordon Parks interview on a local New York City television show, I knew him only as the director of the blockbuster movie, *Shaft*. However, the television program underscored the importance of his photography. Penetrating black and white images flashed on the screen depicting powerful stories of segregation in the Deep South, of poverty in Harlem and Brazil and of the strength of the people of Fort Scott, Kansas where Gordon Parks grew up. The beauty and squalor captured in his prints stirred the pain and joy of my own childhood. By the end of the interview, I was determined to get the artist involved with SNR.

Following the broadcast, I went on a revealing hunt. In addition to filmmaker and photographer, the "Renaissance Man" was an accomplished pianist, musical composer, painter and author. I devoured *A Choice of Weapons*—one of his several autobiographies. His other books included themes of slavery in America, the education of African Americans, and spectacular volumes of photographic prints. Surely, struggling African American and Latino students would be inspired by his art as well as by his journey from overwhelming hardship to astounding success.

The discovery of Parks' broad range of artistic expressions coincided with expansion efforts underway at SNR's South Bronx Campus. In the mid-eighties, the surrounding neighborhood was rebounding from epidemic fires of the previous decade. As one of multiple organizations engaged in renewal projects, the College of New Rochelle refurbished five floors of an office building in the business hub of the South Bronx. Campus Director, Dr. Marguerite Coke, assisted in the design of the facility; and together, we determined the utilization of academic and student service spaces. I envisioned a Gordon Parks Gallery and Cultural Arts Center as an inspiration for adults seeking a second chance to earn a baccalaureate degree.

Dapper and ruggedly handsome in his seventies, Gordon Parks arrived at the opening night reception with family and an array of dignitaries from the art world. Lively conversation bubbled and down-to-earth warmth blanketed the occasion. Photographers with high-powered cameras snapped candid moments; and a wonderful chat with Gordon Parks unfolded until he zeroed in on my name.

"Bessie Blake has the ring of Bessie Smith," he said.

"Oh, did you know her," I asked eager to learn more.

"Yes. I knew her back in the thirties. You remind me of her."

As a musician Gordon Parks probably focused on Bessie Smith's bluesy voice; but I was not impressed by the comparison. The one photo I had seen of her depicted an overly plump singer dressed in an Aunt Jemima costume. Still, it was an honor to speak one-on-one with the unassuming, celebrated *Life* magazine photographer and filmmaker of hit movies like *Shaft* and *The Learning Tree.*

The gallery's inaugural exhibit, entitled *Moments Without Proper Names,* showcased a cross-section of Gordon Parks' work. In a generous act, the photographer selected and personally matted and framed ten of the prints and donated them to start the SNR permanent collection. Gracing the walls of the South Bronx Campus cultural arts center were glossy black and white 16 x 20 and 20 x 30 prints seen on television screens and in prestigious galleries and museums. It was my good fortune to study those photographs whenever at the South Bronx Campus.

The ten images from the show linger in my soul. "Flavio's Father (1961)" captures the horrors of abject poverty in Brazil. "Man and Wife (1949)" summons long ago dressed-in-Sunday-best days when I ached for a father who sat in the church pew next to my mother. Most disturbing though was "Mother and Four Children (1970)." The photograph of a day at the welfare office tells the story of thumb-sucking and sad-eyed children who snuggle close like a cloak of protection between their mom and an apparently humiliating social worker. In conversation with Mr. Parks, I learned the name of the woman in the photograph was Bessie. I pondered, *but for the grace of God, that's me and my four children.*

Opening night provided only a glimpse of the scope and intensity of the full *Moments Without Proper Names* collection housed at Kansas State University. I poured over other images in the catalog but would have to wait to feed my hunger for more of Parks' captivating photography.

On the evening of the inaugural exhibit of The Gordon Parks Gallery and Cultural Arts Center, Toni stood at her father's side. She was a petite woman who carried herself with the elegance of a stately model. Shoulder length hair framed a medium brown face. Knee high black leather boots contrasted a designer dress. Her movements conveyed an ease with celebrity and privilege. On an evening when crystal glasses clinked softly, Toni's deep-throated drawl had a gritty edge. I quickly learned that she was candid or nothing at all.

"We need to talk," she cornered me. "I have lots of ideas for the gallery. When can that happen?"

I pointed to Donna Tyler, "Give me your number and I'll have the Associate Dean call you."

"No. We can set it up now," she replied.

I thought, *Oooh, this is going to be a headache.* I also had ideas for the gallery. It had been envisioned as a student learning center that opened to neighborhood groups by appointment. Instead of talking about my vision, I responded, "Let me find out from Donna when I'm free."

"I'll see you before the evening is over," she replied in a manner that sounded like the threat of an afterschool brawl.

To avoid a scene, I scanned the crowded room for Donna. The sooner the ordeal was behind me the better. "Come, let's set up an appointment with Toni," I said.

"She's downstairs having a cigarette," Donna stated.

"Downstairs smoking!" I was in a panic. "You know how isolated those streets are at night. We don't want anything to happen to Gordon Parks' daughter."

"Calm down Bessie. That girl's been around the block a couple of times," Donna offered in her usual unshakable manner. My eyes widened as I attempted to square the streetwise image Donna evoked with the stylishly dress, sophisticated, assertive woman I had just met.

At the end of the evening Toni and I wrangled over the details of the appointment. She wanted to meet for lunch but it was impossible to clear my calendar. She did not want to travel to my office in New Rochelle and I could not detour into Manhattan. Finally, we arranged to meet for breakfast at a half way point between her apartment in Washington Heights and my house in Southeast Queens.

Two weeks later, I slid into the booth across from her at the LaGuardia Marriott Hotel restaurant. Like most women dressed for business in the late eighties, I wore a colorful blazer, dark slacks, white blouse, and black pumps with a medium heel. Toni was stunning in a white shirt tucked into skinny jeans, a silk scarf elegantly draped around her shoulders and brown leather boots up to the calves.

Before coffee was served, she got right to the point, "Tell me about your plans for the gallery. My father's work deserves a good curator. I can help with that."

Oh, I thought, *This is going to be a game of cat and mouse.* I ducked behind my role as SNR Dean to slow her down. "First," I said, "let me tell you a little about the College of New Rochelle and how the Gordon Parks Gallery fits into the institution." Methodically, I outlined administrative structures of the College and its four schools; explained that the school I headed had seven campuses in metropolitan New York City—one in New

Rochelle and six in New York City proper; and finally I concluded, "As you can imagine, in the governance of such a complex operation, a lot of work is done by committee." On I went...b*lah, blah, blah.*

Toni listened quietly. When I finished she said with earnest candor, "Bessie I don't know how these things function. I don't have business experience, but I would like to curate some exhibits. So, take my request before your committees."

I was stunned by her forthrightness; but before I could respond, she added, "I'm sick," and her perfectly erect posture slumped ever so slightly.

Completely disarmed, I dropped my shield and listened with a compassionate ear. I did not pry for details; I just let her talk. She conveyed anxiety regarding her health but did not say whether she was undergoing any treatment. I supposed she was under a doctor's care for her ailment because of frequent references to a weekly support group.

The meeting ended with my saying, "Toni, my mom is a woman of God."

"A holy woman?" she asked.

"Yes," I said touching her hand gently. "With our prayers, you are going to be just fine."

"Well," she said with obvious skepticism, "if you want to send some positive energy my way, I'll accept it."

Ignoring the profanity tacked to her response, I focused on the dejected tone of her voice and knew she meant no disrespect. She was under a great deal of stress; but my belief in the power of intercessory prayer saw us through the conversation about her failing health.

I was doubtful about Toni's faith but she surprised me the next time we met. Her first question was, "Did your mother pray for me?"

"Yes," I said, "she prayed and told me that you're going to live and declare the works of the Lord." Toni's warm smile launched a friendship that lasted nearly thirty years.

The various academic committees of the school set about incorporating gallery exhibits into students' studies. Research on Gordon Parks revealed a fascinating life. Of his movies, I was most drawn to *Lead Belly* the story of a blues singer from the Mooringsport-Shreveport, Louisiana area where I grew up. *Twelve Years A Slave: Solomon Northup's Odyssey* caught my interest because I had never heard of Africans in America who were enslaved for such a short period of time.

In reading two of Gordon Parks' books—*A Choice of Weapons*, and *Voices in The Mirror*, I discovered a masterful writer whose riveting accounts of his life echoed Maya Angelou's style. The Parks autobiographies could serve as writing models for SNR adult students as they examined their lives and assessed their prior learning in SNR's required educational autobiographies. Furthermore, Gordon Parks' books spoke to my own love of writing and prompted an author's series at the gallery called, Book Talk.

Once each semester, Book Talk highlighted a published member of the SNR faculty, staff or student body. Featured books were reviewed under the capable leadership of Elza Dinwiddie Boyd, chair of the school's Letters Committee and an author and editor in her own right. Associate Dean Donna Tyler handled the logistics of book reading events. Students and staff from the seven campuses flooded to the Gordon Parks Gallery and Cultural Arts Center for evenings of animated dialogue.

I dreamed of one day standing before my colleagues as an esteemed SNR author. Unfortunately, a writing schedule of academic reports frustrated such visions. In the meantime, the joy of sharing ideas among budding writers provided welcomed relief from demanding administrative duties. Book Talk remained a high priority and a popular literary series during my tenure as dean.

*W*hether at literary readings like Book Talk or art exhibits, Toni was faithful in attendance at gallery events. Contrary to our bumpy start, she and I developed an easy working relationship. As planned in our first meeting, she curated two very successful shows. The *I-Sight* exhibit featured her and Adger Cowans' photographs. The second show, *"Cross Sections/PWP,"* included selected prints by members of the New York based consortium, Professional Women Photographers, Inc.

I-Sight was Toni's debut exhibit. In the 1991 show her black and white images dig beneath the surface of daily life. "Twins (1988)" contrasts the forces of good and evil reflected in the faces of sisters in a West Indian Day parade. An indictment of the handling of the Tawana Brawly case screams "Tawana Was Aped (1988)" from the front page of the *City Sun.* Just out of the range of stardom, "The Back-Up Singers (1987)" gyrate in the shadows of stage floodlights. The single color portrait in the show was of her father, whose image conjures the spirit of an aging messiah whose flame will not die.

I purchased several prints from *I-Sight* to start my Toni Parks collection. Among works later secured were "Dance Theater of Harlem Students with Their Teacher, (1990)" and "The Red Umbrella (1990)" in which her statement on race in America is as powerful as Gordon Parks' "American Gothic (1942)." In 2002, my friend, Toni, gifted me an "Untitled" poster that captures frames of an ordinary New York City street scene.

Following a spectacular debut at the Gordon Parks Gallery, Toni exhibited throughout the metropolitan area. The two of us walked through her shows at off hours. She was a fierce self-critic and, though I sometimes offered my opinions, mostly I marveled at Toni's brilliance with the camera.

When not at art shows and receptions, we met for lunch or explored quaint little shops for pottery and jewelry crafted in the backrooms of storefronts on the Upper West Side of Manhattan. On one of our autumn excursion, she gathered twigs, dried leaves and pebbles.

"What are you doing?" I asked.

"Oh, Dad is working on a new project. It's mixed media art." She described his process, "He places an inanimate object on a background he has painted with oil or acrylic on paper and then photographs it." The result was a spectacular collection of Gordon Parks' abstract artwork that was also published in book form in 1994. Images in the volume, *Arias in Silence,* were as splendid as the large prints in the premiere exhibit at the SoHo Greenberg Gallery the same year.

Selected large pieces from *Arias in Silence* later hung at the Gordon Parks Gallery where Mr. Parks graciously signed the companion book. It was his second of two exhibits at the gallery that bore his name. Opening night marked another exhilarating evening of mingling between members of the art world, representatives from the South Bronx neighborhood and CNR students, staff and faculty. At the end of the affair, people left with autographed copies of the book happily tucked under their arms. For the six weeks that followed, I listened to students joyfully express appreciation of the art that transformed their learning environment.

At the dawn of the twenty-first century, Gordon Parks and Toni Parks Parson bridged the artistic gap between father and daughter in an extraordinary collaboration. Toni caught dusty pastel images of the performance of *Martin,* an opera by her father that depicts the funeral of Dr. Martin Luther King, Jr. She captures moments of agony as ballet dancers stretch and strain on the edge of two worlds. "Rosa Parks," "Birmingham Jail," "Letters to the World" and "The Day of Death" are photographs portraying the magnitude of an unspeakable tragedy. Toni selected eight additional prints from the *Martin* series for a 1997 calendar commemorating the 25th anniversary of the School of New Resources. It was the school's most popular publication.

Toni and Gordon Parks opened a door to a world I had long imagined. Music and fine art infused wonderment while revealing objects and events from unique sometimes piercing angles. In addition to sharpening my perspective on teaching and learning, their works opened me to multiple points of views.

The 1998 retrospective of Gordon Parks' photography at the Cochran Gallery in Washington, D. C. illuminated complex social strata from several societies. Scenes of hunger and excess, squalor and splendor and of struggle and triumph co-existed in common spaces. The exhibition was a stroll through Depression Era misery; a flight in courageous battles with World War II Black airmen; a glimpse at high fashion shows in France; and visits with families experiencing heart-wrenching poverty in Brazil and Harlem. Finally, mixed media abstracts, *Arias in Silence,* pricked the spirit and heightened awareness of the interlocking threads between humans and the environment.

The crush of people at the Cochran opening allowed only cursory glances at an amazing display of genius. Thankfully, the full retrospective traveled to New York City where Jimmy and I surveyed the exhibit at an unhurried pace. The boundless trove of Gordon Parks' art offers fresh gazes at everyday scenes often taken for granted.

$\mathscr{B}$reakfast with Toni meant quiet mornings at her father's place. When I arrived at the apartment in one of the twin residential towers of United Nations Plaza, she greeted me in the lobby and escorted me to the unit that overlooked the East River. On the first visit, my eye was immediately drawn to the photograph of a snowy patio scene at the family's homestead in White Plains, NY; and then to the grand piano that stood majestically in front of a wall of windows. On a corner of the mammoth dining room table Toni's specialty of spicy eggs and hollandaise sauce rested on white plates. Such was my entrance on the first of a series of visits to follow.

Usually, her father slept late because of wee hours spent working at his craft or in attendance at a variety of events. On the rare occasion he was awake, he poked his head into the living room for a quick hello. To show respect for his stature as an artist and for his position as an elder, I addressed him as Mr. Parks.

"That's too formal," Toni groaned once her father left the room. "Just call him Gordon."

"Oh, I can't do that," I protested.

She rolled her eyes, "I sometimes call him GAP. You can use it too. It's the initials for Gordon Alexander Parks."

"Well maybe, I said; but I will have to call him The GAP because he's no ordinary Gordon Alexander Parks; he's the one and only."

It took some adjusting but eventually I grew comfortable using, "The GAP," when chatting with Toni about her dad. However, in direct conversations, I continued to address him as Mr. Parks. Besides, he had never told me, *Bessie, just call me Gordon.* Indeed, he seemed to enjoy the respect shown to him.

Times at the apartment were especially relaxing when Toni—an accomplished musician—played the piano. A student of the Boston Conservatory, she sometimes played her own original pieces. The melodies prompted surveys of wall hangings of her father's work as well as small framed photos of friends and family that graced the grand piano.

As the years progressed, Toni and I tiptoed around the apartment. "Dad is working," gradually shifted to "Shhh, dad is sleeping," and eventually to "Dad is not feeling well today." Etched in my memory is the day he dressed especially for me though he was obviously weak. Looking regal in slacks and a dress shirt with a baby blue wool sweater loosely draped around his shoulders, he crooned, "Hellooo, Bessie," gave me a gentle hug and went back to bed. It was my last time seeing him at the apartment.

For a short while, I continued to see Gordon Parks at public functions like the night he played the piano at The Studio Museum of Harlem. Artists from around the metropolitan area swarmed him at the uptown event but, as always, he managed to reach through the crowd and give my hand a squeeze.

As I saw less of The GAP, I saw more and more of Toni. In addition to becoming the official photographer for social events and graduation hooding ceremonies at SNR's seven campuses, she remained a staunch supporter of the Gordon Parks Gallery and Cultural Arts Center. For the school's 25th anniversary, she curated an exhibit of *Martin* photographs and published twelve of them in a calendar commemorating the school's special milestone.

In between visits to SNR campuses and art exhibits around the city, Toni and I raided secondhand stores.

Exploring Goodwill, Salvation Army and little consignment boutiques with her was a learning experience not to be matched. She knew where and when to shop and what brands to buy. In short, she converted cheap into chic.

"I never shop retail. It's more expensive and the quality is usually inferior. I like vintage," she declared as she nabbed a petite designer blouse plus a cute little jacket for less than twenty dollars. I was never that fortunate. My size fluctuated between ten and fourteen and the best styles were always scooped up by store clerks or the proprietors of re-sale shops. Still, those ventures into the secondhand markets of New York City eventually paid off bigtime for both my daughters.

When Kanari decided that she wanted her MamMaw, my mother, to marry her in our living room, an occasion intended for immediate family members quickly ballooned into a November wedding for upwards of thirty people. Once a color scheme of eggshell white and gold was set for the ceremony and reception to follow, Toni and I went shopping.

The search for silverware, china and crystal began at a Salvation Army store in the theater district of Manhattan where the bargains started with free mid-town parking. I supposed the drive-in lot attached to the store was for the convenience of high-end donors who dropped off lightly used garments but my friend and I made good use of the free parking. Once inside the store, I received an advanced lesson in shopping on a shoe-string budget.

"Darrrling," Toni said, without the slightest hint of snobbery. It was simply the way she talked—highbrow with a little profanity interlaced in unpretentious speech. No matter the circumstance, you always got genuine Toni Parks Parson. Consequently, my tutorial on buying chic at basement prices began, "Darrrling, the silverware doesn't have to match; just make sure it's sterling. Look for this little mark on the back of the handle. See. Always look for it."

Turning to a row of mixed stemware and water glasses, "Buy only crystal," she instructed as she thumped a fluted champagne glass and listened for the chime.

"Get white china," she emphasized. "Not those clunky glass dishes. If not porcelain, then get the feel of porcelain. Whether the design matches or not get white. White gleams in any setting."

"How do you know so much?" I asked.

"Honey, I had to learn early. By age ten my mother had left Dad and I was in charge of the household. He was always entertaining and I was hostess for lots of phony people. That's how I learned about all of this... "Oh, look!" she interrupted the trip through dusty corridors of her childhood. "See these, how thin and elegant they are. This is china, baby! And, it's almost a complete set. They have twenty of these dinner plates and one, two, three... only twelve bread plates, but it's good stuff. You can always mix them with other pieces. Get the clerk! Go! I won't let anyone take them."

I rushed off with the sure knowledge that those plates were mine. Toni wore a size one dress and was a five-feet-two-inch "broad," as she sometimes described herself but she was no pushover. In a tight situation she could be a tough cookie. Oh, she was tenderhearted at the core, but with a dismissive sleight of hand and a drop-dead stare, I had seen her hold the fiercest adversary at bay. No, I was not worried that any enthusiastic shopper would lay hands on a single dish that she guarded.

Before we left the store, for ten dollars, she purchased, a little dinner jacket labelled *Saks*. The top would make a splash at any special occasion or could double as a jazzy top for jeans. It made me sick; elegant little pieces that add flare to an outfit were not available in my size.

After hours of exhilarating plundering, my Volvo pulled out of the Salvation Army parking lot into midtown traffic. The trunk was loaded with crystal, sterling silver and fine china.

On Kanari's special day, Toni trudged to outer Queens and took photographs. Thanks to her, I have treasured pictures of my mother and other beloved family members.

A splendid day! A table decked with crystal, silver and porcelain was perfect for a daughter who grew up asking about every gift, "Is it real?" Well, on Kanari's wedding day most everything was "real."

The year after her sister's wedding, RiShana graduated from Syracuse University and moved into a spacious studio with hardwood floors in Sunnyside, Queens. Toni and I hustled my younger daughter into the Volvo and headed to our favorite Salvation Army store in Manhattan. RiShana was instructed on how to choose and care for a leather couch; to recognize the grain of wood that reflects best in a well-lit space; and how to buy inexpensive but exquisite duvets to cover frayed but warming blankets. From times shared with Toni and me, she learned to appreciate antiques.

In the process of furnishing her apartment RiShana developed a sort of second-mommy friendship with Toni. The three of us shopped at little craft stores along Amsterdam Avenue; and my younger daughter sometimes joined me at The GAP's apartment for one of Toni's delicious omelets. I delighted in the interactions of two creative minds—one young and budding, the other seasoned and established. Toni the pianist, RiShana the flutist and Toni the photographer, RiShana the painter, both spoke the languages of music and the visual arts.

Barriers of age, class, and color were strangers to Toni. She accepted people for who they were inwardly. Indeed, her most refreshing attributes were a humble heart and an unpretentious manner. The girl whose childhood spanned the White Plains family homestead in Westchester County, as well as residency in Paris, Hollywood and New York City naturally spoke in high-tone ways but she absolutely detested phoniness.

She liked for folks to get to the point. So, in her usual frank manner she announced, "I'm moving back to England." I was shocked.

"Don't go," I begged at every opportunity. I met her British husband on one of his visits to New York and brazenly suggested that Mr. Parson might want to move to New York City.

Instead of responding directly to my meddling, Toni turned her big eyes on me and said, "Bessie, I don't want to be an old woman in New York." There was no argument against such a desire. I stopped pressuring her.

Toni attempted reassurance. "I'll be back at least twice a year," she said. "There's Dad's birthday in November and the annual summer festival they hold for him out in Fort Scott, Kansas where he was born."

In fact Toni's relocation back to England turned out to be more pauses than interruptions in our relationship. As vowed, she made two scheduled trips to New York City annually. Her stays generally lasted a month; and we spent ample time visiting our favorite re-sale shops. Also, calling cards, unlimited long distance and other 'bundled" phone services allowed us to keep in touch when she was back in England.

While she was away from the city, The GAP and I occasionally chatted on the phone—mostly about recent correspondence or conversations with Toni. During those early days of the new millennium, I moved into a high-rise on the Queens side of the East River directly across from the United Nations Towers. Life is indeed a "marvelous mystery." I had once gazed from Gordon Parks' living room window to the very area where I raised hands, "Lord, bless The GAP today," as I completed my morning walk.

"These books are for Dr. Bessie Blake," I read in one of Gordon Parks' magazine interviews. Around the same time he called to say, "Come pick out a photograph, Bessie, and I'll sign and frame it for you." By the time I got around to responding, his health was failing fast and a group of assistants and managers was handling his affairs. I did not have the heart to push beyond them to him.

It was even more difficult for me to ask him to write the forward to my first book, *Speak to the Mountain*.

"Why not ask?" Toni wanted to know.

"Because... I'm not out to get what I can from your father. I have great respect for his work and for his privacy."

"Well, everybody else does it."

"Like I told you before, I'm not everybody," I ended the conversation. Before she returned to England in 2005 she called to say, "I told Dad about your foreword. Now, it's up to you to phone him."

With coaxing from Jimmy I phoned, and the minute I identified myself, The GAP answered with the usual deep baritone, "Hellooo, Bessie." Graciously, he went immediately to the subject of the foreword and spared my squirming. "Send me a blurb about your manuscript," he said, "...and "I'll be happy to introduce the book." With sheer excitement, I hung up and followed his instruction. The call was among our last conversations. He died on March 7, 2006 and my first book was released on June 7th the same year.

At the repast following the funeral Toni and her family were surrounded by celebrities from the worlds of art, fashion and film. I gave her a brief hug before fleeing to cold winds that whipped the steps of Riverside Church. The Hudson River lashed misty tears against the shore while I reflected on a life well lived.

Toni stayed in New York for several weeks after the funeral. She was understandably busy, but we spoke by phone. When she returned to England, like clockwork, our monthly calls resumed. Several times we planned for my visit to the seaside town of Torquay but neither of our schedules cooperated. We continued to settle for her twice yearly trips to the city.

The last gala opening night shared with my friend was for the exhibit, "Bridging the Gap." At the Castle Gallery on the College of New Rochelle's main campus, art lovers gathered for a nostalgic look at photographs by Toni Parks Parson and her father. For the occasion she presented cut glass bracelets to three of her best friends. As she often did at such events she credited me with launching her career as a photographer. That night she included extensive remarks regarding my role in securing ten Gordon Parks photographs for the College's permanent collection. She ended the public acknowledgement of my efforts to bring artistic and cultural expressions to communities without easy access with a sweep of the hand and a nod in my direction. "Take a bow," she said.

The packed room broke into applause. The moment of ecstasy was not muted by modesty. I waved my cut-glass cuffed wrist as though it were a coveted academy award and thanked God for genuine friendships cultivated in the backyards of life where only a few glimpse their beauty.

My friendship with Toni drifted in relative comfort until her son, Alain, called with the news. Toni passed in

England on September 4, 2015—nine years after her father and over a quarter of a century after my mother prayed a healing prayer.

For the longest, I relived the last phone conversation. We had opened with usual exchanges of questions regarding the welfare of family. Toni started, "How is everybody?" and then, proceeded to ask about Jimmy and each of our children by name.

"Things are fine," I answered. "RiShana is hosting performance-word jams based on her book, *The Gifted Quiet,* and she has composed a couple of songs for the piano and the flute." Toni was always excited to hear that RiShana was keeping up with her music.

She peppered me with questions about the other children and, wanting to get to how she was doing. I answered in brief clips: "Shango is working on his doctorate." "Takbir is finishing his bachelor's degree. He's also a really good homemaker and is involved in every aspect of his boys' schooling." "Yes, Kanari is still teaching school in an American-oriented school in Abu Dhabi. Of course I wish she'd come home."

"Enough about my family; how is Alain?" I finally asked about her son.

"He's good." Toni answered and after a sputtering cough continued, "He spent a week with me in Torquay last month." The coughing turned to hacking and she turned to cursing about the damp weather in the South of England. "I was in the hospital for three weeks that's why I haven't called," she said.

"How are you feeling now?"

"I tire quickly. I'm dragging around the house. Can't go out and take any photographs. Haven't been in the dark room I spent so much time building three years ago. Crap!" More coughing, "Look I got to go."

"Okay, I will write to you."

"Why can't you use the calling card like I told you?" she fails at shouting but mumbles under her breath.

I was quiet for a long while. I had grown use to her outbursts; but my patience was waning. Frustration took the lead and I argued back. "Look Toni, I told you I tried to use them but those calling cards don't work."

"You have a doctorate and you too dumb to use a calling card," she groaned her disgust.

"Nobody uses calling cards anymore," I snapped. "We text, Skype, email! We don't use calling cards!"

"Yeah, yeah, yeah." The muffled reply was wrapped in struggle. Both our nerves were frayed. We knew the big event was imminent.

I managed to check myself and, in a calmer voice said, "Look, Alain must have an email. Next time I can't contact you, I'll email him. Okay?"

"Okay." I heard the plunk of the receiver. In the background papers rattled, and muted curses escaped. She returned to the phone and spelled out her son's email. "I got to get off the phone." She coughed.

"Yes, I pray for you always and I love you."

"Thank you for your prayers. I love you too, Bessie. Bye."

When I got the news from Alain, it was hard to absorb the reality of life without Toni. For months, the ebb and flow of sweet sorrow churned. Eventually, I moved from grief to gratitude and thanked God for gracing me with her warm, honest and enduring friendship.

Unimaginable!

At LaGuardia Airport, (l to r) Elaine Steele (Executive Assistant to Rosa Parks), James Blake (my husband), Mrs. Parks and me (Photo: TBC, circa 1983).

Unimaginable! I never envisioned the Mother of the Civil Rights Movement when Mama said I would entertain royalty.

True to prophesy, Rosa Parks arrived at CNR for an honorary doctorate in the early 1980s. "Will you be in charge of Rosa Parks' transportation during graduation?" the Executive Vice President asked.

"You bet I will!" I responded with glee although, as SNR dean, I was swamped with graduation preparations.

Jimmy was the perfect person to entrust with the job of squiring Rosa Parks. He was a civil rights activist and his charm would immediately put Mrs. Parks and her aide at ease. I wanted the best for the woman who spearheaded the movement responsible for the position I held. With my husband tending the needs of the Mother of the Civil Rights Movement, I relaxed and focused on frantic last minute commencement demands.

At first sight of Rosa Parks on graduation day, I thought, *What a humble little lady for such a big bold legacy.* Jimmy helped her up the stairway of Leland Castle to the Office of the President. In the sprawling reception area outside of Sister Dorothy Ann Kelly's office, two exquisitely dressed round tables were set for a pre-commencement luncheon for four honorary degree recipients: Rosario Manalo, Lillian Vernon, Donna E. Shalala and Rosa Parks. The honorees were joined by one guest each and by select members of CNR's Board of Directors and Executive Staff. Jimmy and my name cards rested next to ones that read "Rosa Louise Parks" and "Elaine Eason Steele."

At annual commencement luncheons, I dined with civil and human rights legends Bishop Desmond Tutu, Charlene Hunter Gault, Ruby Bridges, Ossie Davis and Ruby Dee; but none had the awe-inspiring grip of Rosa Parks. In the presence of her graceful nobility, words failed. Light chatter was left to my husband while I pushed food around the plate and prayed my nerves would settle in time to read the six hundred names of SNR graduates waiting for their triumph moments.

Once under the familiar furls of the tent, I inhaled the fresh air of new beginnings. A plush carpet of cut grass put a bounce in my step as the platform party swayed to French horns of a live brass band. The cheers of hundreds of inner city women and men erupted in a victory shout as I stepped onto the stage. The sweeping vista of black caps and gowns offset by powder blue hoods symbolized spectacular potential of graduates from the college's three undergraduate schools. In the expansive SNR section, the hope of Rosa Parks' struggle beamed on the faces of adult learners who had been afforded a second chance.

At the end of the day, Dr. Rosa Parks, her aide, Ms. Steele, Jimmy and I climbed into the limousine he had secured for the occasion and headed to LaGuardia Airport for their flight home to Detroit.

In an exchange of light banter Mrs. Parks mused, "All those Black students crossing the stage felt like one of the colleges in the South."

"They are older but basically the same as students at historically Black colleges and universities. They come from communities like Harlem," I said.

"It is wonderful that so many adults have returned to school to better themselves," she responded wistfully. I later learned she had wanted to be a teacher. As we rode along, it was as if she were envisioning herself a college graduate.

I promised, "I'll send you a copy of the photo you took with the seventy-two-year old SNR graduate, the one you said is around the same age as you."

"Yes. Thank you," Mrs. Parks answered and then turned to my husband, "Professor Blake, when are you going to have a Black mayor in New York City?" The hint of playfulness in her voice signaled a dare.

"Oh, we're working on it," Jimmy answered.

Her muffled grunt was laced with doubt.

"Mrs. Parks stop trying to needle me. We're going to have a Black mayor," Jimmy defended his city.

A soft chuckle preceded her next jab, "You can't get together enough votes to elect a Black."

"Yes we can. You wait and see."

"I'll wait," she smiled but her meaning was clear: New York City was not yet sophisticated enough to elect a Black mayor like Detroit had done.

She got a kick out of ribbing Jimmy. When he realized he would have to actually produce a Black mayor in order to win any sparring session with her, he shifted to a conversation they had had earlier in the day.

"Now remember, Mrs. Parks, James Blake the bus driver had you dragged off that bus in Montgomery and arrested; but this James Blake is going to put you in a limousine whenever you come to New York."

"Alright," she nodded.

Handing Ms. Steele my business card, I supported my husband's offer with, "Whenever you are in the city call my office if you and Mrs. Parks need assistance getting around."

Goodbyes at the airport ended a preordained day when my husband and I hosted royalty—the "Queen" Mother of the Civil Rights Movement.

$\mathscr{A}$ relentless push moved the Harlem Extension Center to a fully accredited unit of CNR in 1987. The iconic place of Harlem in the life of Black communities across the nation and, indeed, around the world demanded an identity of equal importance. A special name was sought for SNR's newest branch campus.

The other six SNR campuses were named for their community designations. The New Rochelle, Coop City, South Bronx and Brooklyn campuses reflected residential neighborhoods; while the D. C. 37 Union and the New York Theological Seminary campuses signified organization affiliations. The Harlem Campus deserved a name that reflected the deep and rich history of a people and its community. In pondering a name, my mind drifted to Rosa Parks who was often by-passed for honors like the signing of the 1964 Civil Rights Bill. SNR served the needs of bypassed adults who were overwhelmingly African American women returning to school to better the lives of their families. What an inspiration it would be for them to study under the banner of Rosa Parks.

The proposal to change the name of the Harlem Extension to the Rosa Parks Campus was enthusiastically endorsed by President Dorothy Ann Kelly and quickly approved by the CNR Board of Trustees. I received the go-ahead while in Houston, Texas for a meeting of the Executive Committee of the Board of Directors of CAEL. When the session ended, I made a routine phone-in to the office. In a rush of excitement over the news, I hung up and immediately called Mrs. Parks' aide.

The woman on the other end of the line identified herself, "Louise Tappes, Assistant to Mrs. Parks."

I had expected Ms. Steele to answer but continued, "Mrs. Tappes, this is Dean Blake from the College of New Rochelle. We would like to name a campus in honor of Rosa Parks; and to extend an invitation for her to attend the dedication ceremony at the Studio Museum of Harlem."

"Honey," Mrs. Tappes answered, "Mrs. Parks is down sick. The doctor says she's never getting out of bed again but you can send a letter anyway."

I almost dropped the receiver but managed to convey to Mrs. Tappes a few cordial get well wishes for Mrs. Parks. In the moment of sadness that followed, Mama's words floated in: *"You're going to be lifted from the dunghill and set among princes.* Well, Mrs. Parks was my queen. I dialed home in a panic.

"Mama, pray for Mrs. Parks!" I cried without saying hello. "The doctor says she is on her deathbed and..."

Mama's supplication was instant: "Oh God, touch Mrs. Parks! Raise her up! She is your servant and has done much for your people. This I ask, in the Name of Jesus, and I believe you to do it Lord! Amen."

My mother's prayers were never filled with vain repetition and flowery phrases. She got to the point and she got results. With her simple but fervent prayer, I calmed down and spent a few minutes chatting about my desire to honor Mrs. Parks.

"Oh it's a wonderful idea," Mama assured me. "Don't worry. She is going to be alright and I believe she is going to approve the use of her name." After a brief pause, more like an afterthought, she declared, "Rosa Parks is going to attend your opening."

I left Houston confident about the planned dedication. Back in New York my attention turned to preparations for the event. At the new campus, I worked with CNR's engineer, Fred Sullo, on a final punch-list for computer wiring of classrooms, the library reading room, and of the state-of-the-art communications unit with a television studio. There were doorknobs to install, floor boards to paint, light fixtures to mount, and a hundred other nitty-gritty details to address before everything was perfect for Mrs. Parks' arrival.

Months after the Houston phone conversation with Mrs. Tappes, I received a letter from Ms. Steele giving consent to use Rosa Parks' name and indicating that she would be accompanying Mrs. Parks to the dedication. In the follow-up call to make arrangements for the visit, I conveyed regards to Mrs. Tappes; but received the news that she had passed. I offered words of condolence and pondered the mystifying turn of events: *Rosa Parks recovered from her deathbed; and sadly, her friend has died.*

Nervous excitement charged the days leading to the dedication of the Rosa Parks Campus. Back when she was awarded her honorary doctorate from CNR, the quiet and humble Mother of the Civil Rights Movement had not addressed the audience. After her hooding she had simply waved to the roaring crowd. Because executive staff was aware she had been in poor health on that previous visit to the college, they wondered whether or not Mrs. Parks felt up to speaking at the Harlem dedication ceremony. Everybody was in a tizzy.

"Does she do public speaking," a member of the college's public relations staff asked.

Since her hooding, I had only seen Mrs. Parks in still photographs and none of them were at a podium. "Why don't we call and ask if she wants to have remarks," I suggested.

"If she doesn't speak before crowds, we don't want to pressure her into an awkward moment," one of the vice presidents concluded. It was amazing that everyone, including me, knew little about Rosa Parks beyond her courageous December 1, 1955 refusal to give up her seat on a Montgomery Alabama bus.

Unimaginable!

Because my office was not responsible for scripting the short ceremony preceding the ribbon cutting, I returned to inspecting the finishing touches of the renovated facility; as well as finalizing guest lists, catering, security, and the assignment of hostesses for citywide and Harlem VIPs.

September 15, 1987 was a glorious day. Among local leaders who paid tribute to Rosa Parks, was State Senator from Harlem, David Patterson, who would later become the first African American and the fifty-fifth Governor of the State of New York.

As Mistress of Ceremony, I opened the program with welcoming remarks. After describing it as the college's highest honor, Sister Dorothy Ann presented The Pope John XXIII Medal to the seventy-four-year old Mother of the Civil Rights Movement. When the president moved back to let the audience applaud, Mrs. Parks stepped up, gently pulled the microphone to her height and began speaking in a soft deliberate tone about her appreciation of the honor presented to her on behalf of all who struggled and died for freedom, justice and equality.

It would be one of many times I witnessed people mistaking Rosa Parks' quiet manner for diminished capacity due to illness or age. However, nothing was farther from the truth. Though she was not one to engage in unnecessary prattle, she was a keen observer of people and situations. When she did speak, her remarks were thoughtful, penetrating, and inspirational. One such speech occurred eight years later when Mrs. Parks was eighty-two years old.

On the occasion of the fortieth anniversary of her December 1, 1955 stand, Jimmy and I were honored to arrange a visit to Magnetech Intermediate School 231 in Queens, New York. On December 5, 1995 Mrs. Parks addressed an assembly in the school auditorium that was packed with dignitaries, parents, teachers, staff and students. With a warm smile, she began:

> *Good morning and hello everybody. This has been a wonderful morning here in Queens, New York. I am totally surprised and very, very happy to see these young people and the enthusiasm they have. And to the principal of Magnetech 231, Mrs. Melanie Johnson, I am just overwhelmed and I am happy to have experienced this morning. It has given me new life. I am very, very glad to see you, and to hear you [the students] singing and dancing. All those things, I have never been able to do and never will be now.*

She paused as laughter thundered through the crowd.

> *But anyway, I enjoyed seeing and hearing you. So thank you very much.*
>
> *I am grateful that I have been spared to be here. I always have to thank Elaine Steele because she makes these arrangements for me. Along with Mr. Mark Kerin and other people who are really interested. Mr. and Mrs. Blake are very good friends; and I'm very glad they are here.*
>
> *As I spend these few days here, I don't think anything can top this; but, I do hope you will get the spirit and have the courage to finish school. Stay in school. Make good grades and reach your highest potential. Always, as you have been told, be filled with freedom, courage, justice and determination. Go into the new century taking your leadership part. I know you will be very successful. Thank you.*

Yes, Rosa Parks was more than capable; she was an eloquent speaker; and proved it to the CNR community at the 1987 dedication ceremony of the Rosa Parks Campus. We were inspired by the opportunity to express our appreciation of sacrifices she had made for the cause of freedom and justice. However, Mrs. Parks blessed us with uplifting comments. Unfortunately, no tapes were running.

At the reception that followed at her new campus, royal blue and white buttons declaring, "I love Rosa Parks," were perched on, blouses, scarves, purse straps and lapels. The buttons were a big hit and subsequently traveled around the country with Mrs. Parks as a part of her public relations endeavors.

In a teachable moment at the reception, a local junior high school student asked to interview Rosa Parks. A teacher at heart, Mrs. Parks responded with her vision of a future world of fairness achieved through the education of children. She answered all questions posed by the student interviewer but ended with motherly advice: "Always read about the person you are going to interview, and then ask questions that might provide new information about them," she said with a gentle pat on the girl's hand. It was an uncomfortable moment for the teen but the most powerful learning situations are often awkward.

Adult students of the Rosa Parks Campus basked in the aura of the Mother of the Civil Rights Movement. Later, they adopted as their campus motto: "When Rosa Parks sat down, we stood up." My friend, Toni Parks was on hand taking photos of the ribbon cutting ceremony in front of the library. She also took pictures of Mrs. Parks behind the camera in the television studio; and of her with students, staff, elected officials and CNR board members. My favorite snapshot, however, is the one taken by an onlooker of Toni, Rosa Parks and me.

On an otherwise extraordinary day, I regretted my mother was unable to witness the fulfillment of her prophesy of a successful event. I prayed for another opportunity for Mama and Mrs. Parks to meet.

$\mathcal{F}$or more than two decades, memorable moments were shared between Rosa Parks, Elaine Steele and my family. With the dedication of the Rosa Parks Campus, Mrs. Parks became a beloved member of the CNR community; and the college's support of her endeavors became a means of expressing gratitude for the honor she bestowed on SNR's Harlem campus.

Relationships born out of a common commitment to social justice through lifelong learning served the needs of the two institutions. Soon after the dedication of the Rosa Parks Campus, I volunteered for the Rosa and Raymond Parks Institute for Self-Development. The organization— named in recognition of the sacrifices of both Rosa Parks and her husband, Raymond—was co-founded by Mrs. Parks and Ms. Steele in 1987. The goal of the Institute was and remains helping the nation's youth live up to their full potential. The two women viewed their work with young people as the primary route to more equitable and just societies.

Beyond my desire to help Mrs. Parks and Ms. Steele realize their vison, similarities of missions and methods with SNR motivated me as a volunteer at the Institute. Though their target population was teens, and ours adults, both institutions offered community based-learning opportunities. Like SNR, the Institute removed superficial barriers of location. Its programs were offered in local Detroit neighborhoods as well as in designated travel-study sites in Canada and throughout the American South. Interesting programs bridged generation gaps in Institute workshops. Young people reaped the benefits of oral history as they learned civic responsibility and leadership skills from their elders. In a reciprocal fashion, adults gained computer and other technology skills from young people. Indeed, in one such collaboration Rosa Parks learned to use computers.

Especially compatible with the SNR educational model was the Institute's emphasis on actively learning from experience. In its premier program, Mrs. Parks, Ms. Steele, Anita Peek (Director of the Institute) and an array of volunteers from around the country led young people on tours of sites of the Underground Railroad and the Civil Rights Movement. Diverse groups of students traveled with the Mother of the Civil Rights Movement to historical spots in Canada; down the paths of Freedom Riders; and to places of bloody protests in the Deep South. Along the way, they spoke to eyewitnesses to history; and they listened as Mrs. Parks and Ms. Steele dialogued with history makers. Once the full scope of the tours was apparent, I was inspired to name the program: Pathways to Freedom.

With my appointment to the Board of Directors of the Rosa and Raymond Parks Institute for Self-Development in the early 1990s, I served in a number of capacities. When my schedule as Dean permitted, I represented Mrs. Parks and received awards on her behalf when neither she nor Ms. Steele was able to attend east coast events. On the occasions of those appearances, I realized that amazing numbers of people in the New York metropolitan region did not know Rosa Parks was still alive. Though it is probably natural to think that people read about in history books have passed, this blind spot in public knowledge begs for correction. In response, the SNR Dean's staff—especially Donna Spalter and Corrine Olensky—assisted in the design and publication of *The Legacy Lives* brochure that updated Mrs. Parks' activities with a particular focus on the Rosa and Raymond Parks Institute for Self-Development.

In addition to frequent travel to Detroit, I often met up with Mrs. Parks and Ms. Steele at political and civic conferences in Washington, D.C., Montgomery, Philadelphia, as well as in townships of New York and neighboring states of New Jersey and Connecticut. Eventually, SNR's Associate Dean, Donna Tyler, and I ventured to California, Mexico to assist in an international conference sponsored by The Rosa and Raymond Parks Institute for Self-Development. The 1993 trip to Rosita Beach was an early attempt by the Institute to foster global interactions between youth. Though dialogue between Institute youth and young people of various nations did not take place immediately, a series of such forums were fostered through a partnership with the United Nations after Mrs. Parks passing on United Nations Day in 2005.

However, back in the 1990s, much of the time with Rosa Parks and Elaine Steele was spent visiting schools along the east coast and furthering the Institute's work of educating the country's youth about struggles for equal rights regardless of race, gender or economic status.

At the dedication of the Rosa Parks Middle School in Olney, Maryland in 1992, a battery of eager reporters converged for an interview. Anticipating a host of queries about educational issues, Ms. Steele asked me to sit with Mrs. Parks to assist in fielding questions. As it turned out, I was not needed because no one asked about the dedication ceremony or about Mrs. Parks' views on education. All the reporters shouted at once, "Mrs. Parks, what is your position on gay rights? Do you think it is the present-day civil rights movement?"

Mrs. Parks seemed blinded by hot lights from the television cameras as she considered the questions. Just as I was about to respond, she stated in her usual deliberate manner. "Of course, homosexuality is not my sexual preference, but I believe all people should receive equal justice under the law." Silence fell on the room. The press abruptly packed up and left without a single question regarding the newly named Rosa Parks Middle School or the beautiful presentations by students who had just dubbed Mrs. Parks, "Empress of the World."

That day, I learned something about being in the public eye: Just because everyone is in a mad dash for quick and easy answers is no reason for me to speed up too. Pressing issues deserve measured, well thought-out responses. We can all slow down a bit, take time to formulate ideas and deliver them clearly.

Volunteer work has rewards beyond the joy of giving back. Star-studded evenings shared with Rosa Parks and Elaine Steele abounded in 1993. At the April 30th Essence Awards, Jimmy, Kanari, and I spent a spectacular night at the taping of the show aired on ABC.

Jimmy was informal security for the ocassion2. He rapidly guided Mrs. Parks along velvet ropes that separated us from an enthusiastic public reaching out to touch her. It was heartwarming to witness both ordinary citizens and celebrities paying homage to the Mother of the Civil Rights Movement.

Inside the Paramount Theatre in Manhattan, for the second time I sat close enough to touch Aretha Franklin. On the first such occasion, I sat next to her for the unveiling of Carl Owen's oil-on-canvas portrait of Rosa Parks at the Charles W. Wright African American Museum in Detroit. At the end of the ceremony, I turned and said, "Ordinarily, I would not bother you, but please sign this program for my ten-year old daughter. My husband and I listen to your music all the time and RiShana has become such a fan." Graciously, she took the pen I offered; signed, "To RiShana, Aretha," and added a little doodle.

The 1993 Essence Awards was like lighting striking twice. I sat directly behind the Queen of Soul, who was one of the honorees. Had I leaned forward the slightest, I would have nuzzled against her fur wrap. At first it was difficult to keep my eyes on the stage, but as the program highlighted other honorees I become engrossed in African American stories of achievement and captivated by the performers who paid homage to them.

Danny Glover and Patti Labelle were the emcees. Elaine Steele escorted Mrs. Parks to the stage to accept her award. As Eddie Murphy read the citation detailing Rosa Parks' struggles for the human dignity of a people, my heart thumped irregular beats of joy and determination for the distance we had come and the distance yet to travel.

Second to my adoration of Rosa Parks was Dr. Corla Wilson Hawkins. After years of teaching inner city school children of Chicago, Dr. Hawkins started a "Recovering the Gifted" program that addressed the educational needs of poor children. She was praised as an old fashion educator who got results with the problem child, the slow learner and the chronically truant. In her acceptance speech, Dr. Hawkins revealed basic assumptions about teaching and learning that resonated with mine. She believes all children are gifted; teachers just need to know what their interests are. Though called an "unorthodox teacher," she did not mind. To her the term, orthodox, had come to mean ineffective. "The essence of being a teacher is being effective," she proclaimed.

Rosa Parks, Dr. Hawkins and distinguished honorees from the worlds of sports, entertainment and community service were hailed at the Essence Awards as ordinary people who rose above circumstances of race and poverty to do extraordinary things. From backgrounds common to everyday people eight women were chosen as living examples of Gandhi's belief that when we change ourselves, we change the attitudes the world has towards us. He stated, "We need not wait to see what others do." I remain grateful to Susan Taylor and the *Essence Magazine* staff for the untiring years spent annually recognizing the African American woman with public citations, elegantly crafted award statues and jubilant praise-songs.

At the 1993 program, Patti LaBelle's electrifying tribute to the Queen of Soul plunged her into the audience in typical Patti-fashion as she blasted piercing notes of Aretha's hit single, "Ain't No Way." Directly across the aisle from me Tina Turner danced in her seat. I could hardly contain myself!

Following the awards ceremony, Rosa Parks' party of five headed to the private reception. The hotel elevator stopped for a woman to exit and a wide-eyed Mark Curry of the hit television series, *Hangin' with Mister Cooper* wedged his shoulders between the closing doors. With a sweeping bow and a kiss on her hand, he professed gratitude to Mrs. Parks for making his career possible.

At the reception Patti LaBelle approached me about meeting Mrs. Parks. Wow! Patti was stunning. A bejeweled sheer cape caressed her shoulders. Underneath, the bodice of a black dress tapered just above the waistline and flowed to the floor. I cleared the introduction with Ms. Steele and took the legendary entertainer over to meet Mrs. Parks.

Afterwards, Patti delighted me with brief chatter and a big bear hug. "Don't move!" she gasped as she ended the embrace. I thought we were about to pose for a picture until she panted, "Darling, don't move! These are real pearls stuck to your dress."

I looked down. Just beneath my chin a twinkling constellation shimmered against a dark background. I could have lingered forever locked in the euphoric glee of Patti's arms but in a nervous attempt at wit, I quipped, "I won't move; my dress is real lace."

While Patti's husband painstakingly untangled us, all I could think was, *I can't wait to tell Shango about this!* Patti LaBelle was the idol of my teenage son who constantly debated me about whether Patti's or Aretha's was the best version of "Ain't No Way."

What a Cinderella night! I attended the *Essence* Awards with Rosa Parks; sat behind the Queen of Soul and just across the aisle from Tina Turner. If that were not enough I ended the evening with a close encounter with Patti LaBelle. Was I among royalty? You bet I was! Thank you Elaine!

*E*agerly sought after by civil rights organizations, women's conferences, schools and colleges, Rosa Parks made personal appearances throughout her seventies and well into her eighties. Time and again her attendance at events drew overflow crowds with clamoring applause. She stood before the media; gave countless interviews in support of various organizations; and, posed for endless photos with attendees but she ended her evenings exhausted and empty-handed. Institutions raised bundles of money and goodwill for their causes but it did not matter to Mrs. Parks. She was ever ready to advance the social justice agendas of organizations. I, on the other hand, wanted more for her.

To my knowledge, not one of the seemingly civic minded groups she supported had stepped forward to aid in financing her beloved Rosa and Raymond Parks Institute for Self-Development. Determined that the next decade of her life would be different, I decided to mark her 80th birthday with a fundraiser in support of the Institute.

I landed in a hornet's nest. Greedy, egotistical, and ambitious hustlers dropped their masks. A New York City radio personality and socialite in the African American community wanted to take over the tribute for her own glorification. "Honey you way out of your league," she said without asking what I had in mind. Neither did she attempt to determine my background nor the resources available to me. "First, of all" she rattled on in total arrogance and, I must say, ignorance. "You have the wrong venue; the celebration should be at a Broadway theater; and, second, you don't know the right people."

I thought, *If you know the right people, get them behind this effort to help Mrs. Parks*; I said aloud, "Thank you, I will take your ideas before the committee." Of course, there was no formal committee. There was no need for one; CNR's board of trustees, executives, and SNR staff supported the effort whole-heartedly. I could solicit advice and aid from anyone of them at any time.

A series of hustlers—many who professed close friendship with Mrs. Parks—made the most audacious proposals. One person of national prominence schemed, "You should divide the funds four ways—one-fourth for the Institute, one-fourth for the college, a fourth for my organization; and a fourth for..." Well, the organizations will remain nameless. Why reveal the identity of a would-be thief who is now departed? Suffice it to say I did my research and discovered that the fourth installment of funds would be earmarked for one of the schemer's obscure organizations. Anyway, the notable scam artist concluded our conversation, "You do that and I'll pull the people in for your dinner." I politely thanked her and referred her proposal to "the committee."

The most irritating query came from a nationally acclaimed television personality wanting to know, "Who will be at the event?"

By that time, I was so frustrated that I snapped, "Rosa Parks will be in attendance."

Besides worrisome callers, last minute armchair counselors rushed in with advice after the contract had been signed reserving the New York City Grand Hyatt ballroom for December 1, 1993. Committed to an elegant affair, the hotel staff had worked diligently with Associate Dean Donna Tyler in cutting costs because it was an event honoring Rosa Park. Also, CNR had paid a sizeable non-refundable down payment by the time the naysayers started whispering.

Without contacting me, two so-called stalwarts in the fight for justice planted a story in a Black weekly saying the event would be a flop. After the story appeared in the newspaper, it was virtually impossible to get pre-dinner publicity for the planned gala. Though invitations had gone out on schedule, responses were slow even from invitees who had previously cleared their calendars with enthusiasm.

Added to the growing number of challenges, New York City democratic big wigs scheduled a dinner on the same night though December 1, 1993 hold-the-date announcements of the birthday tribute had been forwarded to elected officials nearly a year earlier. It was a great disappointment when Jimmy's political cronies some of whom held the highest elected offices, ignored the invitation to pay homage to Mrs. Parks.

Thank God for encouraging corporate support. Through the college's network of funders and the efforts of friends like George Khaldun major sponsors lined up behind the sizeable contributions from the CEOs of American Express, Con Edison and Toyota. Nevertheless, gossip about a big flop at the Grand Hyatt reached members of the Board of Directors of the Rosa and Raymond Parks Institute for Self-Development. Names are omitted because my intent is not to expose personal flaws but to illustrate how selfish ambition and disloyalty work against the noblest causes.

Three or four days prior to the birthday gala, my home phone rang. "Are you available for an emergency conference call?" the operator asked.

"Emergency? Of course," I responded anxiously. It was an Institute phone number and I wondered what ill had befallen the Institute, one of its volunteers or, God forbid, Mrs. Parks. As soon as I said, "Hello, Dr. Blake on the line," the designated spokesperson got right to the point.

"We can't let our beloved mother suffer national embarrassment at an event that is a flop," he stated.

My mouth fell open. Sitting in the breakfast room gripping the receiver of the wall phone, *I'm the emergency? Oh, I am the emergency!* As he spoke, the thought wobbled through my mind in a continuous loop.

"You have to cancel that dinner," finally jarred me to the next series of thoughts: *I persuaded the College to support this event. Thousands of dollars have been invested. I can't cancel. Several corporate donations have been received.*

Then, without a chance to explain my dilemma, two board members declared they would not attend the event in New York. The convener of the meeting quickly followed up, "Before we end in prayer, we want our beloved mother to greet us."

I did not realize that Mrs. Parks was on the line. The knot in my stomach tightened to aching.

The unassuming motherly voice that I loved began in the usual slow cadence. "Wellll..." Her every word was a jab of anticipation. "All... I have... to say...   is...," she seemed to take deep breaths before completing the sentence, "...I'll see you in New York on December 1st."

My body slumped. I almost wept. Nobody spoke. Dead silence filled the void. A minute passed. Or, maybe it was a few seconds before I forced the lump in my throat to the side and uttered a scratchy, "Thank you, Mrs. Parks."

The promised ending prayer was replaced with hasty goodbyes and clicking phone lines. I held a tight grip on my receiver long after the wailing busy signal had died. After sobbing uncontrollably, I hung up the phone and stumbled upstairs.

The minute Jimmy saw me, he bolted upright in bed. "What's wrong?" he asked in a near panic.

My tears had dried but words failed. Invisible air bubbles rushed from my mouth at every attempt to explain. He jumped out of bed, held me tight and after a while pushed me an arm's length in front of him. "Girl, you better tell me something!"

We stayed locked in an eye-to-eye moment until I whispered, "I want a cup of tea." He released his grip on my shoulders, rushed downstairs and returned with a steaming cup. After a couple of sips, I recounted the trauma I had just experienced. By the time I finished, his quiet promise had ballooned into the emphatic shout: "YOU WILL NOT HAVE A FLOP!" With those words he tied the malicious intent of con artists, naysayers, and doubters into a single bundle and tossed them out of my life. "We are moving forward," he declared. "We are doing this for Mrs. Parks and we don't need any emotional baggage for the work ahead."

By the end of the next day, thanks to my husband, I had the strength to set aside the rancor that was forming against those who abandoned me. In time, the disturbing phone call became a bitter-sweet memory. It saddened but, at the same time, unleashed an untapped tenacity within myself. A valuable lesson was learned: Don't let the offenses of others distract from important goals; nor personal pain strangle empathy for others. In the middle of my own agony, I reflected on the years of treachery Elaine Steele must have faced in her role as Rosa Parks' Executive Assistant. To re-commit to the goals she and Mrs. Parks established for youth or to sink beneath the hurt of betrayal were probably among her daily choices.

In the days leading to the 80th Birthday Tribute to Rosa Parks, Jimmy, a veteran community organizer, shifted into overdrive. He sold tables to civic organizations, community groups, social service agencies and houses of worship throughout the city.

Down the home stretch, three other people—Sister Dorothy Ann Kelly, Toni Parks and Donna Tyler—were unwavering supporters. Sister Dorothy Ann rallied CNR Board of Directors many of whom were CEOs of banks and major corporations. As president of the college, she was an experienced fundraiser and an encouraging ally. "Bessie," she said, "the planning of these affairs never run smoothly, but in the end things work out. By the way," she added, "Carol Jenkins of Channel 4 News has agreed to be the moderator for the evening if you haven't already secured someone." Had it been a face-to-face meeting, I would have kissed Sister Dorothy Ann.

While I continued to work on major donors and the program script, Donna handled logistics at the Grand Hyatt. She chose reception and dinner menus; identified check-in points and crowd flow; and assigned hostesses and other staff duties. Her role of coordinator for annual commencement dinners for upwards of a thousand SNR graduates and their guests had helped prepare her for such a night as the December 1st gala.

Toni Parks rounded out my inner circle of supporters. She arranged for folk singer Odette to volunteer her talents and reserved back-up entertainment if needed. Among her precious gifts was pro bono photography service at a time when I knew she was strapped for cash.

Despite persistent challenges, the December 1, 1993 birthday celebration for Rosa Parks was a star-studded night to remember. Melba Moore performed her famous rendition of "Lift Every Voice and Sing." Phil Donahue, the pioneering talk show host of the eighties, delivered a moving account of Rosa Parks' impact on his life. Odette ended the festivities with an audience sing-along of civil rights anthems and folk songs with freedom themes. It was an evening befitting the Rosa Parks legacy.

As promised, Toni slipped among the crowd taking photos. Watching her dance around the room reminded me of another Parks-on-Parks moment. It occurred at the *International Photography Center's* opening reception for the *I Dream A World* exhibit and book featuring portraits of Black women who changed America. Among the several larger-than-life photographs, in addition to Rosa Parks, were Constance Baker Motley, the first Black federal judge; Dr. Anna Arnold Hedgeman, first woman to serve in the cabinet of a New York City mayor; Dr. Alexa Canady, at age thirty, first Black female neurosurgeon in the United States; as well as Shirley Chisholm, first Black woman elected to the United States Congress and, in 1972, the first woman of any background to make a bid for the Democratic Presidential nomination. Each woman in attendance sat in front of her portrait and autographed copies of the book.

Unimaginable!

Gordon Parks' incredible *Life Magazine* photograph, "Sisters of the Nation of Islam," was among the prints on display but I had attended the function with Rosa Parks and Elaine Steele. Ms. Steele and I took turns assisting Mrs. Parks as she signed her photo and chatted with admirers. I was standing slightly to her left when, without fanfare, a figure emerged from the crowd, knelt on one knee, gently took Mrs. Parks hands and kissed them. Back then they were both nearing eighty but, like a little boy, Gordon Parks gazed up at the Mother of the Movement and spoke in tender tones. I could not hear what either said, but an aura of mutual respect and reverence was evident. As he rose from kneeling, his eyes met mine with the familiar, "Hello, Bessie," and he vanished in the crowd as quickly as he had appeared.

Four years later, Gordon Parks did not attend the Rosa Parks 80th birthday function but his spirit was present in the adeptness with which Toni angled her camera. She produced an amazing photographic record of the evening.

In the end, things "worked out" according to Sister Dorothy Ann's prediction about fundraising. More than a hundred thousand dollars cleared after expenses; and The Rosa and Raymond Parks Institute for Self-Development received substantial on-going donations because of the goodwill and friends cultivated on the night of the gala. In 1993, it was dubbed the largest single amount of money donated to the organization.

Equally as important, Mrs. Parks had a wonderfully relaxing time. Still, I could not help but think: *If every African American man, woman and child donates a dollar, Mrs. Parks' dream of a viable Institute can become a reality in her lifetime.* I would have attempted such a national campaign but was weary from my stint in the shark infested waters of fundraising where bloated egos, greed and ambition are strong swimmers. A few years later, I settled for a "dollar-wave" to Rosa Parks from school children in New York City.

On a professional note, had I cancelled an event with numerous prepaid investors, it would have tarnished the fundraising apparatus of the college. Instead, the affair enhanced CNR's reputation; and, I did not lose my job due to "folly" as distractors had predicted. On an even more personal level, joy flowed from the fantastic evening my family spent celebrating the life of Rosa Parks. My mother traveled from Louisiana and spent time with Mrs. Parks on the days leading up to the amazing night of the "happening at the Hyatt!"

At every opportunity since the gala, I have shared the Rosa Parks legacy with school children. Recently, I asked a class of kindergarteners, "What did you learn about Rosa Parks today?"

"Oh they're too young to understand," the teacher answered for the class. However, a seemingly timid little Asian girl in the back of the room raised her hand and said softly, "Rosa Parks changed the rules."

In simple eloquence, a child captured the essence of Rosa Parks' role in re-shaping the world. Helping children at a tender age to envision kinder societies is worth the time spent telling and re-telling them our stories. When we fail to do so, we fail to secure their futures.

On the threshold of her nineties, Rosa Parks' pursuit of a just and peaceful world continued through her work with young people. Thanks to Elaine Eason Steele, I walked a portion of the way with Mrs. Parks for nearly a quarter of a century.

Old yearnings were aroused by talented students, staff and faculty who chased dreams of becoming fulltime writers.

A featured author in the SNR Book Talk series, Tonya Bolden, inspired my transition from drafting dull academic reports to writing lively family narratives. Even before she started to speak, Tonya's book title, *Tell All the Children Our Story,* beckoned me to times and places where barefoot children listened from porch swings to gripping tales of elders in straw bottom rocking chairs.

In 1993, the year of Rosa Parks' birthday gala, I approached Mama: "I must've heard you share the testimony of your miraculous healing a thousand times. Why don't I write about it in honor of God's favor on your life? You have been on the battlefield preaching, praying for the sick and winning souls for Christ since your healing fifty years ago. You were only twenty-one when you vowed you were going to live to be seventy. Aren't you excited? He's about to fulfilled His promise of *'three-scores and ten.'*"

"Yes, that is His promise," she mused.

"And, your Saturday radio broadcast has been on the air for thirty years."

"A little more than thirty," she said.

"Maybe we can read something on the air. Send me an outline and I will write a brief sketch when I get back to New York. It will be a keepsake for your children, grands and even great grands who will know about the angel God placed in our family."

"Oh that sounds wonderful," she agreed.

I had barely returned to New York before a manila envelope backed in Mama's beautiful calligraphy-style penmanship arrived. At the end of a busy workday, I opened it and pulled out a black and white speckled composition tablet—the kind used in elementary school. Without taking off my heavy sweater, I sat in the living room and read the thirty-one-page hand-scribbled draft that began eerily like my high school English class autobiography:

> *I, Tommie Martin Waites, was born in Jefferson, Texas to Bessie Ross Martin and Tommy Martin. I have three brothers Herman, Major and Alfred and three sisters Emily, Earlene and Minnie...*

The sketchy narrative contained bare-bone facts of Mama's life story. I called her, "Do you want me to write your biography?"

"That is what we are talking about, isn't it?" She sounded as if she dared me to disagree. Her insistent tone set off an internal struggle between the anecdote I was preparing to write and the biography she was proposing. Mama won out. After all, my desire to write had been seeded in her kindergarten when I was age five. Though absorbed in duties as wife, mother of four, and dean, I decided to give her biography a try. The project honoring Mama started me down a road of exploration of the oral history of my East Texas family.

While home doing research for the book, my mother was busy planting spiritual seeds. "Brother Scott is preaching at the First Church anniversary over in Lakeside this afternoon," she announced after dismissal from Faith Tabernacle—one of three churches she had founded. "Want to get a bite to eat and then drop by to support him?"

That Sunday, thoughts of the long ride back to New York by myself overwhelmed me. In thirty years, Jimmy had visited my hometown only three times. Naturally, I was ecstatic when he decided to tag along on the summer of 1994 research trip. I looked forward to sharing with him people and places of my youth. Together we were to uncover crucial facts for Mama's biography. It did not happen. Two days into what had been planned as a two week stay, he abruptly returned to New York for a Million Man March organizing meeting. I was livid.

Ordinarily, I flew home but Jimmy did not like planes. To keep him company, I had taken Amtrak north along the Hudson River, West to Chicago and South into Louisiana; and he had the nerve to leave me stranded with no good choices. I could take a train ride plagued by delays; or, fly back and lose the money already spent on a sleeper compartment that costed far more than an airline ticket. I decided on the train but anger flared at every thought of the reversed zigzag and lonely route back to New York.

If it weren't for the children and my job I wouldn't go back, I was thinking when Mama asked again, "You want to go support Brother Scott?" The invitation was her attempt to pull me out of a brooding slump.

"Yes, let's go," I answered. "Brother Scott's preaching always brightens my day."

I strolled into First Church dressed in all white. The straw hat covered natty box braids sorely in need of re-doing and the eyelet dress with matching one inch high white pumps were attempts to keep cool in the intense August heat.

During "Choir Selection A" my eyes scanned the walls and rested on a green banner with gold lettering that declared: "Forgetting those things that are behind, and reaching forth unto those things which are before." I thought. *That's what I'm doing: pressing forward.*

The anniversary program moved quickly. The pastor provided a brief church history; an offering was collected; and "Choir Selection B" ushered Brother Scott to the podium. Lively as ever, he began reading his text but paused mid-sentence to study the congregation. "There is someone here today who thinks they are not saved because it's been a long time since they spoke in tongues. I'm going to pray for you before I leave," he said and then returned to his text.

That's me! Oh my God! I don't want to go up in front of all these strangers. I don't want to confess that I'm not saved; but I need the peace that surpasses understanding that people are always testifying about. I was in a quandary.

Brother Scott must have delivered a rousing sermon. "Amen!" "Hallelujah!" rang throughout the congregation as he ended. My heart beat wildly but, to my great relief, he sat down. There was no altar call, no mention of speaking in tongues. I relaxed.

Brief announcements preceded the pastor's instruction, "All rise; we're going to dismiss."

"Wait!" Brother Scott jumped to his feet and rushed back to the microphone. "Please be seated," he said. "That person who hasn't spoken in tongues for a long time, come on up for prayer."

I walked nervously down the center aisle determined not to stumble. Brother Scott shouted praises to the Lord as he came down from the pulpit to where I stood. As he reached out, sounds of a swishing ocean rushed from his cupped hands. I drifted like a feather in gentle winds. Next thing I knew, three women I loved dearly—Mama, Sister Rock and Sister Lee of Hollywood Church of God In

Christ—joyfully hovered over me. I felt an after-the-rain freshness in body and soul when they finally lifted me from the floor.

Thank God, Jimmy had returned to New York. Had he been present, he would have bolted from his seat, scooped me up and dragged me out of that church. Instead, I was surrounded by people familiar with the Biblical Pentecostal experience described in the second chapter of *Acts*.

On the way home, Mama, Honorene, and Brother Scott teased me. "Ole Sister Bessie didn't wait for me to lay hands on her before she fell under the power of a MIGHTY rushing wind," he playfully emphasized the entrance of the Holy Spirit.

In gleeful laughter I responded, "Yes, I felt like chiffon collapsing in soft folds."

"Chiffon? Noooo, Dr. Blake! You hit that floor straight as a board," my sister, Honorene, poked at me. "And you spoke pure tongues." She was referring to the evidence of the presence of the Holy Spirit recorded in Mark 16:17, "And these signs shall follow...they shall speak with new tongues."

As Brother Scott got out of the car, I quipped, "From now on, I'll have to call you 'Daddy.' You're twenty years younger but God used you in my spiritual rebirth."

That day at First Church, a fog lifted. Gone were the days when sporadic periods of research were followed by brief episodes of writing my mother's story. I wrote with renewed vigor and without condescending intellectual overtones about religious zeal. I committed fully to capturing the point of view of a fiery evangelist minus my own perspectives and commentaries.

In between writing sessions, I huddled in planning meetings with Honorene and our dear sister-friend, Lessie Felton. We organized the 70th birthday celebration that blossomed into a magnificent banquet thanks to the dedicated work of many volunteers. Kudos to Sister and Brother Lars of Faith Tabernacle who oversaw the purchase, preparation and serving of food; and to my friend Minnie V who helped secure the right venue.

On January 2, 1995 Mama's church and East Texas families gathered in jubilant praise for the miracles wrought in her life. Empowered by the Holy Spirit, I forgave Jimmy for his premature departure from Shreveport and I am glad I did. It freed him to join our four children, their spouses, and our first grandchild, Ameer, and me in the birthday festivities of a truly remarkable woman—my mother, Evangelist Tommie Waites.

Forgiveness of Jimmy also galvanized family support for his leadership role in organizing the Million Man March in which Black men from around the nation converged on Washington, D. C. They expressed brotherly love for one another and vowed to work to improve their communities back home. As it turned out, the historic October 16, 1995 march set the bar for a series of subsequent marches. There was the 1997 Million Woman March in Philadelphia (750,000 strong according to organizers); and the 1998 Million Youth March in New York City (estimated by police at 6000 and by organizers at 20,000). Though few of the nineties protests reached the magic number, marches aiming to attract a million people continued into the new millennium.

*T*wo loves vied for my attention. Though life's circumstances led me first to the joy of teaching, writing was always an equal passion. While pursuing Mama's story, writing sank its hooks into me and my job as dean lost some of its luster. I adopted a schedule of weekends, holidays and vacations in hotel rooms clicking out tales of yesteryear. Weekdays, I rose at three and four o'clock in the morning to knock out a page or two before going to work. Increased numbers of hours were devoted to writing but daily agendas were shaped by obligations as SNR Dean.

For six years I worked part time on my mother's biography. All the while Mama lamented, "I hope Bessie finishes that book before I go home to meet the Lord." Her constant nudging made it difficult to avoid the possibility that it might be time to leave SNR.

Oh, there were other signs that I had fulfilled my potential at the job. I had reached a plateau of predictable events that rolled around in a methodical fashion. Another Middles States or State Education Department visit; one more out-of-town stay in a luxury hotel away from family; and, the retirement of a truly visionary president pointed to a season of change.

Actually, my resignation was overdue. I probably should have left the College of New Rochelle in 1997 when Sister Dorothy Ann Kelly retired as President. Though she, Jimmy and I maintained a schedule of monthly lunch dates, the absence of her on-the-job encouragement and guidance tilted toward my departure. The needed push came when talk about making the college catholic with a large "C" led to discussions about ending the partnership with protestant-based New York Theological Seminary. I was a builder not a closer of campuses. It was time to go.

Besides, enthusiasm at the dean's desk had been overshadowed by growing excitement at the writer's desk. I was no longer satisfied with drafting academic reports; teaching an occasional writing course; or, cramming creative writing into narrow margins of my life. Effective June 30, 2001, I resigned and exited with a glad heart and silver, if not a gold, parachute.

During twenty years as dean, I had the pleasure of working with a staff whose infectious love of teaching and learning made the job easier. With the aid of committed colleagues, the school grew from four to seven fully accredited campuses; and from an annual enrollment of roughly 3000 to a student body of approximately 6000. More than 10,000 adults earned the baccalaureate degree; and ninety percent of them were women and men from marginalized communities like Harlem, Bedford Stuyvesant and the South Bronx where disparities in resources act as barriers to higher education.

At the time of my departure, students whose intellectual abilities had been underestimated earned advanced degrees at Columbia, Princeton, Harvard, New York University and the graduate schools of the City University of New York. Alumni were pushing beyond barriers of race, class and gender to enter careers as teachers, social workers, clergy, attorneys, elected officials, and as civic leaders bent on transforming society. Like the impact my mother's education had on me, SNR graduates were setting achievement markers for future generations in their families and communities.

At the School of New Resources, I had been the first Black in every academic position I held. The College of New Rochelle was by no means unique in its hiring and promotion practices. The institution simply reflected a broader pattern of discrimination in an American educational system that had carved a space of cultural isolation for me long before I was hired at CNR. At best I had worked in settings with a hand full of African Americans. At worst, I had been the only Black in a White work environment. Fortunately, as SNR dean, I had also been positioned to address some glaring employment inequities.

The Ocean Hills Brownsville struggle for community control of schools had provided a penetrating look at how the lack of diverse role models limits students' abilities to succeed academically or to set and measure life goals. One of my many aims as dean was to ensure that all SNR students saw themselves reflected in some aspect of the academic leadership of the school. I worked to eliminate the glib excuse, "We can't find a qualified Black applicant." Time and again I discovered, hired, cultivated and promoted talented workers who had been languishing in unemployment or in positions where their skills were grossly under-utilized.

In sharp contrast to my 1979 arrival at SNR as the only Black academic administrator, when I resigned in 2001 the school's instructional and executive staff included a talented group of women and men who reflected the composition of the student body of the school. Among the ten-member Executive Committee, four were African American women with doctorates; and, indeed, my successor was a talented woman of African descent, Dean Elza Dinwiddie-Boyd. I resigned confident that future leaders would not encounter the same pitfalls I endured as the first woman dean of SNR and the sole Black at the helm of one of CNR's four schools.

People asked after I left the college, "Don't you miss the busy life of a dean?"

I answered, "I do miss the wonderful SNR staff and students. Otherwise, it's a good miss because I'm pursuing my passion for writing." Then, I thought, *The essence of my calling is unchanged. Writing is simply another way of learning and teaching.*

Shortly after I left CNR, Dr. Ellen McGovern, Director of the New Rochelle Campus, sent me a beautiful handwritten note that began, "Once upon a time, we had Camelot." At the time, neither Dr. McGovern nor I could have foreseen that, due to financial problems, the entire College of New Rochelle would close its doors in 2019.

$\mathcal{I}$n 2001, I left the School of New Resources as a fan of lifelong learners. I believe that learning at every phase of life should excite the awe of a well-run kindergarten classroom. Like children at play or flowers being watered, each lesson should leave the learner thirsty for more. At age fifty-six, research for my mother's biography was that kind of amazing learning experience.

I began with interviews of elder members of my East Texas family and moved outward to seniors in the village. Those old people were reluctant to talk about themselves. They ducked painful questions, "Oh that was too long ago; I can't remember that far back," and then a wave of the hand ended conversations before they started. My inexperience as an interviewer certainly contributed to the flights of memory. After many blunders, informal chats peppered with gentle probing replaced stark questioning.

The best stories are told over food—whether preparing or eating meals. In my mother's case, storytelling shortened the hours spent over hot stoves. Spontaneous kitchen talk and songs were gateways to precious nuggets of oral family history. With my knees in a jackknife position, I lay on top of the four-foot long deep freezer and listened to the blues lyrics, *"My Mama done died/My daddy is po'/Ain't gon' wear clothes no mo'/I'ma be naked, naked, naked."* This little ditty led to stories about a mother who died young and a father who paid little attention to Mama's tattered clothing when she was a child.

Eventually, I carried a scratchpad and captured the juiciest tales before they lost their fleshy details. Incidental scribblings contained embers that caused the sight and smell of smoke to curl from the written page. For instance, on a summer visit to New York, a buggy ride through Central Park with my mother and cousin opened gates to memory lane. The minute we turned off busy city streets with honking horns and onto a tree-lined path of greenery, Mama and Tomprell sighed and settled back in their seat. The *clop, clop* sound of the horse's hooves against pavement, the poignant odor of steamy droppings took them down bygone roads of hard red clay. Oblivious to the Manhattan skyline peeking over regal tree tops, my mother and cousin had escaped to Smithland, Texas.

Tomprell asked, "Aunt Tommie, you remember Pie Crust, don't you?"

I grabbed my pad and began writing. The driver wanted to give us our money's worth and started his routine, "That's the Tavern on the Green restaurant over there; and just ahead...

"Shhhhh," I tapped him on the shoulder; landmarks would have to wait.

"Sho' Prell. Who could forget Ole Pie Crust?" Mama answered. "She loved that tree swing in front of Papa's house. You remember the swing, don't you?"

"Oh yeah, but Pie Crust went too high. Every day that swing would throw her like a bucking mule."

"Yep, but no matter how many times she landed on her backside, she climbed right back on the swing and went at it again," Mama chuckled.

"Oooooo, we used to laugh at Ole Pie Crust and try to make her stop."

"Yes, yes," Mama agreed and then added, "but she wasn't really harmed. It just goes to show you; no matter how bumpy the ride, if you truly like a thing keep at it."

Mama and Tomprell rode along telling tales of their childhoods and enjoying nature's symphony. Birds tweeted love songs; squirrels rambled in the bushes; and I jotted down the details of murder-suicides, descriptions of a favorite horse named Johnny Boy and stories about how my Great Grandpa Ross (a freedom during slavery) had "the biggest buggy—larger than any White man in Smithland." No questions were necessary. East Texas reveries glided on city asphalt.

I never knew whether or when a tale from my scratchpad would be used. Stories that did not edge their way into one manuscript surfaced in another. The Pie Crust yarn did not make it into my mother's biography, but pops up here as an illustration of how to enliven writing through the use of dialogue and description.

The biographer teases out precious gems of truth in likely and unlikely places. In addition to impromptu conversations, Mama's electrifying Sunday morning sermons and recordings of her weekly radio broadcast were gold mines. During frequent visits home, sweet nectar was dripping from a branch of the family tree without a bucket in place to catch it. Since my mother was accustomed to microphones, I began switching on my tape recorder at Saturday radio broadcasts; during Sunday sermons at Faith Tabernacle; or in the praise services at the Rock Mission. Even at the amazing team taught Bible studies at Hollywood Church of God in Christ, the recorder rolled while Mama and young Brother Scott delivered The Word.

Team-teaching? Yes, but never had I witnessed team-preaching until I watched Mama and Brother Scott. In front of the offering table just beneath the pulpit, the two of them marched back and forth passing one another in the two lanes their feet trampled. Mama with Bible in hand and him swinging his arms loosely, "God is love," he stated.

The minute she started speaking he stopped in his tracks, "Yes, mother," and *click* went my tape recorder.

She completed the thought, "For God so loved the world, He gave His only son."

"True, mother, true," he responded and they resumed the march.

As he expounded on God's love, she encouraged him with "Amen," and "That's right anyhow, Brother Scott."

The entire Bible lesson was delivered in cycles of marching, pausing with "Yes, mother," and followed by commentary or a scripture she inserted. It was odd that they never collided. Their delivery of The Word was a beautifully synchronized dance that fascinated. Most amazing was the clarity of the message captured on a hand-held tape recorder.

Over time, my taping extended beyond church services to any conversation that held promise for the book project. A crucial story slid from the lips of Mama's oldest sister while we feasted on a plate of hot fried fish. Aunt Emily had grown accustomed to the click that captured their conversations. When she did not want a record of what was being said—especially her cursing— she snapped, "Girl, turn that thing off!"

The day of the fish fry, she asked in a lazy soothing voice, "Tommie, you remember how Mama used to put pretty ribbons in your hair after she combed it?"

"Naw, I can't say I do," my mother answered just like I expected. There was a long pause where the tape recorder captured indistinct sounds of the stalled conversation. Silence and patience were less distracting than my scrambling for scraps of paper or grabbing napkins when the chat resumed. While waiting we sipped home brewed iced tea and enjoyed the East Texas breeze that stirred among the zinnias beneath the kitchen window of Aunt Emily's trailer house.

Without warning, conversation resumed. "Yeah, Mama made one big plait in the top of your head and two in the back. She tied a ribbon on each braid. You looked pretty, unnn-huh."

"I remember the Christmas I was three," Mama offered with a vacant look as if she had drifted back in time. She surprised me by plunging into details about the day her mother knelt for prayer before crawling into her deathbed. While breaking bread at Aunt Emily's house, I recorded the gripping story that opened my mother's biography.

Indeed, during the year of recording exchanges between her and her sister, Mama released the pain of her most traumatic childhood experience; and a new fluency entered conversations about her life. Like an unclogged facet, she started talking and did not stop until the completion of the first draft of *Speak to the Mountain; The Tommie Waites Story.*

The meticulous hunt for the right word is like tracking an elusive but prized prey. In drafting *Speak to the Mountain,* the endless pursuit of exacting words that convey meaning and mood inflicted a torturous joy. In an attempt to best reflect the character of my mother's life, I embarked on tireless vocabulary searches. Then, just short of ripping the manuscript to pieces, I forced myself to move forward.

Fact-checking was another wondrous phase of revising the original manuscript. Months were spent confirming or disavowing my mother's recollection of specific events. Elders in the family, church members, and random people from the community told their versions of what happened "way back when." Days in county court houses pouring over leases and deeds verified the accuracy of dates and places. Government offices and libraries yielded birth, death, school, military, marriage and census records. Old homesteads provided bundles of funeral programs with short narrations of individual lives. Family Bibles contained records of baptisms, weddings and additional important names and dates.

In a quest for accuracy, I trampled off the beaten path; squinted at headstones in overgrown cemeteries; read historical roadside markers; and photographed cornerstones of crumbling churches. As a roving researcher with camera in hand, I documented scenes and characters from shotgun houses that were fast disappearing as "the bottom" areas of towns were cleared for freeways and other so-called "renewal" projects.

Clueless about the disturbing nature of time capsules, in 2004 I headed to the outskirts of Shreveport for snapshots of the Gilliam plantation. I had fled those fields in the middle of the night fifty-three years earlier. Once again life as a sharecropper's daughter overwhelmed me. The freshly whitewashed big house with its grand entranceway screamed, *Unconquerable!* Shacks with caved in roofs and weathered buildings with peeling paint whispered, *"Gilliam Cotton,"* while the little girl lying on a rickety porch listened—still alive, still yearning to be free. I had never really escaped Gilliam. Its effects had chased me for a lifetime. In truth, the horror of the sharecropper experience had been an ever-present force in my struggle for empowerment through education.

Standing at the foot of a cotton row that disappeared over the horizon, I realized Gilliam was more than a place; it embodied blatant lies about poverty in the richest country in the world. Return to the plantation was reminiscent of my visit to Senegal's slave dungeon at Goree Island. In a flash, my story told the history of persistent racial division in America.

Despite the best efforts of well-meaning people, none of us have escaped the crippling impact of horrible episodes of history that linger as strong as ever. Millions of Gilliams are still strewn across the landscape of America yearning for justice. The magnitude of unfinished work is evident among those who still labor in fields of despair as well as those cloistered in big houses of government bodies and corporate board rooms fixed on greed.

Sure, individual and collective pockets of success have been realized in addressing racial disparities in education, employment and general social wellbeing. However, nearly three-hundred years of slavery followed by Jim Crow and systemic denial of human rights are not easily undone. The Gilliams of America cannot be escaped by fleeing. Until we have the courage to talk honestly about the hard things and to face one another repent and forgive, the entrenched legacy of slavery will continue to imprison people at every social and economic strata of society. There has to be kinder-gardens than sharecropper plantations, drug-induced wastelands and entrapped neighborhoods of poverty.

On a picture perfect January day, a new millennium that should have been bursting with hope sent me fleeing from the Gilliam plantation for a second time. Rosa Parks' words rang in my ears: "As long as people use tactics to oppress or restrict other people from being free there is work to be done." Thoughts of Mrs. Parks reminded me of how Christian faith had sustained her quiet strength through more than seven decades of activism for civil and human rights. Indeed, the Joy of the Lord in the middle of struggle was one of the common bonds between her and me. Joy generates strength to continue to do the work. No wonder spiritual hymns and praise songs were pistons that energized the Civil Rights Movement of the sixties and seventies.

After the second flight from Gilliam, I felt like throwing up my hands and surrendering to defeat but faith quieted my troubled spirit. I refocused on the progress already attained and was strengthened for the miles left to travel. I resumed unfinished fact-checking tasks hopeful that the book I was writing about my faith-filled mother (who approached every person as a child of God) would help all of us value one another as deserving of compassion. Truly, it will take love to lift us out of the quagmire of a divided nation. With that thought I moved forward.

While on the road collecting data, a network of newfound relatives graciously shared records of family history. Among the contributors was Belzora Cheatham, a prolific researcher and writer who was treasurer of the Afro-American Genealogical and History Society of Chicago (1992-1997) and president of the organization (1999-2001). My beloved Cousin Bell and I share the same great grandmother, Hattie Taylor Johnson Martin—a former enslaved African in America. At a Martin family reunion in Lodi, Texas, Mama mentioned to her first cousin, Hattie Brown, that I was writing a book about the family. Cousin Hattie introduced me to her daughter, the genealogist who became an invaluable resource in documenting the family tree of my Martin ancestors. Cousin Bell's computerized database contained thousands of entries about families with East Texas roots. She remains a one-woman clearinghouse as she cross-references and connects countless African Americans to branches in their family trees.

Through Cousin Bell, I met Nzinga Asantewa, a California genealogist who had done extensive research on my paternal ancestors, the Waiteses. Nzinga is the daughter of my father's long lost brother, Johnnie, who had been missing for thirty years and presumed dead by our family. In the aftermath of World War II, Black men—especially veterans—walked away without a backward

315

glance at the racial horrors of the Deep South. Meeting Cousin Nzinga was a double blessing. First, it was a pleasure to inform Daddy's four sisters that their brother was alive and residing in California. Second, Nzinga became a road buddy as we crisscrossed East Texas counties uncovering hidden trails of the Waites and Martin clans.

Nzinga Asantewa and Belzora Cheatham enriched the writing of *Speak to the Mountain* beyond my wildest expectations. They shared kinship charts, family photos and tidbits of information about the daily lives of African Americans in East Texas. Their devotion to resurrecting family histories sent a host of ancestors back to my desk for each revision of the *Speak to the Mountain* manuscript. At the computer, faded images in dusty yellow pages of old Bibles and funeral programs sprang to life in vibrant colors.

CRED

A Texas Goodbye is filled with tall tales and longings for frequent family gatherings.

At the last reunion with my East Texas relatives, a blood red sun hung above the treetops waiting to set. Jimmy moaned, "Not another one of those Texas goodbyes." As a native New Yorker, my husband did everything at lightning speed including farewells. He glanced impatiently back and forth between the setting sun and the ritual unfolding in my brother's front yard. A Texas goodbye, the distinguishing feature of all reunions of the Martin-Waites clan, was in full bloom.

"Well, I guess we better go," an uncle announced and, on cue, everyone swarmed the front yard.

"Sho' enjoyed seeing you," a cousin offered.

My brother Edgar, the proud host, beamed, "It don't get any better than this!"

"Yes, we need to do this more often," his wife Hellen chimed.

"Well, let me get a hug before I go," said the uncle who had been poised to leave for ten minutes but his request kicked off another round-robin of hugs and kisses.

"How is Billy?" someone remembered to ask and set in motion a chain of replies: "Pretty good considering he is getting up in age." "Ain't seen him in months; tell him I said Hello." "Sho will and you tell Pearlie Baby I send regards." "Will do. Ummm... Think I'll get me another hug before I go; might not get down this way for another year or so."

By then, it was dusk and the entire clan stood swatting mosquitos, laughing, and dredging up just-remembered tales. Finally, the aging uncle and his wife corralled their grandchildren into the car. As the taillights disappeared around a curve, flagging hands waved farewell.

Another relative declared, "Guess I better get on down the road too," and the hugging and back-slapping ritual repeated itself until the last person left well after nightfall. Such was the nature of my family's goodbyes.

At the time, no one had an inkling we were on the brink of Texas goodbyes of greater magnitude. Whenever genealogy explorations took me to Smithland, Mama made popcorn calls on relatives. She prefaced one visit to her brother's house with the puzzling comment, "Your Uncle Major is sweetly confused."

I knew nothing of his confusion but sweetness had always been a hallmark of my favorite uncle. I spotted him under a tree at the edge of the yard. With a small pocket knife, he was prying meat from the hard shell of a hickory nut. Though in his seventies, when I walked over he began feeding me marcels from the hickory shell the way he had done when I was five. I opened my mouth as if receiving a holy sacrament.

Friendly banter from Mama and Uncle Major's wife, drifted from inside the house to where we stood.

"Girl, I might be past my prime but I know I'm pretty," Mama teased.

"Yeah, but-but y-y-your hair is not as nice," my aunt stuttered.

"Sister Annie," Mama addressed her sister-in-law as a Holy-Ghost-filled follower of Christ even when kidding. "I got this smooth black skin. You know what they say, 'The blacker the berry the sweeter the juice.'"

I could not resist joining in play with two old women teasing like teenagers. "I'm the prettiest," I shouted toward the window.

"Beautiful," Uncle Major corrected me with a soulful gaze that said: *I love you, Bessie.* We stood holding hands. Neither of us wanted to let go.

"He doesn't seem muddled to me," I said once back in the car with Mama.

I soon learned, though, that my sweet uncle was indeed confused. In a series of long distance phone calls, Mama reported: "Annie says he can't remember what he ate for breakfast." "He always forgets where he puts his glasses." "He repeats what he said a minute ago." Finally, on a chilly October morning, the news, "Major is missing," shocked me.

In Mama's blow by blow accounts I learned the circumstances surrounding my uncle's disappearance. A World War II veteran, retired farmer and county fireman, my uncle had a definite sense of manhood. He did not clean house or cook; he chopped wood, plowed the fields and did other he-man jobs. It was no surprise when he had refused to use the indoor facility his children installed in the seventies when septic tanks rapidly replaced the outhouses once common in the vibrant farm community. Uncle Major thought no self-respecting man would do his business inside the house. Only womenfolk used indoor chamber pots; and, to him, the shiny new commode was nothing more than a glorified chamber pot. Because his outdoor wooden toilet had caved in well before the nineties, whenever nature called, he grabbed a roll of tissue and headed for the bushes at the edge of the woods near his house.

On the day memory failed him, he finished his business and walked away from the house deeper into the forest. Since he knew every inch of those woods, Aunt

Annie thought he had gone for a stroll. When he did not return in an hour, she called two of her sons. They left work and began the search. By noon worry grew to panic and the authorities were notified.

Uncle Major was well-liked and the whole village of Smithland, Blacks and Whites, turned out. Howls of dogs and shouts of frantic neighbors floated skyward among thick pines. At night the men fanned out with lanterns and flashlights. With no signs of his whereabouts after three days, the search was called off.

On the fourth day, around noontime, my uncle was spotted walking barefooted alongside Highway 43. His shirt was tattered and he was unable to explain where he had been or how he ended up seven miles from home. The incident was a sobering reminder of how fragile the mind can be.

I worried from afar but made no connection between my "sweetly confusion" uncle and dementia or any memory challenges associated with aging. Nor did I realize that the three-day disappearance signaled his demise. When he passed a few weeks after the incident, his death struck a hard blow. Goodbye must have been a lengthy ordeal for his immediate family; but, from afar, it seemed Uncle Major had been snatched away abruptly. I stopped visiting Aunt Annie whenever I traveled to Shreveport.

During my hiatus from East Texas, I was comforted by a precious family heirloom passed from my beloved Grandpa to his son, Major, and from my Uncle to his daughter, Belvie. She had loaned the nineteenth century tin photograph of our Great Grandma Hattie to me as an inspiration for writing. Clad in the high-collar fashion of the day, Grandma Hattie sat erect. Her posture said, *I am strong* but eyes void of light steered final drafts of *Speak to the Mountain* toward difficult truths about our family's America odyssey.

*A*fter completing the *Speak to the Mountain* manuscript in 2004 the focus shifted to finding a publisher. For months, I read tear-stained rejection letters before signing a one-year contract with an agent. James Schiavone, who had clients on the *New York Times* bestselling list, circulated my manuscript widely in America and abroad. Rejection notices kept coming. Praise for my craftsmanship did not alter the response. With slight variations in wording they said, "There is no market for the story of a Pentecostal Black woman preacher."

"I have failed as a writer. Everybody can't be wrong," I groaned.

"Bessie, everybody is wrong," Schiavone was quick to reply. "It's really a good piece of work."

I did not believe him nor did I renew his contract at the end of the year. I shelved the manuscript and wondered what to do with the rest of my life.

Jimmy, still an "added resource" in all my endeavors, did not give up. He shared a copy of the manuscript with a colleague at Borough of Manhattan Community College. Jack Estes ran a small publishing company, Pleasure Boat Studio.

"I can't get your mother's voice out of my head," he said. Though his authors were mostly poets and mystery writers, he wanted to publish the biography.

I asked, "Why Pleasure Boat Studio? It sounds a bit risqué."

He chuckled, "Yes, I know; but isn't reading a good book like embarking on a pleasure cruise."

"Yes it is," I said. From that moment, Jack and I had frank but easy ways of talking. I trusted him with my mother's story and he did not disappoint. His help was invaluable in editing the text, designing the book block and providing financial support once the book was released.

Speak to the Mountain: The Tommie Waites Story was finally published in 2006. A year later, the volume received the *U.S.A. Book News* "Best Book Award for Religion and Christianity." At age sixty-four, a lifelong passion for writing brought elation over the publication of my first book and flooded me with hope of fulfilling other dreams. A phone conversation would not do. I boarded a plane to Shreveport.

The long awaited biography was a bittersweet accomplishment. My thrill over sharing the book with kinfolk mingled with yearnings for relatives who could only be visited in the pages of family history. Still, I gathered strength to go back to Uncle Major's house and return Great Grandma Hattie's photograph to Belvie. While there, I expressed gratitude to my cousin for her loving patience.

When, I placed *Speak to the Mountain* in Mama's lap, "Ummmm," she moaned; and, for the longest, she held the book between palms that rubbed up and down in a prayer position. Then, turning it over, she stared at her photo on the front cover as if she were trying to remember where she had seen that woman before. Mama lived back behind a door somewhere on the edge of eternity.

"That's your book," I broke the silence. "See, I finished it before you went home to be with the Lord."

"What? It's about me!" she exclaimed before fading again.

I eased the book from her hands and began reading. Immediately, Mama bounced back with animated you-can't-tell-it-let-me-tell-it testimonies. Fully alert, she completed every passage I started. As soon as she finished speaking, she disappeared again.

In her early episodes of detachment, I described my mother as "frayed around the edges." By the time I presented the book to her, the door to a world of silence was left only slightly ajar. Yet, there were reasons to be thankful. Back when she was alert and vibrant, Mama had been blessed to read and comment on the completed first draft of the book manuscript.

She loved the title, *Speak to the Mountain.* "That's me," she said. "I've spoken to many mountains too high to climb."

Her feedback regarding the narrative was couched in diplomatic language. "Oh, I wouldn't say it like that, do you think?" Or, "That's too smart for me; it sounds more like you, doesn't it?"

At the end of the reading she declared, "I don't want to hurt anyone, especially relatives who are still living. The purpose of the book is to help others; and you're not likely to help people by hurting them. A little sugar, a little humor will do more to draw them." Where there were harsh comments about others, with few exceptions, Mama had said, "Don't you think maybe we can delete this passage?" I followed her instructions.

The countdown to publication of *Speak to the Mountain* had coincided with the final stages of the longest Texas goodbye. When memory loss began to pose a danger, Edgar moved our mother in with him and his wife. When she said she wanted to live with me, I brought her to New York. After several months, she cried to go home. Edgar and Hellen arrived on a snowy day to carry her back to the warmth of Louisiana.

On the frigid New Year's Eve they were scheduled to leave, the pain of separation was almost too much. Because I was unable to witness my mother's departure, Kanari was hostess to her uncle and aunt. Jimmy and I spent the day wandering in the emptiness of a blocked off Times Square where people would be celebrating within hours. Though reluctant to hand over caregiving responsibilities, I knew in the depths of my heart it was right for Mama to return to the familiar surroundings of Shreveport.

I ached for her presence but slowly came to grips with the fact that healthcare was not my assignment. I thought: *I have a new mission. After all, Mama opened old wounds to make her biography possible.* Completion of the book project became my life raft in a stormy sea.

One family member lamented, "Why would God allow such a devoted servant to suffer such a horrible illness?"

I was quick to respond, "Mama isn't suffering; she is content in yesteryear. We're the ones suffering. This is our trial, not hers." My siblings and I shared a common anguish. Loss of our mother's companionship seemed to us a "mountain too high to climb."

Unlike Sister Lessie Felton who gave Mama regular facials and Sister Pearlie Pea who anointed her weekly with blessed oil, most people spoke of my mother as if a catastrophic change had not occurred. "How's Mom?" they chimed like she was off somewhere running a revival.

I would tell you if I knew where the heck she is, exploded in my head but, "Fine, thanks for asking," became an automatic response.

Mama lived mostly in the distant past by the time of *Speak to the Mountain's* publication. Thankfully, the book provided a means of connecting with her. She was energized whenever I read about the Depression, World War II or her callings as nurse and then preacher. She even surprised everyone and joined me in a book reading at the nursing home where she lived after she needed twenty-four-hour care.

Every able-bodied patient at the nursing home gathered in the cafeteria. Mama, Honorene and I sat across the front of the room. My younger sister got us started with a rousing solo. I read the chapter from the book entitled, "I Still Have Joy." Awakened by memory of gospel songs from the old days, Mama led a hand-clapping sing-along. Gaiety blanketed the once somber cafeteria; and both patients and staff marveled at our mother's charisma.

Evangelist Tommie Waites had not lost the gift of song or the gift of healing. On my visits to the nursing home she responded every single time I grabbed her frail hands and asked for prayer. The fact that her petitions continued to get answers reminded me of one of her favorite sayings: "God doesn't give a gift and then take it back. We might leave him but He never leaves us." I tucked the thought in my heart, relaxed and began to enjoy precious moments of the longest Texas goodbye.

Stress free days resulted from the combined efforts of Edgar, his wife, Hellen and my sister, Thelma. During the last six of twelve years of illness this team of three provided coordinated care for our mother. Hellen visited the nursing home daily with stacks of washed, mended, ironed and even new outfits she had sewn for Mama. My sister-in-law also kept an inventory of supplies and purchased, as needed, toiletries and disposable items along with fresh fruit and spring water that augmented the nursing home diet.

A Mama's boy, Edgar had once boasted, "I'm never moving away from Shreveport. If I fall I want to be close enough to grab her apron string." True to his vow he always lived within ten minutes of her. Once she was in the nursing home, though he spent grueling hours on the road, his overnight runs as a truck driver always ended at Mama's bedside.

Edgar also handled her business affairs; arranged for her to have a private room; and made sure all nursing home staff performed at the highest level. No distinction was made between position and rank. The message was the same for the facility director, doctors and nurses as it was for the cafeteria and janitorial staff. He wanted Mama's room spotless; her food delivered hot and on time; and he wanted all treatment delivered with the utmost respect and dignity. My brother got what he wanted or else they heard from him loud and clear.

Thelma, an excellent nurse, took the lead in caring for Mama's day to day medical and personal needs. She relocated from California back to Shreveport; moved into the room with Mama; and provided around-the-clock private duty nursing. As she cared for our mother, my sister sprinkled tiny but blissful goodbyes into my life. The phone would ring in New York, "Hey girl, you got a minute? Tommie is having a good day. Let me put her on with you." Conversations unfolded as if Mama and I were having coffee and carrot cake at her breakfast room table.

As Alzheimer's took greater control, Mama stopped coming to the phone. That did not stop Thelma's calls with lighthearted anecdotes. "You want to hear something funny?" she would say before jumping into the drama of the day. "Tommie busted my top lip. I asked her, 'Mama you tired of me hovering over you?' She drawled, 'Yeeess,' in her sweet little voice but I kept dressing her. Next thing I knew she had popped me in the mouth. So, I'm going to take the day off and give Tommie a rest." Thelma always ended those accounts with laughter—as if she never grew weary in well-doing.

My sister and brother took good care of Mama while I toured and hosted readings of *Speak to the Mountain*. In marketing the book, networking was a prime activity. The majority of my appearances and readings were hosted by colleagues, friends, classmates and contacts that acquaintances provided. In addition, Mama's vibrant network of churches held readings.

Any cross country trips always included Shreveport on the itinerary. Hometown readings included a gathering of Booker T. Washington's class of 1960 hosted by longtime friends, Armanda Clarkson and Minnie Fontenot; as well as by Minister John James of Faith Tabernacle Revival Center, Reverend Ted Scott of Harvest Temple COGIC, and Pastor Johnny David Banks of Word of Faith Christian Fellowship.

In addition to Shreveport readings, my publisher, Jack Estes, shipped books and funded the cost of appearances at multiple venues in Southern California, Las Vegas and North Carolina. Not only did his support build my confidence as a writer, he became a mentor.

With my second book, *God's Bad Boy*, I joined a growing trend of author-publishers. *If I could run a school as complex as the School of New Resources, surely I can publish my own books*, I said and self-directed learning rose to a new level. Jack generously assisted me in understanding the intricacies of the publishing process. At his suggestion, I read Dan Poynter's *The Self-Publishing Manual, Volume II;* chose other guides on my own; and later benefited from the wisdom of friends like Gregory L. Hudson who had experience as a self-publisher.

Becoming a publisher forced me to examine my abilities; to review accomplishments; and to identify key players who might share my interests. I called on friends and associates to assist with editing, computer graphics and other technologies. Transferrable skills from previous phases of life reshaped my world. I chose the name Lit Lore which means knowledge or wisdom handed down—usually in the form of stories. With the birth of the small publishing imprint, a dual career of writer-publisher emerged as I continued to tour with *Speak to the Mountain*.

All the while, Thelma encouraged me with humorous tales of Mama's activities until a frosty mid-December day. She called, "Hey girl my job is finished. I didn't come for a death watch. Mama ain't getting out of bed anymore; and people are crowding in to sit around with the shades drawn. I came for the living; I can't stay for the dying."

Thelma's decade of loving devotion to Mama helped me endure the goodbye years. Had my mother died suddenly, I would have been paralyzed with grief. When Alzheimer's first robbed me of daily interactions with her, I cried rivers of tears; but the ultimate call on Christmas Eve of 2011 brought peace instead of agony. Mercifully, God had allowed an adjustment period that carried me slowly through the transition. On Christmas morning, I envisioned Mama receiving the biggest gift of all: She woke up in the Throne Room of Heaven. Among a host of angels, I still hear her singing, "Holy, holy, holy is the Lord God Almighty." I praise God for my sixty-eight years with Mama and thank my dear sister for the comfort she provided our mother as well as for me.

Back in grade school, classmates quipped, "Goodbye? Well, every goodbye ain't gone!" It was wisdom from the mouths of babes. My mother's goodbye certainly is not gone. Her vibrancy lives in the thirty years of audio tapes of her radio broadcasts; in the pages of *Speak to the Mountain;* and on the days when I bake her walnut-raisin carrot loaf; slice off half a banana; pour a cup of hot black coffee and salute Mama—my first love, my first teacher.

ope and a future is God's promise. So, Mama planted a spiritual seed.

Fourteen years prior to her passing and two years before turning down Alzheimer lane, she asked, "Is one meal a week enough nourishment for your physical body?"

Of course the answer was, "No, I can't survive on one meal a week."

"Then, how do you think you can stay healthy on one spiritual meal a week even if that meal is a Sunday feast?"

I shrugged.

She continued, "You need to get into a good Bible-based church where you get daily square meals and healthy snacks in between."

The exchange was profound in its simplicity. Yet, I entered the new millennium as a church-hopper. Sunday to Sunday, I circulated among two to three churches but never settled anywhere. It was difficult to transfer my membership from Faith Tabernacle where my mother had pastored to a house of worship in New York. I wanted her to emerge from the fog of dementia and resume the role as my spiritual leader. Fellowshipping at a variety of churches created the illusion of holding her inevitable departure at bay.

During those disconcerting years, my daughter, Kanari, repeatedly invited me to visit her church. She lived in Woodbridge, New Jersey but was a member of Agape Family Worship Center located in the nearby town of Rahway. I dreaded the out-of-town trek from Queens, New York. Nevertheless, I accepted her invitation because I had been taught from a child, "The family that prays together stays together."

In the spirit of family unity Jimmy, our youngest daughter, RiShana and I rose at five on a Sunday morning in 2002. We had breakfast on the move; and took two subway lines and the New Jersey Transit commuter rail to Rahway where Kanari waited to shuttle us the few blocks to church.

I intended to rotate my daughter's church into my schedule of houses of worship, but Agape put me at ease. Visitors were welcomed without an intimidating request to stand and greet the congregation. I liked the way first-timers were described as guests who could attend as often as they liked. The emphasis was on saving souls rather than membership drives. Without the pressure to join, I relaxed and a spirit of unrestrained worship took over.

Every aspect of the service was devoted to worship. Praise songs swelled to God in adoration. Gone was the frequent passing of the collection basket. Instead, giving was a form of worship where each person presented offerings in joyful recognition of the Creator and Provider of all things. Most of all the Gospel of Jesus Christ was taught boldly. On the first visit, I entered the sanctuary hungry and left well-nourished. Divine encounters drew me back to Agape every Sunday but it took two years before I officially joined.

Committing to a church home is as scared as the marriage oath. Membership represents a vow of love and support in good times and bad times. Union with a church family should not dissolve because of petty disagreements and judgements of one another's faults. As with marriage, prayer and study of scripture sustain religious commitment. However, I did not ask God if Agape were the right fit. Previous experiences guided my decision. In the Pentecostal churches of my youth, I had observed joyful worship and heard powerful sermons followed by bickering and backbiting that scattered members at the first sign of trouble. I wanted to avoid such experience.

However, most members at Agape Family Worship Center remained faithful through times of challenge. Though I did not ask, God in His mercy revealed I had finally found a church home. My name might not have been on the membership roll the first two years but my heart was with the Agape family from the very beginning.

"There is nothing like a live Agape experience!" Dr. Lawrence Powell enthusiastically proclaims. Nothing could be truer. For twenty years, unrestrained worship and a loving congregation has drawn my family from New York City to Rahway, New Jersey. We feed on the Biblical exhortations and pearls of wisdom of Dr. Odessa McNeil, a devoted teacher of the gospel. We relish the friendship of Minister Clinton Miller, who prior to my arrival at Agape invited me to Elizabeth High School to speak to his students about Rosa Parks. In addition, I am always happy to see Ralph Stowe, his wife Flora, and their son Matthew. Ralph is one of my sons who grew up in Jamaica, Queens with my children.

Among the fellow believers, who never fail to greet me and my family with hugs that energize are Sisters Pam, Mamie, Mia, Lori, Patricia, Doris (and her mother) along with Minister Denette. Then, there is a special love between Sister Carol Matthews, her son, Josiah and me. Their enthusiastic worship repeatedly inspires me to higher praise. Also, during the three years Kanari worked abroad, the thoughtful generosity of Sister Lisa Rodriquez, Sister Lolanda Hooper, (fondly called Landi), and Dr. Yvonne Wesley spared my family the hardship of walking or waiting for cabs. These three women faithfully shuttled RiShana, Jimmy and me to the New Jersey Transit Station for the train back to New York City. Because of the warm and giving natures of these and others who show their love with a nod and a wave, I have affectionately dubbed Agape, "The Little Big Church." Some describe the assembly as a mega church but genuine unpretentious worship has fashioned a close-knit intimacy once experienced in small town and country churches of my youth.

Dr. Powell may not describe himself as a songster but the pastor certainly carries a tune that quickens the Holy Spirit. I am especially blessed, though, by his un-compromising delivery of the gospel of Jesus Christ. He does not tickle the ears with popular or trendy notions but says what is most needed and backs it up with scripture. Not only do I grow in knowledge, but in wisdom of how to apply what is learned to daily living.

In his role as a standard-bearer, Dr. Powell maintains a sense of humor. He often weaves funny anecdotes into his sermons. Humor helps us swallow the medicine of sober messages. In the middle of a sermon, entitled "What to Do with Your Problem," the pastor led the congregation in a brief prayer.

"Close your eyes," he instructed.

We obediently closed our eyes.

"Now repeat after me: "Lord, help me to see what or who is at the root of my problem."

In unison the congregation prayed, "Lord help me to see what or who is at the root of my problem."

"Amen." He ended with a raised eyebrow and asked, "How many of you saw your own face while you prayed?"

Laughter rang throughout the congregation. Prayer with a hint of humor opened hearts to receive the tough message: "Stop hacking at the leaves and go for the roots; sometimes you bring problems on yourself."

Pastor Powell's unique brand of humor is augmented by occasional laugh-out-loud Sundays where

Christian comedians minister to the assembly. They remind everyone that laughter is a part of God's design for human beings. Indeed, Ecclesiastes 3:4 says there "is a time to laugh;" and Proverbs 17:22 declares, "A merry heart does good like a medicine." Scientific evidence also shows that laughter reduces stress and releases natural feel good chemicals called, endorphins. Who knew that cheerfulness increases immune cells that fight infections and relieves pain? No wonder I am rejuvenated at the end of a Laugh-Out-Loud Sunday service.

Kanari says, "Pastor is just plain ole nice," and I agree. Dr. Powell is a natural born encourager who passionately pronounces: "I believe God!" "Every trial has an expiration date!" "God loves you!" Finally, in a forthright expression of affection for the congregation, he frequently declares, "I love you and ain't nothing you can do about it." Such exhortations continually move me from trial to triumph.

During the first few years at Agape Family Worship Center, I feasted heartily on Sundays but virtually starved during the week. Evening travel from New York to New Jersey was a barrier to attendance at mid-week services. Thank God for modern technology. Today, nourishment is available on Agape's daily 6:30 AM *Morning Prayer* phone line; and the 7:30 PM streaming of Wednesday services on YouTube and at agapecenter.org.

My mother would have been pleased to know I stopped church-hopping and settled in a Bible-based house of worship that provides "daily meals with healthy snacks in between." Indeed, my Agape experience has been a higher education that unifies mind, body and spirit.

Along with links to Agape ministries, I am blessed with additional sources of spiritual food. Eight years ago, I joined with my cousin, Tomprell in California and my sister, Honorene in Texas on a weekly Thursday noon prayer conference call. On Mondays, childhood girlfriends, Armanda and Minnie V. and I study the Bible on a three-way phone line between New York and Louisiana. Great strength is drawn from fellowship with these four women.

The more I read the Bible, the more I understand my mother's excitement over "feasting daily on the good sweet Word." Early in my life, she instilled a love of scripture. Actually, a longtime goal since childhood has been to read the Bible from cover-to-cover but I stumbled at every attempt. Either I started in Genesis aiming to reach Revelation or in Matthew hoping to finish the New Testament. Both strategies failed until ten years ago.

For an unexplainable reason, the book of *Acts* seemed a plausible place to begin. While sitting at my desk reading Jesus' instructions to the Apostles before His ascension, the phone rang.

It was my girlfriend, "Hey Bessie Waites Blake, what you doing?

"Hi Armanda, I am doing morning devotion."

"I'll call you back."

"No, I can talk. I just started reading the Book of Acts."

"Oh, we're studying Acts in Bible study."

"Really? I wish I were there; I would go to church with you."

"I don't study at my church; I go to Bible Study Fellowship. We call it BSF for short. Are you familiar with the organization?"

"Nope, never heard of it."

"They have study groups in every state in the country and many major cities around the world. Who in your family is good with computers?"

"Me. I just finished the manuscript for my second book, *God's Bad Boy,* and I'm in the process of establishing my own publishing company. It involves a lot of computer work. My nephew John helps when I need technical assistance."

"I remember John. How is he?"

"He moved from Shreveport to Houston where he has a big information technology job with the city's utilities or something like that.

"That's wonderful. John is such a nice respectful young man."

"Yes he is. I told you he'll help you with your computer needs. His father still lives in Shreveport. I can ask him to stop by whenever he's in town."

"We are not talking about my computer needs, Bessie Waites Blake! Let's get back to your Bible study. You can search on the computer for BSF; or, let me see. It is called International Bible Study Fellowship. Look it up; there has to be a class in a city the size of New York."

Sure enough, there was a Manhattan class a short subway commute from my apartment. I noted the schedule and enrolled the same week.

Close to ten years, from September through May, I have gathered once a week for two-and-a-half hours of prayerful study of scripture with BSF women of diverse backgrounds. I get off the uptown 6-train at Lexington and 86th Street and a delightful crosstown walk is waiting. I proceed up 86th beyond the breathtaking floral malls of Park Avenue; make a right turn on Fifth Avenue and stroll along the beautifully landscaped fronts of mansions perched across the street from Central Park. Depending on the season, I pause to pluck fists full of purple pansies and bundles of rousing red tulips with my cellphone camera, of course. At the corner of 90th and Fifth, I enter the Church of the Heavenly Rest invigorated by nature's beauty.

Following a thought provoking lecture; lively group discussions of scripture; and fellowship with the BSF ladies, I head home around noon. On the way, I stop off for "Bean Soup Tuesday," at the Greek restaurant in my neighborhood. I arrive at my apartment motivated to begin the analysis and personal reflection required in the first of six daily homework assignments. Thanks to BSF, detailed examination of scripture is now a revitalizing force in my life.

In my eighth year at BSF, I came full circle back to the study of *Acts*. In the second reading, fresh perspectives were shaped, in part, by new sets of personal circumstances as well as by deeper understanding of scripture. Some wonder if the time spent studying, praying and worshiping leaves room for anything else. Others flatly state, "It doesn't take all of that!" For me it does. Spiritual pursuits expand and enrich every aspect of my secular undertakings.

God, who strengthens, provides boundless energy to participate in a variety of activities. I am now retired but I am in no ways tired. As my children mature and grandchildren come of age, family obligations keep me busier than ever. In addition, I discipline myself to a four-hour daily writing schedule. Woven into book readings are occasional television appearances and guest speaking engagements on educational and civil rights topics. Sometimes I become engrossed in larger projects like the semester spent volunteering at the Cicely L. Tyson Community School of Performing and Fine Arts.

My phone rang on July 4th weekend, 2009. On behalf of Cicely Tyson, Lois Harris, whom I met through

Elaine Steele, extended an invitation to accompany the actor on a tour of her brand new multi-building campus in East Orange, New Jersey. Ms. Tyson and I strolled along the corridors of the school; discussed the importance of library services; and brainstormed ways the arts can serve as platforms to motivate learning in all academic areas. She spoke with passion about a future where children "articulate confidence regarding their choices whether as artists, scientists or mathematicians."

Cicely Tyson's name on the school complex represented much more than a distinctive honor; it meant she would be available for students. "As often as I can," she said, "I head to New Jersey to be with my children." Indeed, as she escorted me through the main building, she constantly engaged students in dialogue and knew several of them by name.

At the end of the tour, she asked me to serve as liaison between her and school staff during preparations for the October 24, 2009 reception and dedication of the campus named in her honor. She also sought my ideas regarding enrichment of the educational environment. In a subsequent memo to her, I shared some of my thoughts about curriculum and offered to curate an inaugural exhibit in the new school's empty gallery space.

Six months earlier, in a one-on-one meeting on the set of *Law and Order* she had said: "I'm the only actress in the world who carries the history of her people in her soul. The arc spans from *Roots* to *Jane Pittman*, with me intersecting." Her comment provided the exhibit focus: *An Arc of Freedom: Depictions of the African American Experience from Slavery to the New Millennium.* It was a theme befitting Cicely Tyson's decades of relentless portrayals of penetrating truths about Black life in America.

Though the school's founding principal, Mrs. Laura Trimming, was on leave during preparations for the dedication, she and I spoke by phone a couple of times. The onsite supervisor, Assistant Principal Debra Boone, assigned a group of talented staff to work with me on the gallery project. By the October 19ᵗʰ countdown, prints from various movie sets had been matted, framed and hung in the museum. My personal favorite photograph was of Cicely Tyson in a "mock antebellum" gown with her co-star Paul Winfield arriving for the New York opening of *Sounder.* About the frock, Ms. Tyson reflected, "I wanted the dress Rebecca Morgan might have purchased if her sharecropper family could have afforded it."

Also mounted in the show was a step-by-step photographic depiction of how makeup transformed Ms. Tyson from a beautiful young actress to a hundred-year-old woman for her role in *The Autobiography of Jane Pittman.* For her riveting 1974 performance she received two Emmys—one for best actress in a leading role and the second for the coveted actress of the year award.

In an amazingly short time, Mr. Jefferson Wolf's students screened major Cicely Tyson television and movie roles and produced a video montage that ran in a continuous loop. On the afternoon of the reception, four young men helped their teacher installed two glass cases that sparkled in the center of the gallery awaiting the arrival of the two Emmys. The incomparable designer B Michael delivered and fitted on display stands two costumes: the antebellum gown worn by Ms. Tyson to the opening of *Sounder;* and the dress she wore as Flora Palmer in *Mama Flora's Family*—a CBS mini-series based on the Alex Haley novel of the same title.

October 24, 2009 was a rainy night but the stars shined at the Cicely L. Tyson Community School of Performing and Fine Arts. Glamorous luminaries like

Oprah Winfrey, Susan Taylor, BeBe Winans and Nick Ashford & Valerie Simpson flocked to the dedication. Among elected officials were Governor Jon Corzine of New Jersey and Mayor Edward Bowser of East Orange. As hostess in the gallery, I did not witness the red carpet arrivals that my husband and daughter, Kanari enjoyed. I delighted, though, in sounds of gaiety that drifted from the reception as Ms. Tyson ushered celebrity guests in and out of the gallery at frequent intervals. She was absolutely stunning in a floor length couture gown by B Michael.

My enchanted moment came at the intimate dinner that followed the formal program emceed by Soledad O'Brien. I chatted with Angela Bassett on the way to the dining area where Jimmy, Kanari and I were seated next to Terrence Howard's table. In pre-dinner chatter, Kanari introduced me to him and he responded, "Oh, Bessie is my mother's name." My family fell into easy conversation and he shared grief over the recent loss of his mother. He seemed comforted by my name and was such a gentleman. Whenever I needed to leave the table for one or another duty, he jumped to his feet and helped me out of my chair.

Dinner with theater royalty was one of several gratifying days as a volunteer at The Cicely L. Tyson Community School of Performing and Fine Arts. I have the warmest memories of school staff; and enjoyed the array of student talents that exploded on the auditorium stage. Finally, courtesies extended to me by Ms. Tyson and her aide during and since preparations for the school dedication are priceless. I am especially grateful for the sisterly relationship that developed with Lois Harris—a woman of grace, compassion and boundless generosity. Lois' friendship is rooted in an infectious humility that reflects the love of God in all that she does.

$\mathscr{A}$ disciplined writing schedule continues to shape the frequency and scope of new projects. However, I do not decline volunteer work in an off-handed fashion. With each request or proposal, the decision is guided by the scripture: *"I know the plans I have for you,' declares the Lord, 'plans to prosper and not to harm you, plans to give you hope and a future."* So, I live in prayerful anticipation of work arising from places traveled, people encountered, and students served. My expectations exceed all past achievements. A glorious season is ahead. Like Pastor Mike McClure, Jr., I claim, *"God is going to open the windows of heaven and pour me out a blessing... and it's gonna to be BIG!"*

I look forward to sharing a magnificent future with Jimmy. He remains my best friend and we still enjoy one another's company more than anyone else's. A few evenings ago we dined at one of those breezy New York City "open restaurants" of the 2020 pandemic. After a gust of wind I asked, "How does my hair look?"

"Black," he winked and whispered, "When I look at you I still see the girl I first laid eyes on."

"Ooooo, you smooth," I blushed.

How sweet is that? A fresh romance after fifty-eight years of marriage! God is truly amazing.

"He who does not know love, does not know God, for God is love." 1 John 4:16 NJKV

$\mathcal{My}$ *photo gallery* presents people, events and places that molded me.
Images of my earliest beginnings are drawn from memories of age seven. The sketches below provide the context for photos on the subsequent pages.

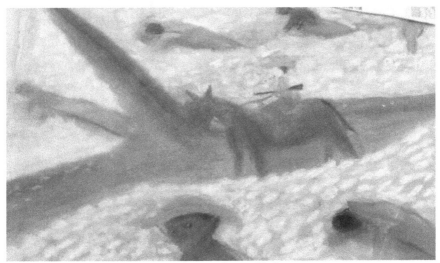

"Plantation Life"

"Self Portrait"   *"Portrait of Mama"*
(Photos of "Pastel Series" by Bessie W. Blake, 2004)

341

The Motto: "*Make* every child's potential a reality!"

Above left: Mr. Holt, my Math teacher at Union Street Junior High School *(Photo: TBC [The Blake Collection], 1957)*. *At right*: Booker T. Washington High School - Shreveport, LA *(Photo: BTW Lion Yearbook, 1959)*.

Above: My mentors were typing and shorthand teachers at BTW: *(left)* Mrs. James S. Hall; *(right)* Mrs. Blanche H. Milloy.

Above (l to r): Mrs. Theola B. Pryor, Math; Mrs. D. M. Barnes, Physical Education; and Mr. Herbert D. Webb, Social Science. *(Photos of the five power teachers above, BTW Lion Yearbook, 1959)*.

*H*igh School pals and college chums...

Above (l to r): Best friends always, Minnie V. Lee (Fontenot), Armanda Clarkson and me. *(Lion Yearbook, 1959)*

Above: Yearbook photo of the Student Union Building at Southern University, Baton Rouge, LA *(1961)*.

I am standing 6th from left in photo of residents and the matron of Cottage 5, a Southern University cooperative for young financially needy coeds *(Photo, TBC, 1962)*.

Family and work...

Above left: Master's Degree from North Carolina College (*Photo, TBC, 1964*). *In wedding snapshot (l to r):* Jimmy's granny, Essie Toomer; sister, Carol Patterson; the happy couple; Jimmy's dad, Joseph Blake; and my maid of honor, Scottie Cunningham (*Photo: RBA [Ruth Blake Archives], 1964*).

Above: Pictured in center with my English class at IS 59 Q. *(Photo, TBC, 1972)*

At right: The Blake Family *(clockwise)* Bessie & Jimmy, Kanari, Shango, RiShana, Takbir *(Photo, TBC, 1977)*.

*F*riends and family...

At left: friends Carole Hysmith, Adrienne Green and me *(TBC, 1970)*. At *right*: Carole and I relax at home *(TBC, circa 1972)*.

Above left: Son, Takbir, cheers; *at right*, my mother, RiShana & Kanari pose after the award of my doctorate, *(TBC, 1979)*.

RiShana dances at Family Day *(TBC, circa 1980)*.

𝒞reating settings for adult learners...

Above: As new Director, I oversee renovations of the Yellow Schoolhouse for the Coop City Campus of the School of New Resources-College of New Rochelle *(Photo, TBC, 1980).*

Above left (l to r): Coop City Campus staff Frank Graves, Joan Henry, Anna Green and I, *(1980). Above right;* SNR students dine in Senegalese village, (1981).
Below: Goree Island Slave Dungeon and bush village *(1981).*

"Rebellious Captive" "Children of Dignity,"
(Photos this page, TBC).

𝒢od delights to see the work begin.

Above left: Family looks on as I assume duties of SNR Dean at CNR commencement; *at right (l to r)*, I pose with colleagues and friends, Yvonne Heyes and Linda Ebinger *(Photos, TBC, 1983)*.

Above (l to r): SNR Campus Directors, Carolyn Wiggins, Louis deSalle and Celestine Johnson with Bishop Desmond Tutu, President Dorothy Ann Kelly and me after a special academic convocation honoring Bishop Tutu *(Photo, TBC, 1990)*.

*C*ollage of SNR graduates from my first commencement as dean...

(Photos, courtesy of Sonja Brown Clarke, 1983)

𝒢ordon Parks, photographer, filmmaker, author, composer:

Above left: I am pictured with *Gordon* Parks and featured photographers Toni Parks and Agar Cowan at their *I-Sight* exhibit. *Above right:* Gordon Parks signs a copy of his book, *The Learning Tree,* for Mary Kennedy Bloom *(Photos, Johnna Paladino, 1992).*

Above left: Gordon Parks signs his book, *Arias in Silence,* for me while photographer, Toni Parks, waits for her next shot *(Photo, TBC, 1994). Above right:* husband, James and I with Gordon Parks at Corcoran Gallery's retrospective exhibit, Washington D. C. *(Photo, Toni Parks, 2005).*

$\mathcal{R}$osa Parks, Mother of the Civil Rights Movement...

Above (l to r)*:* After receiving honorary degree from CNR, VP Yvonne Heyes and I watch as Mrs. Parks greets SNR Campus Director, Celestine Johnson *(Photo, TBC, 1983)*.

Above (l to r): I join Mrs. Parks and President Kelly for ribbon cutting at the dedication of the Rosa Parks Campus in Harlem *(Photo, Margaret Garri, 1987)*.

*ℛ*osa Parks' deepening relationship with CNR...

Above left: Toni Parks, Mrs. Parks and I at the Harlem campus named in her honor. At the book event, she signs a copy of *Rosa Parks: My Story* for me *(Photos: TBC, 1992)*.

At Rosa Parks' 80th birthday gala, *(standing* l to r)*,* C. Delores Tucker, a schoolgirl, Betty Shabazz, Odetta and me; (seated l to r), Elaine Steele, Mrs. Parks, and the CEO of Toyota, Shoichiro Toyoda – son of the company founder *(Photo: Toni Parks, 1993)*.

Above left: My mother, Tommie Waites, at the gala with my daughters, RiShana and Kanari *(Photo, Toni Parks, 1993)*. *Above right (l to r):* Donna Tyler, Renee Vaughn and Donna Spalter serve as greeters at the gala *(Photo: Johnna Paladino, 1993)*.

$\mathscr{M}$y mother celebrates her 70th Birthday.

Above (l to r): RiShana, Takbir, Martin, John and Shango at the 70th birthday party for their grandmother, Tommie Waites. *Below left*: Mama delights in the occasion. *Below right*: She and I leave the celebration at the end of a joyful day.

Photos this page, TBC, 1993

*G*olleagues and friends...

Above left: Dr. Louis deSalle (Director of the New York Theological Seminary Campus) and I are flanked by hosts from the Scottish Department of Education on our trip to Glasgow (circa, 1992). *Above Right*: Dr. Marguerite Coke-Maxwell Terrell and I at a fundraiser for college-bound youth of Queens, NY *(Photo, TBC, circa 1995)*.

Former colleague and friend, Dean Elza Dinwiddie Boyd, begins her tenure of leadership at the School of New Resources in 2001 *(Photo, TBC)*.

*H*ope and a future...

Above: Jimmy and I enter new millennium, (*Photo: Ruth Blake, 2000*).

Below: (l-r) Beloved daughter-in-law, Fritza Blake, and son Takbir stepping out to celebrate second anniversary, (photo: TBC, 2009).

Above: A reading of *God's Bad Boy* at the home of Dr. Charles Loveday & wife, Peggy Shepard, (*Photo*, Elroy Williams, 2014).

Below: (l to r) Jimmy and I, Takbir, Sharifah, Maisha and Shango celebrating two members of CNR's class of 2016.

Above: Jimmy & I with grandchildren (*on our laps, l to r*) Noah and Matthew; (back row, l to r) Najah, Na'im, Ameer, Nadirah and Bilal (Photo: *TBC, 2016*).

At right: Son, Takbir *(in rear)*, grandson, Noah, and I *(center front*) share the hope of Rosa Parks; then pose with 6th graders at PS 98 Queens NY (*Photo, PS 98 Yearbook, 2019*).

Abbreviated Chapter Index

Acknowledgments

I am grateful to the many people who generously supported the publication of three volumes of the Martin-Blake-Waites family history saga. As editor, my daughter RiShana gently guided the writing process with clarity. The critical insights and encouragement of Elza Dinwiddie-Boyd, Jack Estes, Tony Gronowicz, and Bob Mendelson are also immensely appreciated. Jonathan Banks, James Carter and Ruth Blake provided technical assistance and artistic input regarding designs for interior book blocks and covers.

With each publication, the weight of marketing has fallen to Team Blake. My four children, husband and grandsons (Ameer and Bilal) have lugged books to libraries for readings; hosted book talks at their homes; and involved friends in the effort. Finally, to the host of everyday people who provide remarkable inspiration, *Thank You!*

About Lit Lore

Lit, guided by light; on fire. **Lore** is experience, tradition, knowledge or wisdom about a subject. True to its root meaning, Lit Lore books explore private problems and public issues that ignite passions for self-discovery and societal renewal.

Readers of *Love Lifted Me ...from Sharecropping to Harvard!* may also enjoy *God's Bad Boy: James Blake and the System*—another Lit Lore publication by Dr. Bessie W. Blake.

CPSIA information can be obtained
at www.ICGtesting.com
Printed in the USA
JSHW031437041222
34254JS00002B/4